Light & Healthy
Chinese Cooking

LIGHT & HEALTHY CHINESE COOKING

*The Best of
Traditional Chinese Cuisine
Made Low in Sodium,
Cholesterol, and Calories*

Daniel N. Jue & Teresa Chew, R.D.

The Bobbs-Merrill Company, Inc.   Indianapolis/New York

Published by The Bobbs-Merrill Co., Inc. Indianapolis/New York
Manufactured in the United States of America

First Printing

Designed by Sheila Lynch

Library of Congress Cataloging in Publication Data

Jue, Daniel N.
    Low sodium low cholesterol Chinese cooking.

    Includes index.
    1. Salt-free diet — Recipes. 2. Low-cholesterol diet — Recipes. 3.
Cookery, Chinese. I. Chew, Teresa. II. Title.
RM237.8.J83 1984   641.5′632   83-3837
ISBN 0-672-52776-6

We would like to acknowledge the following for their encouragement and help in tasting and evaluating the recipes in this book: Rose Chew, Teresa's mother; Elaine, Dan's wife; and Sharon and Brian, Dan's children. We would especially like to recognize Andy Yee for his invaluable technical help.

Above all, we dedicate this book to the Alpha and the Omega.

"O taste and see that the Lord is good!"

(Psalms 34:8)

Contents

Preface

Light and Healthy Chinese Cooking is written to enable everyone — even those who wish to cut down on sodium and cholesterol — to enjoy the best of Chinese food. The gourmet recipes in this cookbook are easy to prepare in an American kitchen, tantalizing in flavor and good for your heart and health. Containing delicious adaptations of Chinese favorites that maintain authentic flavor while limiting sodium and fats, the recipes represent all of the regional styles of Chinese cooking, and utilize the many special sauces that make this cuisine so distinctive. *Light and Healthy Chinese Cooking* provides you with a dietary plan that will please the heart and body while enabling you to enjoy the full range of recipes that have made Chinese food America's favorite ethnic cuisine.

Ingredients and condiments are selected and used in moderation so that Chinese specialties may be enjoyed without excessive sodium, cholesterol and calories. You'll learn how to use Chinese cooking to enhance coronary health, while controlling hypertension and weight. The weekly menu plans for weight loss and sodium modification build our *Light and Healthy* recipes into your style of eating, automatically making sensible fat and sodium allowances a part of a zesty, satisfying diet. Beneath each recipe, suggested modifications to further reduce the sodium level of each dish are supplied for those who need to strictly control their intake.

Chinese cuisine is already known as one of the world's most healthful styles of eating. Our low-sodium, low-cholesterol *Light and Healthy* recipes will dramatically increase the benefits of Chinese cooking, promote a sound heart, and a trim body.

1

Why Another Chinese Cookbook?

The proliferation of Chinese cookbooks in the marketplace is a positive indication of America's fondness for Chinese food. Many of these books are quite authoritative and provide tasty authentic recipes. "If this is so," you may ask, "why have you written another Chinese cookbook?"

First, *this* Chinese cookbook emphasizes the many beneficial aspects of Chinese food. Second, unlike others, it modifies the seldom-mentioned shortcomings of Chinese cookery. (These modifications will help trim excess weight and reduce the dietary risks of high blood pressure and heart disease.) Third, the recipes are arranged in a clear and logical format to make the preparation of the food less confusing.

HEALTHFUL QUALITIES OF CHINESE CUISINE

Let us examine some of the health-promoting aspects of Chinese cooking which were incorporated into the planning of this cookbook.

Plant Food–Based Rather Than Meat–Based

For centuries, the Chinese have wisely practiced a healthful dependence on the produce of the earth. Unlike the typical American meal, the major portion of Chinese meal consists of fresh vegetables and starches, with meats playing only a supporting role. Often, as little as 2 ounces of meat may be the individual portion at a meal. The emphasis on plant foods, rather than on meats, probably evolved from economic necessity. Yet, what would seem an unfortunate hardship at first glance, is, in reality, a blessing. Clinicians and researchers now recognize the benefits of reducing the amount of meat in the diet. They have found that meat and other

1

animal foods are the major sources of cholesterol and saturated fats. These substances are the suspected culprits in the development of heart disease. Plant foods, on the other hand, foster heart healthiness because they contain no cholesterol and are low in saturated fat.

It is unfortunate that many of us continue to believe that the more meat we consume the healthier we are. Granted, meat is a very important source of protein, but, surprisingly, our daily protein needs can be met with as little as 4 to 6 ounces of meat, fish, or poultry along with 2 cups of milk or the equivalent in dairy products. The total protein consumed daily by Americans adds up to twice the amount necessary for good health. This excess consumption is more than a drain on the pocketbook: It escalates the risks of heart disease, as 40 percent of this protein is from animal sources high in cholesterol and saturated fat. Also, much of the excess protein will probably end up being stored in those ugly fat cells known as adipose tissue!

Sufficient Fiber Intake

Another health-promoting aspect of Chinese cuisine is its potentially high fiber content. Researchers recommend a high-fiber diet for the prevention or treatment of such conditions as constipation, hemorrhoids, irritable bowel syndrome, cancer of the colon, and high blood cholesterol levels. Although the benefit of additional fiber in the diet is not conclusive, population studies have indicated a positive connection between increased fiber intake and reduced incidence of heart disease and cancer of the colon. Data additionally suggest that the common American diet can benefit very well from more fiber. Fiber requirements are easily met in Chinese cooking because fresh vegetables, which make up a significant part of most meals, are very good sources of dietary fiber.

Vitamin Retention

The techniques used in Chinese cooking, such as stir-frying, also encourage healthy eating. Vegetables are excellent sources of vitamins and they should be cooked in a manner which will retain these nutrients. Cooking vegetables for a prolonged period and in an excess amount of water contributes greatly to vitamin loss. Stir-frying minimizes this loss because the vegetables are cooked for only a very short time to maintain crispness and very little water is used in the process.

UNIQUE FEATURES OF THIS BOOK

We obviously agree with what the authors of other Chinese cookbooks say about the delectability of this great cuisine. What we have chosen to do differently, however, is to confront the deficiencies of Chinese cookery and to correct them. These deficiencies include high sodium and excess calories in many dishes and high cholesterol and saturated fat in the more traditional recipes. To rectify these flaws, we have introduced modifications that uniquely blend the art of Chinese cooking with the science of nutrition. Together, we (one with a background in cooking and chemistry, and one a registered dietitian) have collaborated to offer you the best of two worlds: the delectable tastes of Chinese cuisine and a healthier lifestyle tailored to reduce excess weight and the dietary risk factors of heart disease.

Taste was a major consideration in planning the dietary modifications. We tested the recipes until they met our strict standards for flavor, texture, and variety.

To conquer the problem of excess weight and to reduce the risks of developing heart disease requires the establishment of sound, nutritious eating habits. Specifically, calories must be lowered for weight loss; cholesterol, saturated fat, and sodium must be lowered for heart health.

Lower Calories

Calories have been reduced to help those who are burdened with the problem of excess weight. Alterations in ingredients, cookware, and techniques were made to accomplish this.

The ingredient which contributes an unnecessarily high proportion of calories in Chinese food is fat, including cooking oil. Since fat, saturated or unsaturated, is a highly concentrated source of calories, we have deliberately limited its use. For example, cooking oil has been decreased and the use of leaner cuts of meat is encouraged. Trimming away all animal fat and eliminating chicken skins are also stressed.

The standard round-bottom metal wok is the cookware generally suggested in Chinese cookbooks. We find that this kind of wok requires a relatively large amount of oil to prevent ingredients from sticking during cooking. Also, the wok's round bottom is not suitable for electric stovetops, as the heat transfer between the heating element and the wok is insufficient to maintain the necessary "sizzling hot" temperature for stir-frying. Therefore, we do not recommend the metal wok for use in the American kitchen and for fewer calories in cooking. Instead, we recommend that you use a 10-inch or larger fry pan, treated with nonstick coatings such as Silverstone® or T-Fal®, or the newly available flat-bottom nonstick woks for stovetop cooking. An alternative to these would be an electric nonstick wok. Even without the round bottom, the nonstick surface of the pan or wok will allow you to use less oil, therefore less calories, and will still enable you to get excellent results in stir-frying.

The technique of deep-fat frying has been modified to cut down fat and calories. An alternative method using a combination of baking and broiling was developed and proved successful in retaining much of the fragrance and texture of deep-frying, while eliminating greasiness and fattening calories.

These modifications in ingredients, cookware, and techniques will reduce calories. To further assist you in a total weight-loss program, a week's set of low-calorie menus is included in Chapter 8.

Low Cholesterol and Saturated Fat

Next, because foods of animal origin are the only sources of cholesterol and the major sources of saturated fat, we have reduced their use. Each recipe limits the meat portions to no more than 2 to 3 ounces per serving. Practical sample menus in Chapter 8 have been designed so you can enjoy typical American breakfasts and lunches along with two-course Chinese dinners consisting of a meat and a vegetable dish. Of course, you will occasionally want to indulge in a meal high in cholesterol and saturated fat, which is only human. Realizing this, we have included selected recipes relatively higher in these substances. You will find them in a special section designated for "discretionary use."

Lower Sodium

Population studies show a strong positive correlation between high sodium intakes and the incidence of hypertension (high blood pressure). Being aware of this and mindful of the substantial amounts of sodium in Chinese condiments and foodstuffs, we set out to reduce the sodium content of each recipe to more acceptable and safe levels.

Even though we do use Chinese condiments in the recipes, we still maintain a safe, sensible sodium level. The sodium data on many of these condiments were simply not available or obsolete. Paucity of this information probably prevents many people who want to limit sodium from enjoying delicious Chinese food. To make this book truly valuable to you, the health-conscious consumer, we analyzed the sodium values of frequently used Chinese condiments in a laboratory. This data then enabled us to carefully calculate the sodium content of each recipe and the values of each serving portion. It is now possible for you to know how much sodium you are consuming when you cook and eat Chinese food!

Each recipe contains less than 400 mg. of sodium per serving. This ceiling was established so that the maximum sodium intake could be kept to 2,000 mg. of sodium per day. Medical authorities recommend this sodium level as a preventive measure against developing or precipitating high blood pressure.

People with high blood pressure are often instructed to eliminate Chinese condiments from their sodium-restricted diets. This is not always necessary. It is the total sodium consumed each day which must be of greatest concern. We are convinced that Chinese condiments may be used in limited quantities on a sodium-restricted diet, provided it is done with discretion and under professional guidance. Why subject yourself to bland meals when a little careful planning can offer satisfaction, enjoyment, and a variety of tastes? To stay within the recommended sodium level, salt and MSG (monosodium glutamate) were eliminated from our recipes to permit use of the Chinese condiments. Because shellfish are relatively high in sodium, dishes containing shrimp, scallops, oysters, and similar foods have been placed in the discretionary section of the recipes.

As a further aid, one week of sample menus was planned at the 2,000 mg. sodium level for those who desire a sensible sodium intake. For those who are on a restricted sodium diet, a one-week menu is outlined at the 1,000 mg. sodium level. The sample menus are devised to include typical American breakfasts and lunches with the evening meal containing two of our specially created dishes.

Easy-to-Follow Recipe Format

Have you ever had the frustrating experience of following a recipe only to find, at a crucial moment, that an ingredient, a sauce, or a preparation step is missing because the instructions were too vague or wordy? To prevent such a crisis, we have designed an easy-to-follow recipe format. Rather than have you wade through many, many words to figure out what to do, we have coordinated the ingredients and instructions into clear, logical steps. When the actual preparation and cooking begins, you will be able to tell at a glance where you are and what must follow.

SUMMARY

Much thought, time, and effort have gone into this health-oriented cookbook for your dining pleasure and general well-being, and you will find that good taste and good nutrition can coexist. As you cook these recipes, you will be pleased to discover the natural, subtle flavor in foods which was once masked by excessive salt and grease.

This Chinese cookbook can become your trusted diet guide, to help you to trim off excess weight and please your heart in more ways than one. Begin today by cooking a heart-healthy Chinese meal and enjoying it with friends.

2

The Heart of
the Matter

The jury is still out in the case of the People versus Diet. Can the woes of the People, specifically the 4.4 million Americans afflicted with coronary heart disease, be blamed on diet? Many specialists in the fields of medicine, research, and nutrition believe so. They say diet may cause or precipitate high blood cholesterol and high blood pressure, which, along with cigarette smoking, are major contributors to coronary heart disease.

Valuable time may elapse before final judgment is handed down in this case against diet. In the meantime, should we alter our eating patterns? An overwhelming amount of convincing data seems to lean toward diet modification as an effective means of controlling high blood cholesterol and high blood pressure. A brief review of the facts along with some background information on heart disease will help you understand just why diet could be the key to heart health.

ATHEROSCLEROSIS

The most common condition that results in disease to the major arteries of the heart (coronary heart disease or CHD) has the tongue-twisting name atherosclerosis or "hardening of the arteries." Atherosclerosis is characterized by deposits of fatty materials, cholesterol being a major component, within the lining of blood vessel walls. Not only arteries of the heart but also those which supply blood to the brain can be affected. As fatty deposits, known as plaque, accumulate within the blood vessel walls, the vessels become hardened, less elastic, and the free flow of blood to vital organs is obstructed. A *heart attack* or *"coronary"* occurs when part of the heart muscle is deprived of oxygen and nutrient-rich blood because of a blockage in one or more of the coronary arteries. A *stroke* takes place if a similar situation occurs in a vessel leading to the brain.

Since atherosclerosis occurs in both the young and the old, the attention is focused on the degree and the rate of plaque buildup rather than its mere presence. The more advanced atherosclerosis is in arteries of the heart, the closer we edge toward a heart attack. The exact cause of atherosclerosis is unknown. What is known, however, is that when certain conditions or risk factors are present, atherosclerosis may be accelerated and the probability of heart disease is increased.

HEART DISEASE: WHAT ARE THE RISKS?

Unlike the inevitable risks we face in our daily lives, the risk factors associated with heart disease, namely cigarette smoking, high blood cholesterol, and high blood pressure, can be avoided or at least controlled. If they are ignored, they can shorten an otherwise productive healthy life. The probability of developing heart disease may increase from 2 to 6 fold, depending on the number of risks present in our lives. Fortunately, we can improve our odds by taking positive steps to prevent or correct the dangers of impending heart problems.

The risks associated with cigarette smoking are avoidable by simply quitting. Many will attest to the fact that kicking the habit is no easy task, but the rewards for doing so are tremendous. Stopping can have a significant impact on the smoker's life expectancy and quality of life. Studies have proven that people who quit the habit have fewer incidences of heart attacks. Their chances of having a heart attack may even come down to that of nonsmokers. This is promising news and should be an incentive to smokers who normally have a 50 to 200 percent greater frequency of death from heart attacks.

Diet modification is favored to control the two major risk factors, high blood cholesterol and high blood pressure. This is why we have devoted a chapter on heart health and the importance of diet. In addition, challenging fun quizzes have been designed to give you an opportunity to compare your knowledge and eating habits with those recommended by heart experts.

HIGH BLOOD CHOLESTEROL: CAN DIET MAKE THE DIFFERENCE?

Cholesterol has been spoken of so often in a negative sense that one would wonder if it has any redeeming values. Our bodies seem to think so. Not only do we ingest cholesterol, but our bodies make cholesterol in the liver to perform many vital functions. Cholesterol is a component of bile acids, essential for digestion of the fat we eat. Cholesterol is also crucial for production of our body's sex hormones (we all need these!). Life would not be possible without some cholesterol.

The negativism stems from the discovery that cholesterol is a major component of plaque. Also, there is a greater incidence of heart disease, especially heart attacks, among persons with high blood cholesterol levels.

Recent studies show that not only the level of blood cholesterol is significant, but how cholesterol is transported in the body also matters. In the blood, cholesterol can be found in various forms in combination with protein. These cholesterol-protein compounds are called lipoproteins. Two lipoproteins are particularly interesting because they transport most of the cholesterol in the body and determine their destination. LDL, or low-density lipoproteins, are often called the "bad guys" because they contribute to atherosclerosis by depositing cholesterol where the plaque is. HDL, or high-density lipoproteins, are the "good guys" because they have a protective effect by acting as scavengers to take cholesterol away from the plaque buildup.

To guard against or to lower elevated blood cholesterol and LDL levels, researchers recommend that *Americans reduce their intake of saturated fats and cholesterol.* It is also advised that a greater proportion of the fat we do eat come from a polyunsaturated source. Raising the level of protective lipoproteins, HDL, is not as easy. Losing weight may help increase HDL slightly. A more effective means is to follow a rather strenuous exercise program under medical supervision.

Decreasing the cholesterol in the diet involves cutting down on the consumption of egg yolks, organ meats, and some shellfish. Saturated fat is generally found in animal and dairy products, such as meats, whole milk, cream, butter, ice cream, and cheeses. Many baked goods and a few vegetable products are also high in saturated fat. Vegetable oils are a good source of polyunsaturated fats. The quiz that follows will reveal more specifics about a blood cholesterol and LDL lowering diet.

Reducing the total fat in our present diet by over 30 to 40 percent is advisable for several reasons. As total fat decreases, saturated fat intake is less. Also, fat is a very concentrated source of calories which adds considerably to our caloric consumption and often contributes to obesity — a risk factor in heart disease. A third reason to decrease total fat is based on the evidence surfacing that cancer of the breast and colon occurs more frequently in individuals on high-fat diets.

Many Americans accustomed to their daily dose of 450 mg. to 500 mg. cholesterol may find the suggested level of 300 mg. or less per day hard to adjust to. Likewise, they may find it difficult to reduce total fat intake by

25 percent. "Is there a sound basis to warrant making these changes in my life?" Studies of individuals, populations, and animals provide a strong case for reducing total dietary fat, especially saturated fat and cholesterol.

The Ni-Hon San study is an excellent example of what can happen when individuals from a country having typically low blood cholesterol levels immigrate and become acculturated to our society with its rich diet. This study compared the diet and number of deaths from CHD among Japanese in their native country with Japanese immigrants in Hawaii and San Francisco. It was discovered that the blood cholesterol and number of CHD deaths rose as the proportion of dietary saturated fat and cholesterol increased. In contrast to the cholesterol and saturated fat intake of Japanese natives, those in Hawaii and San Francisco consumed 12 and 21 percent more, respectively. Deaths from CHD were 1.7 times higher in Hawaii and 2.8 times greater in San Francisco.

In 1981, two significant findings were published following a 20-year study of 1,900 middle-aged men employed at the Western Electric Company in Chicago: (1) blood cholesterol levels tended to rise as saturated fat and cholesterol rose in the diet, while polyunsaturated fats had a blood cholesterol lowering effect; (2) the risk of death from coronary heart disease was directly related to the amount of saturated fats and cholesterol consumed, whereas polyunsaturated fats had a decreasing effect.

Studies on the vegetarian population further substantiate these findings. Their intake of saturated fats and cholesterol is normally less than that of the general public, as animal flesh, the major source of these two substances, is eliminated from their diet. This dietary lifestyle is often credited for their lower blood cholesterol and LDL levels and heart disease rate. The same holds true for primitive populations whose diets are low in fat.

The feeding of cholesterol and saturated fat to animals has produced cases of accelerated atherosclerosis. Particularly interesting is the halting and even reversing of atherosclerosis in some primates when these fats are withheld from their diet.

DIET RECOMMENDATIONS

The above studies and others over the decades have led such renowned groups as the American Heart Association, the Senate Select Committee on Human Nutrition, the U.S. Department of Agriculture, and the U.S. Department of Health and Human Services to advise Americans to *avoid excess fat, especially saturated fats and cholesterol.* Some specifically suggest that no more than 30 percent of our total calories come from fat and that cholesterol be restricted to less than 300 mg. cholesterol per day.

The "diet-heart" controversy has existed for years and may not be resolved for years to come. Although the evidence demonstrates a strong positive association between diet and heart disease, a definitive cause and effect cannot be established. Other factors, such as stress or heredity, may also contain pieces to this complicated jigsaw puzzle. What steps should we take?

The wise approach is to determine the possible avenues opened, survey the risks and the benefits of each, and then choose the most prudent course of action. There are currently no known risks associated with reducing total fat, including saturated fat and cholesterol. In fact, in many countries, the population consumes half the fat Americans do without detrimental consequences. The Japanese diet derives 10 to 15 percent of its calories from fat and their life expectancy is greater than ours at every age level compared.

The studies mentioned earlier are only a few examples of the overwhelming data supporting a low-fat diet, particularly one low in cholesterol and saturated fat for reducing the incidence of heart disease.

Such a diet is also recommended for the obese, who currently make up more than 30 percent of the adult population. As fat is the most concentrated source of calories in our food, a drop in fat intake can mean a drop in weight.

With the mounting evidence connecting high-fat diets to cancer of the breast and colon, we again see additional valid reasons and benefit for choosing a modified-fat diet.

Finally, let us not forget that atherosclerosis begins early in life and advances in varying degrees with age. We can be positive influences on children, whether they are our own or those of relatives or friends, by adopting a low-fat eating pattern. So be good to yourself and the next generation by making the switch today to a more heart-healthy diet.

SATURATED FAT AND CHOLESTEROL CONSCIOUSNESS QUIZ

We invite you to complete the following quiz and review the answers as step one toward making your heart a happier one.

1. Cholesterol is:
   a. found only in foods of animal origin.
   b. present only in egg yolks.
   c. found mainly in foods of animal origin but small quantities are also present in plant foods.
   d. equally present in foods of animal and plant origin.

2. A rich source of saturated fat that I need to be aware of is:
   a. egg yolks.
   b. luncheon meats.
   c. Cheddar cheese.
   d. b and c.
   e. all of the above.

3. I can reduce my saturated fat intake by limiting hidden sources found in:
   a. angel food cake.
   b. commercial crackers.
   c. spaghetti or noodles.
   d. commercial white bread.
   e. none of the above.

4. Monounsaturated fats in the diet:
   a. may cause my blood cholesterol level to rise.
   b. may cause my blood cholesterol level to fall.
   c. will probably have little effect on my blood cholesterol level.
   d. will probably raise my cholesterol and triglyceride levels.

5. The vegetable oil highest in polyunsaturated fat is:
   a. corn oil.
   b. peanut oil.
   c. sunflower oil.
   d. safflower oil.
   e. olive oil.

6. (The following are ingredients commonly seen on package labels.) I can be assured of a higher polyunsaturated intake if I choose packages labeled:
   a. 100 percent pure vegetable oil.
   b. All natural vegetable oil.
   c. 100 percent vegetable shortening.
   d. none of the above.
   e. all of the above.

7. The American Heart Association recommends a diet which:
   a. limits egg yolks to 1 per week.
   b. limits egg yolks to 2 per week.
   c. limits egg yolks to 3 per week.
   d. limits egg yolks to 4 per week.
   e. eliminates egg yolks.

8. On a heart-healthy diet, I should avoid all:
   a. egg yolks.
   b. red meats.
   c. organ meats.
   d. all of the above.
   e. none of the above.

9. The following are good choices to reduce saturated fat and cholesterol
   except:
   a. chicken, fat and skin removed.
   b. veal, well trimmed.
   c. Cheddar cheese.
   d. duck, fat and skin removed.
   e. scallops.

10. To modify my diet in order to reduce the risk of heart attack, I should:
    a. include liberal intakes of polyunsaturated fats to lower blood
       cholesterol.
    b. maintain my total fat intake at 30 percent of my daily calorie needs.
    c. maintain my total fat intake at 40 percent of my daily calorie needs.
    d. a and c.
    e. b and c.

11. Two servings daily from the *Milk and Milk Products Group* are recom-
    mended for good nutrition. Which group of foods should be used
    judiciously due to their higher content of saturated fat and cholesterol
    and low nutrient value?
    a. 2 percent cottage cheese, fortified skim milk.
    b. dietetic ice cream, nondairy creamers.
    c. farmer cheese and mozzarella cheese made from skimmed or
       partially skimmed milk.
    d. low-fat yogurt, fortified low-fat milk.
    e. none of the above.

12. Two servings daily from the *Meat and Meat Substitute Group* are
    recommended for good nutrition. Which group of foods should be used
    judiciously due to their higher content of saturated fat and cholesterol?
    a. chicken, veal, fish.
    b. crab, clams, well-trimmed and lean cuts of pork.
    c. shrimp, well-trimmed beef ribs and rib steak, and squid.
    d. dried beans and peas, unlimited egg whites.
    e. none of the above.

13. Four servings daily from the *Fruit and Vegetable Group* are recommended for good nutrition. Which group of foods should be used *judiciously* due to their higher content of saturated fat and cholesterol?
    a. papaya, mango, sweet potatoes.
    b. oranges, kale, carrots.
    c. rutabagas, green peas, escarole.
    d. bananas, potatoes, squash.
    e. none of the above.

14. Four servings daily from the *Bread and Cereal Group* are recommended for good nutrition. Which group of foods should be used *judiciously* due to their higher content of saturated fat and cholesterol?
    a. commercial white bread and cold cereals.
    b. rice, spaghetti, whole wheat flour.
    c. commercial biscuits, muffins, and pancake mixes.
    d. homemade sweet rolls made with recommended ingredients.
    e. none of the above.

15. The following commercial dessert generally contains some saturated fat:
    a. ice milk.
    b. imitation ice cream.
    c. sherbet.
    d. apple pie.
    e. all of the above.

Answers to the Saturated Fat and Cholesterol Consciousness Quiz

1. **a.** Egg yolks are one of the richest sources of cholesterol but not the only. Organ meats such as liver and kidney contain substantial amounts. Shellfish are generally low in cholesterol except for shrimp and squid which should be used with discretion. Cholesterol is a component in all animal tissues, whereas plant sources do not contain cholesterol.

2. **d.** Fatty meats (bologna, sausage, fatty cuts of meats, such as ribs) and products made with whole milk or cream (half-and-half, whole milk, many cheeses, butter) contain rich sources of saturated fat. Egg yolks are high in cholesterol.

3. **b.** Most commercial crackers, pies, cakes, and cookies contain lard, coconut oil, and/or palm oil, rich sources of saturated fat. Many commercial products contain them because they are relatively inexpensive to use.

4. c. Popular oils, such as olive and peanut oil, contain large amounts of monounsaturated fats. Unlike polyunsaturated fats, which lower blood cholesterol, monounsaturated fats have little effect. Thus, they are recommended for flavoring only. The regular cooking oil should be one that is high in polyunsaturated fats.

5. d. Safflower oil is highest in polyunsaturated fats. Other oils also considered high include sunflower, corn, soybean, cottonseed, and sesame oils. Peanut and olive oils are high in monounsaturated fats. Coconut and palm oils are high in saturated fats.

6. d. Unless the specific vegetable oil is listed, one cannot be assured that vegetable fats high in saturated fats are not being used.

7. c. Egg yolks need not be totally eliminated, just limited. They are an excellent source of protein, iron, and other nutrients.

8. e. A heart-healthy diet involves reducing total fat, including saturated fat and cholesterol intake. It is not possible or wise to eliminate these foods entirely because many contain essential nutrients needed for good nutrition.

9. c. Whole milk dairy products like Cheddar cheese are high in saturated fat. Fish, light meat of chicken and turkey, and veal are highly recommended as the meats to be eaten most often. Red meats, such as lean beef, lamb, and pork can be used but less frequently. Shellfish, such as clams, scallops, crab, lobster, and oysters, are relatively low in cholesterol, whereas shrimp and squid contain higher amounts. Fatty meats, such as ribs, luncheon meats, and organ meats, should be used sparingly (except liver which may be eaten occasionally, as it is very rich in nutrients). Well-trimmed duck may be used in moderation. When the fat and skin is removed the fat and calorie content is comparable to that of dark chicken meat.

10. b. It is important to lower the total amount of fat in one's diet. A greater proportion of the fat allowance should be from a polyunsaturated source.

11. b. Dietetic ice cream is often made with cream and may contain other substances high in saturated fats. Its high caloric content limits it to occasional use. Most nondairy creamers are made with coconut or palm oil and are a poor source of nutrients.

12. **c.** Shrimp and squid contain relatively large amounts of cholesterol and should be used on a limited basis. Fatty cuts of meats, such as beef ribs and rib steaks, contain much fat marbling which would be extremely difficult to trim well. Egg whites do not contain cholesterol.

13. **e.** Fruits and vegetables do not contain cholesterol. Very small quantities of saturated fat may be present in some fruits and vegetables but need not be of concern. The only exception is avocados which are relatively high in total fat as well as monounsaturated fat and should, therefore, be limited.

14. **c.** Commercial quick breads often contain eggs, lard, butter, whole milk, palm and/or coconut oil.

15. **e.** All of the commercial desserts listed contain one or a combination of cream, lard, coconut oil, and palm oil.

We hope this "tricky" quiz has been informative and will help you during your future trips to the supermarket!

HIGH BLOOD PRESSURE

High blood pressure is the "silent killer" that strikes without clear warning and when least expected. It can cause stroke, heart failure, or kidney damage in an individual who appears healthy and in peak physical condition.

Hypertension, or high blood pressure (HBP), is a condition in which the blood flow exerts an excess amount of pressure along the blood vessel walls. The dangers that accompany this increased pressure can be far-reaching.

First and foremost, hypertension is one of the major contributors to heart disease. The persistent pressure against the blood vessel walls reduces their elasticity so that the process of atherosclerosis (hardening of the arteries) is accelerated. In addition, the resistance of the blood vessel walls to the blood flow strains the heart, forcing it to pump harder than usual. One or a combination of these factors often leads to a heart attack.

Second, since HBP speeds up atherosclerosis, plaque buildup in the arteries of the brain progresses faster. This is possibly why there is a greater incidence of stroke among those with hypertension than those free of the condition.

Finally, kidney failure and even loss of vision can result from the damaging effects hypertension has on the blood vessels. Without a doubt, HBP poses a risk to many vital organs including the heart. Unfortunately, HBP is not completely avoidable because evidence also points to a genetic factor: It tends to run in families, and some ethnic groups are more often afflicted than others. Luckily, several risks of hypertension are avoidable or controllable. Our chances of preventing HBP is greatly enhanced if we eliminate high-sodium diets, obesity, and smoking, and if we control stress and alcohol consumption in our lives. Because this book's emphasis is on heart-healthy eating and weight control, the remainder of this chapter will focus on sodium. Obesity will be covered in the next chapter. Many excellent self-help books are available on the subjects of stress, smoking, and alcohol, and you may wish to take advantage of them.

HIGH BLOOD PRESSURE: CAN A LOW-SODIUM DIET MAKE A DIFFERENCE?

Sodium is a nutrient that is essential to keep our muscles and nervous system functioning at the optimum. A healthy person requires as little as 250 mg. of sodium per day to carry out these activities. To say we easily meet these requirements would be quite an understatement, for we surpass the minimum need by as much as 30 fold!

This overindulgence of sodium is primarily due to our growing dependence on commercial foods, such as cured, smoked, and canned foods, as well as to our excessive use of high-sodium seasonings and condiments, such as salt. Salt contains a substantial amount of sodium, nearly 40 percent, and is often used synonymously with the term sodium. *Salt is not sodium.* Merely decreasing our salt intake may not be enough. A sufficient reduction in sodium also requires a cutback in foods containing sodium compounds, such as monosodium glutamate. Will less consumption of sodium prevent HBP? There is no conclusive proof, but strong correlations from results of population studies and animal experiments lead us to believe so.

Observations on the diet practices of various societies may go a long way to unraveling the cause-and-effect relationship between high-sodium diets and HBP. Primitive societies which consume low-sodium diets are virtually free of hypertension. In direct contrast, societies with high-sodium intakes, such as northern Japan, report the highest incidences of the disease.

Animal and human studies demonstrate a genetic element which causes some to be susceptible while others remain resistant to HBP. Interestingly, animals identified as susceptible to developing hypertension when fed a high-sodium diet, showed no signs of HBP when kept on a restricted-sodium diet. Humans display a similar response. Those who are susceptible will also have elevated blood pressures on high-sodium diets. Their pressures drop as dietary sodium intakes decrease.

Approximately 17 percent of the American population will develop HBP on the current intake of 3,500 mg. to 5,800 mg. of sodium per day. Levels as low as 2,800 mg. of sodium may also precipitate HBP in hypertension-prone persons. For the fortunate Americans resistant to HBP, the condition may not occur at present levels. It seems simple then to adopt a low-sodium diet only if you are the unlucky 1 in 6. If only life were that predictable! Hypertension is found in men and women, blacks and whites, young and old, and "hyper" and sedate persons. It often strikes those who expect it least.

DIET RECOMMENDATION

We suggest you live on the prudent side by following the recommendations of the Senate Select Committee on Nutrition and Human Needs: *Reduce your sodium intake to 2,000 mg. per day.* We believe foods can still be very palatable at this level. Possible benefits from maintaining a low-sodium diet could include cutting down your chances of developing HBP and its devastating consequences, not to mention a greater peace of mind and heart.

The advantages may be even more dramatic for those who have hypertension. Some individuals with borderline HBP may achieve normal blood pressure from diet alone. Those who must take anti-hypertensive drugs can benefit, too. Studies show the helpfulness of low-sodium diets in strengthening the drugs' effectiveness and possibly allowing a reduction in drug dosage.

Of course, it is always advisable to consult a physician before beginning any diet program. A low-sodium diet can be dangerous for a select few. They include persons with disorders of the kidneys or adrenal glands or those who lose an unusual amount of sodium from profuse sweating, diarrhea, or vomiting.

SODIUM CONSCIOUSNESS QUIZ

It's time again for another fun quiz. Again, we hope the answers and accompanying notes will assist you in your desire to reduce sodium.

1. Fresh meats are typically low in sodium *except:*
   a. beef liver.
   b. pork.
   c. fresh salmon.
   d. lamb.
   e. none of the above.

2. On reduced sodium diets, the following fresh produce should be avoided:
   a. celery and tomatoes.
   b. avocado and apricots.
   c. broccoli and carrots.
   d. beets and yams.
   e. none of the above.

3. I am aware of the substantial amounts of sodium in:
   a. fresh roasted peanuts.
   b. avocados.
   c. baked potatoes.
   d. quick-cooking cereals.
   e. none of the above.

4. On a 2000 mg. sodium per day diet, I should avoid all:
   a. soy sauce.
   b. salt.
   c. ketchup.
   d. all of the above.
   e. none of the above.

5. All of the following spices and flavorings contain negligible amounts of sodium *except:*
   a. curry powder.
   b. mustard powder.
   c. chili powder.
   d. paprika.
   e. none of the above.

6. The mineral most often replacing sodium in salt substitutes is:
   a. magnesium.
   b. potassium.
   c. calcium.
   d. chloride.
   e. none of the above.

7. Individuals on drug therapy for hypertension are often instructed to increase their potassium intake. Which of the following foods contains the greatest amount of potassium?
   a. medium banana.
   b. large baked potato.
   c. ½ cup orange juice.
   d. 4 ounces of cooked flank steak.
   e. 1 cup low-fat milk.

8. Of the condiments listed, the one containing the most sodium is:
   a. 1 tablespoon dark soy sauce.
   b. 1 teaspoon salt.
   c. 1 teaspoon monosodium glutamate (MSG).
   d. 1 teaspoon baking soda.
   e. 1½ tablespoon sweet bean sauce.

9. The beverage containing an unsuspected amount of sodium per 12-ounce serving is:
   a. beer.
   b. cola.
   c. club soda.
   d. instant iced tea.
   e. all of the above.

10. The over-the-counter drug containing a surprisingly large amount of sodium is:
   a. Tums.
   b. Alka-Seltzer.
   c. Milk of Magnesia tablets.
   d. all of the above.
   e. none of the above.

11. A nutritious diet consists of 2 servings from the *Milk and Milk Products Group*. Which food contains a considerable amount of sodium and should be used *judiciously?*
    a. American cheese.
    b. instant pudding made with low-fat milk.
    c. low-fat cottage cheese.
    d. none of the above.
    e. all of the above.

12. A nutritious diet consists of 2 servings daily from the *Meat and Meat Substitute Group*. Which food contains a considerable amount of sodium and should be used *judiciously?*
    a. fresh pork.
    b. water-packed tuna.
    c. legumes.
    d. tofu.
    e. none of the above.

13. A nutritious diet consists of 4 servings daily from the *Fruit and Vegetable Group*. Which food contains a considerable amount of sodium and should be used *judiciously?*
    a. frozen peas.
    b. olives.
    c. frozen mixed vegetables.
    d. none of the above.
    e. all of the above.

14. A nutritious diet consists of 4 servings daily from the *Bread and Cereal Group*. Which food contains a considerable amount of sodium and should be used *judiciously?*
    a. frozen waffles.
    b. baking powder biscuits.
    c. granola cereals.
    d. a and b.
    e. all of the above.

15. The commercial dessert highest in sodium is:
    a. 1 slice of apple pie.
    b. 4 oatmeal cookies.
    c. 1 slice of angel food cake.
    d. 8-ounces strawberry low-fat yogurt.
    e. ½ cup tapioca pudding made with low-fat milk.

Answers to the Sodium Consciousness Quiz

1. **e.** Pork is often thought of as "forbidden." Fresh pork, like most fresh meats, is low in sodium (25 to 30 mg. per ounce). Popular smoked, canned, and cured meats and fish should be avoided because they are prepared with large amounts of salt.

2. **e.** Fresh fruits and vegetables are generally low in sodium. Celery contains slightly more sodium (50 mg. per stalk). It need not be eliminated, just limited. Fresh tomatoes contain only 5 mg. of sodium per medium tomato and can be eaten freely. Unlike the fresh tomato, substantial amounts of sodium are found in tomato products, such as tomato sauce (1,414 mg. per ¼ cup) and tomato juice (243 mg. per ½ cup). Tomato paste canned without salt makes an excellent substitute (26 mg. per ¼ cup).

3. **d.** Quick and/or instant cereals often contain salt. Most regular, slow-cooking hot cereals contain little sodium. Always read the ingredient label to be sure.

4. **e.** A trained professional in nutrition can plan a diet for you which could include a limited amount of any of the condiments mentioned. See our sample menus in Chapter 8 for examples. Also look at answer 8 for further explanation.

5. **c.** Most chili powders contain some sodium and average 26 mg. of sodium per teaspoon. Herbs and spices that may be used freely, as they contain only trace amounts of sodium, include: allspice, almond extract, anise, bay leaves, caraway seeds, cinnamon, curry powder, fresh garlic and ginger, garlic and ginger powder, green chili peppers, lemon extract, mace, marjoram, mustard powder, nutmeg, fresh onions, onion powder, paprika, parsley, pepper, pimiento, rosemary, sage, sesame seeds, thyme, turmeric, vanilla extract, and vinegar.

6. **b.** Salt substitutes contain a substantial amount of potassium. Since diuretics can deplete the body's supply of potassium, salt substitutes can replace this loss. Salt substitutes should be used only after consulting a physician.

7. **b.** Bananas are frequently considered one of the few rich sources of potassium. On the contrary, rich sources of potassium can be found in foods from the fruit and vegetable group, meat group, and milk

group. Choose from a variety of potassium-rich foods for added nutrients. Baked potato and orange juice provide potassium as well as vitamin C. Beef and milk provide protein also. Other rich sources of potassium are dates, figs, prunes, raisins, apricots, cantaloupe, broccoli, winter squash, brussels sprouts, sweet potato, lentils, and non-fat milk.

8. b. Salt is a concentrated source of sodium (1,938 mg. per teaspoon). Lesser amounts of sodium per larger quantities of a seasoning are seen in the following: dark soy sauce (1,000 mg. per tablespoon), MSG (492 mg. per teaspoon), baking soda (821 mg. per teaspoon), sweet bean sauce (743 mg. per 1½ tablespoon). We have used this principle to allow Chinese condiments (in limited amounts) in our recipes.

9. c. Club soda contains 90 mg. sodium in each 12 ounces as compared to 5 mg. in iced tea, 22 mg. in regular colas, and 25 mg. in beer.

10. b. Alka-Seltzer contains 532 mg. of sodium per tablet. It is highly recommended that one check with his or her physician or pharmacist before taking over-the-counter drugs.

11. e. Dairy products can be quite high in sodium but they are good sources of protein, calcium, and vitamin B_2. Cheeses such as American cheese (400 mg. per ounce) and cottage cheese (350 to 460 mg. per ½ cup) are very high in sodium. Non-fat or low-fat milk (125 mg. per 1 cup) and low-fat yogurt (130 to 160 mg. per cup) contain moderate amounts of sodium. Dairy desserts, such as instant pudding, can contain a surprising quantity of sodium (400 mg. per ½ cup).

12. b. A product packed in water does not guarantee it will be low in sodium. Water-packed tuna may contain broth, salt, or both and often averages 275 to 400 mg. sodium per 3 ounces. One can be sure an item is low in sodium only by reading the ingredient label carefully.

13. e. All fresh fruits and most fresh vegetables can be used freely because they are low in sodium and high in nutrients. Canned vegetables are usually packed with salt or brine and average over 500 mg. per cup. Many frozen vegetables such as frozen peas, lima beans, and mixed vegetables average 200 mg. per cup. Canned fruits generally do not contain sodium.

14. d. Baking powder (339 mg. per teaspoon) and products with baking powder, such as commercial waffles (438 mg. per 2 frozen waffles) and pancake mixes (456 mg. per 3 plain pancakes), are often high in sodium. Most granola cereals are fairly low in sodium (60 mg. or less per ⅓ cup) but are very high in sugar. Ready-to-eat cereals lowest in sodium are shredded wheat, puffed wheat, and puffed rice. Most ready-to-eat cereals contain from 250 to 400 mg. per serving. Most slow-cooking hot cereals have only 5 mg. sodium or less per serving such as regular Cream of Wheat or grits, Malt-O-Meal, Wheatena, and Quaker Old Fashioned oatmeal. Quick and instant cereals can be high in sodium.

15. a. Commercial desserts range in sodium from 100 mg. to 500 mg. of sodium per serving. On the average, however, they contain 200 mg. to 250 mg. of sodium per serving.

Refer to the Appendix for the specific sodium content of various foods. The week's menu pattern, in Chapter 8, will help you plan your own low-sodium diet.

3

The Trials and Tribulations of Excess Body Fat

The pressure is on. Society's constant reminder that fat is unsightly and socially unacceptable has consumers spending billions of dollars to wage an all-out attack on fat. The victory scene often depicted is one of a multitude of envious eyes ogling a slender, lithe figure confidently strolling by. Medical science paints a more realistic picture: Lose excess fat now if you want to be around long enough for the opportunity to lose weight and parade a new physique.

Evidence abounds that the obese suffer to a greater degree from such health disorders as cardiovascular disease, high blood pressure, diabetes mellitus, kidney disease, gallstones, and some cancers than the nonobese do. It's no wonder the life expectancy of the obese is less than optimistic. This does not imply that one should resign oneself to a short, bleak, pudgy life. On the contrary, when an obese person takes on the challenge to lose weight and succeeds, his medical outlook improves remarkably. High blood pressure drops and individuals diagnosed with diabetes mellitus have been known to be freed from its symptoms or find medication no longer necessary.

Whether excess fat is moderate or extreme, physical, social, and psychological limitations are frequently encountered. With excess fat, one's reduced flexibility and agility have social repercussions. The inability or unwillingness to participate in group activities and embarrassment or self-consciousness may hinder the desire to socialize with others. Psychologically, excess fat causes many to lose their self-esteem.

WHO ARE THE OBESE AND OVERWEIGHT?

For years, persons have been classified as "obese" if they were 20 percent above the ideal body weight (IBW) on height-weight tables published by insurance companies. The "overweight" were those 10 percent over these standards.

Another guideline for establishing ideal body weight and defining these terms has been the following:

IBW for women = 100 pounds at 5 feet plus 5 pounds for every additional 1 inch.

IBW for men = 106 pounds at 5 feet plus 6 pounds for every additional 1 inch.

Adjust 10 percent up or down depending on large or small frame. Obesity and overweight would again be determined as those over 20 and 10 percent of the IBW, respectively.

These methods can still be used to give us a rough estimate of our desirable weight (the term "ideal" body weight is unrealistic and will be replaced with the term "desirable" weight). For greater accuracy of one's desired weight, bone structure or body frame and muscle build must be considered as well.

An individual with greater bone and muscle mass may weigh well over the standards set in various charts but could hardly be defined as overweight or obese. For example, a linebacker on the 49ers may weigh 250 pounds yet possess 15 percent or less body fat. True obesity or overweight, therefore, must be defined as the percentage of excess body fat. Muscle and bone are essential for health; excess fat is not. Total body fat in excess of 30 percent in women and 24 percent in men is the criterion commonly used to classify obesity.

A precise analysis of total body fat requires costly laboratory testing. Since this is not feasible for most people, a combination of simple tests follow which should help you to determine your fat status.

First, determine your desirable weight from an insurance table readily available in many books or use the 100 pounds at 5 feet plus 5 or 6 pounds for each added inch as a guideline. Then determine your body frame or bone size to adjust this weight. We may have been created equal in many ways, but we do not all have large frames!

Second, if you find your weight exceeds that recommended in the tables, consider your muscle tone. Do you frequently participate in a vigorous exercise program (at least 3 times per week) such as weight training, jogging, aerobic dancing, or similar muscle toning and building activities? Then those extra pounds may be muscle mass. If you are above the desired weight or even within the range but hold an 8 to 5 job and only occasionally participate in sports on weekends, your excess weight or present weight may be hard to justify. Muscle mass diminishes if demand is not placed on them by exercising regularly. It is possible for an individual to live a sedentary life for years and not gain weight. Such a person may have a decline in muscle weight due to disuse but compensate for this loss in weight with an increase in body fat weight. The reason some have gained weight over the years is because they have exceeded their caloric needs.

The moment of truth arrives after the initial determination of your desirable weight. If you have any doubt, try these simple tests to determine your degree of "fatness":

- Stand naked in front of a mirror. Fun house mirrors may lie but household mirrors reveal all.

- Pinch the fat from the back of your upper arm or from the back below the shoulder blades. If you can pinch an inch, excess fat resides.

- Compare your waist and chest measurements. If the former exceeds the latter, it's time to lose fat.

CALORIES DO COUNT

Were your test results far from favorable and have you decided it's time to lose fat weight? Then the first step is to face the sad but undeniable fact that calories do count. The popular weight-loss diets promising the incredible — from "eat anything and lose weight" to "shed 10 pounds in two days" — are just that, incredible.

Calorie is the unit of measure used to indicate the amount of energy foods provide to maintain vital body functions and to do work. Calories consumed in excess of the amount we expend is deposited as fat. Only the nutrients, carbohydrates, proteins, and fat from foods provide calories. Vitamins and minerals assist in releasing energy from these nutrients. They do not provide calories or energy per se.

Carbohydrates are primarily found in breads and cereals, fruits and vegetables, and dairy products. They provide 4 calories per gram. Protein also provides 4 calories per gram and is mainly found in meats, fish, poultry, eggs, dairy products, legumes, tofu, nuts, and seeds. Fats provide a whopping 9 calories per gram. Obvious sources are butter, margarine, oils, salad dressings, and gravies. Other sources include dairy products high in fat (cream, half-and-half, whole milk, whole milk cheeses) and protein foods high in fat (sausage, luncheon meats, fatty cuts of meat, nuts, and seeds). Unsuspecting sources of fat are avocados, olives, and baked products, such as Danish pastries and croissants.

Knowing the nutritive and caloric content of carbohydrates, proteins, and fats and applying these facts knowledgeably can help you enormously in your weight-loss efforts. For example, it is unwise to eliminate breads and starches from a dieter's meal plan because grain products provide essential nutrients. Also, as a carbohydrate, they contain less than half the calories of fat. Only a small quantity of fat is needed for good health. Therefore, reducing excess fat would not deprive the body of nutrients and could greatly decrease your calorie intake. Cutting down fat additionally decreases the saturated fat consumed.

A pound of fat equals approximately 3,500 calories of stored energy. To lose 1 pound of fat each week, the daily calorie intake must be reduced by 500 calories (500 calories by 7 days = 3,500 calories). A 2-pound weight loss each week would require a deficit of 1,000 calories each day. Popular diets that advocate an imbalance of nutrients, such as high-protein, low-carbohydrate diets initially seem successful, but weight loss is from water loss and the elimination of many nutritious foods from the diet. After all, one can only eat so much protein. In the long run, such diets are medically unsound, and most dieters regain the weight they have lost — and sometimes more.

The most effective way to lose body fat is through a planned exercise program in conjunction with a low-calorie diet. Regular exercise burns calories not only during the activity but for several hours after the exercise is completed. An hour of brisk walking every day expends 250 calories a day which adds up to about 26 pounds a year, provided the calorie intake remains unchanged. Exercise has several other benefits, including a decrease in appetite, reduction in high blood pressure, muscle toning, and improved heart and respiratory function. Before beginning an exercise plan, you should consult with your physician.

In addition to an exercise program, a well-balanced and nutritious low-calorie diet is indispensable. Calorie requirements differ from one individual to another. A 1,200-calorie diet for women and a 1,500-calorie diet for men will usually meet their nutritional needs and allow a 1-to 2-pound weight loss every week.

GETTING THE MOST OUT OF WHAT YOU EAT

Merely adhering to a 1,200- or 1,500-calorie diet is not enough. How you spend those calories is crucial. Just as a person must budget his expenses on a limited income, so you, the dieter, must wisely purchase all the essential nutrients on a limited-calorie allowance. This concept of purchasing foods high in nutrition but relatively low in calories is known as *Nutrient Density*. To get the most out of what you eat, choose foods from the Basic

Four Food Groups that are low in fats and in concentrated sugars, such as sugar or honey.

The following chart is based on the Basic Four and gives you a guide for good nutrition. By fulfilling the recommended servings per day, your calorie intake will be approximately 1,200 to 1,300 calories per day. This includes 1 tablespoon of vegetable fat needed by women for good nutrition. Men should add an additional tablespoon of vegetable fat. The Basic Four chart assumes you will select a variety of foods low in fat and sweets and in the portion sizes suggested. For example, 2 servings from the Milk Group would mean choosing 2 items low in fat, such as 1 cup of non-fat or low-fat milk and 1 cup of plain yogurt. Also, 4 servings from the Bread Group assumes your choices include 1-slice portions of plain whole grain or enriched breads, ½-cup servings of noodles or rice, or ¾-cup servings of plain ready-to-eat cereals, rather than a croissant and ¾-cup of granola as two of your 4 servings from the Bread Group.

Men on 1,500 calories or more per day are encouraged to get the extra calories from within the Basic Four. Composition tables in the Appendix list the calorie content of various foods. We suggest you use these lists to plan for those extra calories. In addition, a week's menus have been planned for 1,200, 1,500, and 1,800 calories per day with a sensible or low-sodium level.

A sensible weight-loss program is extremely important to stay in good health and maintain a permanent loss. A quick weight loss through crash diets, fasting, or similar methods may result in as much muscle loss as fat and does not foster good eating habits. Your weight-loss plan should help you look and feel good inside and out.

RECOMMENDED
   SERVINGS   **BASIC FOUR FOOD GROUPS**
   EACH DAY   **(Portion Size Equals One Serving)**

      2   **MILK AND MILK PRODUCTS GROUP**

     1 cup non-fat or low-fat milk
     1 cup plain low-fat yogurt
     1 cup custard, made with non-fat or low-fat milk and egg allowance
    1½ ounces low-fat cheese*
     ½ cup low-fat cottage cheese*

*Cheese contains a substantial amount of sodium and should be used with discretion.

2   **MEAT AND MEAT SUBSTITUTE GROUP**

2–3 ounces fish, poultry (without skin), or lean meat**
2   eggs (limit to 3 eggs per week)
1   cup cooked beans, peas, or lentils
1   cup tofu

4   **FRUIT AND VEGETABLE GROUP† including:**

One *VITAMIN C* source
½   cup orange or grapefruit juice (unsweetened)
¾   cup or more of strawberries, papaya, orange, cantaloupe, deep green leafy greens, such as collard or mustard greens, cauliflower, broccoli, bok choy, brussels sprouts, or green bell pepper

One *VITAMIN A* source
¾   cup or more of deep green vegetables, such as spinach, collard or mustard greens, broccoli, or deep yellow-orange vegetables and fruits, such as carrots, sweet potatoes, pumpkin, winter squash, cantaloupe, apricots, or papaya
2   additional servings of fruits and vegetables

4   **BREAD AND CEREAL GROUP‡**

1   slice of whole grain or enriched bread
1   plain roll, biscuit, muffin, or tortilla (made with minimal amounts of fats and sugars)
4   crackers
½   cup cooked cereals
¾   cup ready-to-eat cereals without excess amounts of sugars added
½   cup cooked rice, noodles, or potatoes
3   tablespoons wheat germ without added sugars

A small quantity of fat, preferably from a polyunsaturated vegetable source, should be included in one's daily diet. Women need approximately 1 tablespoon and men need 2 tablespoons per day. Do keep in mind the fat used in cooking.

**Fresh fish, poultry, and meats are low in sodium. Canned, cured, and smoked fish and meats are very high in sodium. Frozen entrees are also high in sodium.
† Canned fruits should be packed in water or their own juice. They contain minimal amounts of sodium. Canned and some frozen vegetables contain considerable amounts of sodium.
‡ Avoid crackers, cereals, and quick breads high in sodium.
Refer to the composition tables in Chapter 8 for further assistance.

CALORIE CONSCIOUSNESS QUIZ

Take a few moments to complete the quiz (yes, another one!). It will give you additional facts and hints on good nutrition and weight-loss techniques.

1. A successful weight-loss plan should include:
   a. only 800 calories per day.
   b. acidic foods to assist in the burning of fat.
   c. vitamin and mineral supplements to burn off fat.
   d. all of the above.
   e. none of the above.

2. A situation that may cause you to eat more than you should is:
   a. eating fast.
   b. eating in front of the television.
   c. skipping meals.
   d. all of the above.
   e. none of the above.

3. Many foods contain hidden sources of sucrose (table sugar). Which of the following foods contains the most sucrose?
   a. ½ cup sherbet.
   b. ½ cup Jell-O.
   c. 12-ounce can of cola.
   d. 1 slice (4 ounces) of cheesecake.
   e. 1½-ounce milk chocolate candy bar.

4. Which ready-to-eat cereal contains the lowest percentage of sugar?
   a. All-Bran.
   b. Cheerios.
   c. Shredded Wheat.
   d. Quaker's 100% Natural.
   e. Special K.

5. Which ready-to-eat cereal contains the greatest percentage of sugar?
   a. Sugar Smacks.
   b. King Vitamin.
   c. Apple Jacks.
   d. Cocoa Pebbles.
   e. Cinnamon Crunch.

6. Fructose contains:
   a. less than half the calories of table sugar.
   b. less than one-third the calories of table sugar.
   c. about the same number of calories as table sugar.
   d. twice the calories of table sugar.
   e. none of the above.

7. A food labeled "dietetic" must by law contain no more than:
   a. 10 calories per serving.
   b. 15 calories per serving.
   c. 25 calories per serving.
   d. 50 calories per serving.
   e. none of the above.

8. The concentrated sugar which provides essentially "empty" calories is:
   a. granulated sugar (table sugar).
   b. honey.
   c. powdered sugar.
   d. a and c.
   e. all of the above.

9. Which food has the greatest amount of hidden fat?
   a. 1 ounce of American cheese.
   b. 10 giant-size ripe olives.
   c. 1 cup whole milk.
   d. ½ of an avocado.
   e. ½ cup (small scoop) of rich ice cream.

10. Which fat contains the fewest calories?
    a. 1 tablespoon of bacon fat.
    b. 1 tablespoon of chicken fat.
    c. 1 tablespoon of corn oil.
    d. 1 tablespoon of cottonseed oil.
    e. none of the above.

11. Two servings a day from the *Milk and Milk Products Group* are recommended for good nutrition. Of the following foods, which should be used *judiciously* because of its lower nutrient density?
    a. low-fat milk.
    b. cream cheese.
    c. low-fat cottage cheese.
    d. Swiss cheese.
    e. plain yogurt with fresh berries.

12. Two servings a day from the *Meat and Meat Substitute Group* are recommended for good nutrition. Of the following foods, which should be used *judiciously* because of its lower nutrient density?
    a. eggs.
    b. tofu.
    c. chicken.
    d. bacon.
    e. squid.

13. Four servings a day from the *Fruit and Vegetable Group* are recommended for good nutrition. Of the following foods, which should be used *judiciously* because of its lower nutrient density?
    a. banana.
    b. frozen orange juice concentrate.
    c. fortified orange drink.
    d. dried apricots.
    e. carrot–raisin salad.

14. Four servings a day from the *Bread and Cereal Group* are recommended for good nutrition. Of the following foods, which should be used *judiciously* because of its lower nutrient density?
    a. tortilla.
    b. french fried potatoes.
    c. whole wheat bread.
    d. white enriched bread.
    e. whole wheat pancakes.

15. Alcoholic beverages:
    a. contain more calories than carbohydrates (weight for weight).
    b. contain less calories than fat (weight for weight).
    c. contain empty calories.
    d. all of the above.
    e. none of the above.

Answers to the Calorie Consciousness Quiz

1. e. A weight-loss program should contain preferably 1,200 calories per day for women and 1,500 calories for men from the Basic Four Food Groups. A slightly lower calorie plan may be utilized under medical supervision. There are no special supplements, foods, or combination of foods that will promote faster weight loss through the burning of fat.

2. d. To successfully lose weight, a person should eat three nutritious meals per day and enjoy every morsel. Poor eating habits such as eating in less than 20 minutes, eating while doing other activities (watching television, reading, walking) and eating out of boredom or anxiety can cause a person to overeat, feel guilty, and even binge.

3. a. The number of teaspoons of sugar in ½ cup sherbet (9 teaspoons), ½ cup Jell-O (7 teaspoons) and 12-ounce can cola (7 teaspoons), is quite amazing. A slice of cheesecake (2 teaspoons) and 1½-ounce milk chocolate candy bar (2½ teaspoons) are relatively low in total number of teaspoons of sugar but are significant in calories because of their high fat content.

4. c. The percentages of sugar in these items are: All-Bran (19 percent), Cheerios (3 percent), Shredded Wheat (1 percent), Quaker's 100% Natural (21 percent), Special K (5 percent). Other cereals containing 5 percent or less sugar are: Wheat or Corn Chex, Wheaties, Corn Flakes, Instant Quaker Oatmeal (regular), Cream of Rice.

5. a. The percentage of sugar in all these cereals exceeds 50 percent, specifically, their sugar content is: Sugar Smacks (61 percent), King Vitamin (58 percent), Apple Jacks (55 percent), Cocoa Pebbles (53 percent), Cinnamon Crunch (50 percent).

6. c. Fructose and sucrose (table sugar) contain 4 calories per gram. Fructose is sweeter than sucrose, so less may be used.

7. e. The term "dietetic" does not guarantee any level of calories per serving. For example, "dietetic" ice cream can contain 100 to 180 calories per serving. Since items labeled "dietetic" generally indicate the caloric content, read the label to be sure.

8. e. Honey, raw sugar, and brown sugar are often promoted as being superior to table sugar. When one considers the trace amounts of nutrients in all these types of sugars, all can be considered a source of "empty" calories.

9. d. The fat content of these items is: 1 ounce cheese (8.5 gms.), 10 giant-size ripe olives (9.5 grms.), 1 cup whole milk (8.5 gms.), ½ of an avocado (18.5 gms.), and ½ cup rich ice cream (11.9 gms.) of fat. One cannot totally eliminate all foods high in fat. Some, such as avocados, can be enjoyed occasionally. Substitutes should be used when available such as low-fat milk and low-fat cheese and low-fat frozen yogurt.

10. **e.** All contain 126 calories per tablespoon. However, the type of fat makes a considerable difference. Bacon and chicken fat are high in saturated fat and should be avoided. Whereas, liquid vegetable oils, like cottonseed and corn oil, are higher in the more desirable poly-unsaturated fats. Some rich sources of fat may contain fewer calories because of ingredients added to "dilute" the calorie content. For example, diet margarine may have water and air whipped into it and mayonnaise has eggs and vinegar mixed in.

11. **b.** Cream cheese is 92 percent fat and is, therefore, considered a very low nutrient density food. Non-fat milk, low-fat milk, and low-fat plain yogurt rate high in nutrients and low in calories. These make excellent choices to meet the two required servings from the Milk Group. Cheese, such as low-fat cottage cheese and Swiss cheese, are nutritious but quite high in sodium. They should be used judiciously.

12. **d.** Bacon is 82 percent fat and not a wise choice to meet protein needs normally supplied by this group. Poultry, fish, lean meats, and eggs are excellent nutrient-dense protein sources. Eggs and squid should be limited due to their high cholesterol content.

13. **c.** Fortified fruit drinks should not be mistaken for fruit juices. Fortified means a nutrient such as vitamin C has been added to essentially a sugar-based fruit-flavored beverage. Carrot–raisin salad is very nutritious and can be low in calories if an excess amount of mayonnaise is not used.

14. **b.** The potato is a nutritious food, but the deep-fat frying more than doubles its caloric value without adding nutrients. Pancakes are also a good choice. It's the butter and syrup one adds that reduces its nutrient density.

15. **d.** Alcohol contains 7 calories per gram as compared to 4 calories per gram in carbohydrates and proteins and 9 calories per gram in fat. It provides minimal amounts of nutrients and is considered a source of empty calories.

4

Condiments and Foodstuffs Used in Chinese Cooking

Chinese cuisine is distinguished not only by cooking techniques but also by the artful use of interesting spices and sauces. The condiments used in the recipes of this book are from the South (Cantonese), North (Peking and Shantung), East (Shanghai and Chekiang), and the West (Szechwan and Hunan). While many of the condiments are common to all Chinese regional cooking, some are used prominently in certain regions. In the descriptions of the various condiments, we will mention this point where applicable.

DRY CONDIMENTS

The dry condiments described in this section may be kept indefinitely without refrigeration, as long as they are kept in sealed or airtight containers. They should be stored in a dry, cool area of the kitchen, where there is no direct sunlight. (See Preparation Techniques for preparation of some of these condiments for cooking.)

Dried Mushrooms

Chinese dried mushrooms are very different from the familiar button variety. These crusty parasol-shaped mushrooms are hard, black on top, and light brown underneath. They must be soaked before cooking. The stems are cut away and only the caps are used. The mushrooms have a pleasing herbal flavor and the texture is velvety soft and smooth when cooked. These mushrooms are commonly used in a variety of meat and vegetable dishes.

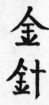

Dried Red Chili Peppers

These small red peppers are spicy hot and indispensable for Szechwan and Hunan dishes. They may be used whole or flaked. Usually stir-fried in hot oil to bring out the aroma and zestiness, a few peppers will add sparkle and tingle to any dish (if flaked use even less)!

Dried Shrimp

These are small shrimp that have been dried. When these shrimp are minced and stir-fried in hot oil, they impart a distinctive "sea breeze" flavor to vegetable dishes. Dried shrimp must be soaked before cooking (see Preparation Techniques).

Five Spice Powder

Consisting of powdered star anise, Szechwan pepper, cinnamon, mandarin orange peel, and clove, this condiment is mild and very fragrant. A quarter teaspoon generally is enough to add fragrance to a dish. Five spice powder goes well with meat dishes.

Gum Jum (Dried Lily Flowers or Buds)

The translation of gum jum is "gold needles." Golden brown and string-like (3 to 4 inches long) in appearance, gum jum have a mild, appealing herbal taste. They have to be soaked before cooking (see Preparation Techniques). They are often used in vegetarian dishes and also with Moo Shu Pork.

Salted Black Beans

This Cantonese condiment is used in a variety of dishes to impart a distinctive beany, salty taste. Salted black beans are usually mashed and accompanied by fresh garlic in cooking. The beans should be rinsed several times before being mashed to get rid of impurities and excess salt.

Star Anise

A hard, star-shaped brownish seed, star anise has a distinctive licorice flavor. One or two of these seeds would give a stewed meat dish an exquisite flavor.

Szechwan Peppercorns

Reddish brown and somewhat resembling ordinary black peppercorns, this spice adds a flowery fragrance and sharpness to a dish. Sometimes used to help eliminate the strong odor of some meats and fish, a few of these peppercorns give a subtle fragrance; a lot will be mouth-tingling hot. Since biting into this spice is an unpleasant experience, Szechwan peppercorns should be wrapped in cheesecloth for stewing dishes, or filtered out if used for flavoring cooking oil.

White Ground Pepper

The main difference between white and black pepper is that the white variety has the black hull milled out, and the flavor is less pungent. Most Chinese dishes are seasoned with the subtler white pepper. It keeps as well as black pepper.

Wood Fungus (Mook Yee)

Mook yee means "wood ears," as they grow on the bark of trees. Hard, wrinkled, and black-gray in appearance, they are in the mushroom family. Mook yee must be soaked before cooking (see Preparation Techniques). When soaked, they expand to two or three times their original size. Any remaining hard parts should be cut away. Mook yee are neutral in taste but are valued for their crispy texture. They are used in both vegetable and meat dishes.

FRESH CONDIMENTS

Garlic

Fresh garlic is used to add fragrance and zest to foods, especially to meat dishes. Often, garlic is browned in oil before the main ingredients are put in for frying or braising. Garlic cloves are first smashed with the broad side of the Chinese cleaver and peeled prior to browning. For stronger flavor, garlic is sometimes minced before it is added to the hot oil in the pan. The garlic should not be scorched during browning. It may be discarded if desired.

Ginger

Because of its tangy taste and ability to neutralize strong odors and tastes, fresh ginger is employed in many Chinese dishes. A slice of ginger in one of our recipes is defined as a piece about 1 inch in diameter by ⅛ inch thick. Like garlic, ginger is peeled and then smashed with the broad side of the cleaver to release more flavor. If it is used to flavor the cooking oil, the ginger may be discarded after browning.

花椒 白胡椒粉 木耳

Green Onion (Scallion)

Often utilized as a garnish because of its pleasing bright color, fresh green onion is valued in cooking for its aromatic flavor. The green part has a stronger flavor than the white. Slivers, lengths, or sections of green onions are often called for in meat and vegetable dishes.

OILS

Cooking Oils

Safflower, corn, or soybean oils may be used to turn out great Chinese dishes. Although it is true that peanut oil is commonly used in Chinese cooking, nutritionally, safflower oil is the best, as it contains the least amount of saturated fat and the greatest amount of polyunsaturated fat. We prefer not to use fully or partially hydrogenated vegetable oils because of their relatively higher degree of saturation and tendency to impart a distinctive taste to the food.

Flavoring Oils

Sesame Oil Valued for its unique nutty fragrance, sesame oil is frequently used in marinades and sprinkled on meat or vegetable dishes as a flavor enhancer immediately before the dishes are taken out of the cooking pan. It is seldom utilized for frying because it becomes smoky and pungent at high temperature. For a full-flavor sesame oil, be sure you purchase the Oriental type which lists sesame oil as its first ingredient. Please read the label carefully so that you get the sesame oil you want. There is nothing like pure sesame oil for that appetizing nutty flavor!

Chili Oil This red, spicy hot oil may be purchased in most Chinese grocery stores. The oil is made from deep-frying red chili peppers. It is used as a table seasoning and also for cooking Northern and Western Chinese regional dishes. If chili oil is not available, you can prepare your own by heating ¼ cup of oil over medium-high heat. Then put in 4 dried red chili peppers and stir. When the peppers turn black, keep stirring for another minute. Remove the pan from the heat and let the oil cool. The color may not be red but the oil will be peppery hot. If redness is desired, add ⅛ teaspoon of cayenne pepper while the oil is still hot. When the cayenne also turns black, let the oil cool. Then filter the oil through cheesecloth to remove the solids. The oil will keep for about a month or more if kept in an airtight bottle or jar.

SAUCES AND PASTES

Bean Sauce

This mild sauce is the fraternal twin of the Szechwan hot bean sauce, except it contains no chili. If spicy hotness is a problem, this sauce is an excellent substitute for the hot bean sauce (see Hot Bean Sauce). Should be refrigerated in an airtight jar.

Chee Hou Sauce

Made of sugar, vinegar, soy beans, water, salt, garlic, sesame seeds, chili, and spices, this Cantonese sauce has a sweet, mild garlicky flavor. Since very little chili is employed, you can hardly feel the hotness. Chee hou sauce imparts a pleasant flavor to meat and tofu dishes. Should be refrigerated in an airtight jar.

Fermented Bean Cake (Furu)

Made of fermented soy beans, salt, and alcohol, this Cantonese condiment is used in both meat and vegetable dishes. The taste is uniquely winy and slightly pungent. Does not need to be refrigerated but should be stored in an airtight jar.

Ground Bean Sauce (Mien See)

Consisting of soy beans, salt, flour, and sugar, this Cantonese sauce is used in steamed or stewed fish and meat dishes. Since it contains no spices, the taste is salty and beany. Should be refrigerated in an airtight jar.

Hoisin Sauce

Made from sugar, vinegar, soy beans, water, salt, flour, garlic, sesame seeds, chili, and spices, this Cantonese sauce is sweeter than the chee hou sauce and has a tangy taste to it. It is great for meat dishes. Should be refrigerated in an airtight jar.

Hot Bean Sauce

This Szechwan sauce, made of soy and kidney beans, fresh chili, flour, sesame oil, salt, sugar, and spices, is peppery hot and tasty. A half to a teaspoonful of this sauce will make most meat or tofu dishes tingle with flavor. The key Chinese character to look for on the label is 辣, which means spicy hot! Should be refrigerated in an airtight jar.

豆瓣醬 柱侯醬 腐乳 麵豉 海鮮醬 辣豆瓣醬

蠔
油
南
乳
沙
茶
醬
芝
麻
醬
鹹
蝦
甜
麵
醬

Oyster Flavored Sauce

Called oyster sauce in this book, it is a popular Cantonese condiment. Consisting of oyster extracts, salt, water, and cornstarch, it does not taste like oysters. It has a delicious meaty, sweet-salty taste. Fantastic with meat and tofu dishes. Need not be refrigerated but should be tightly covered.

Red Fermented Bean Cake

Consisting of fermented soy beans, salt, wine, and red rice, this close cousin of fermented bean cake is also fairly close in flavor. The taste is sweeter and fuller in flavor. It is good with meat dishes and imparts a reddish color to the ingredients. Need not be refrigerated but should be kept in an airtight jar.

Satay Sauce

A Cantonese sauce that may have its origin in the Malay Peninsula. It has an interesting barbecue flavor to it. Made of soy sauce, sugar, oil, peanut, chili, onion, garlic, shrimp, and spices, this sauce is terrific with meats stir-fried with onions, shallots, and/or green bell peppers. Should be refrigerated in an airtight jar.

Sesame Paste

A popular paste used in Northern and Western Chinese regional cooking, it is made of pureed sesame seeds and sesame oil only. This paste has a rich nutty flavor, wonderful for cold dishes. Keeps as well as peanut butter. If sesame is unavailable, peanut butter may be used as a substitute.

Shrimp Sauce

Perhaps the most exotic of the common Chinese sauces, this Cantonese "soul" sauce is made from fermented shrimp extracts and salt. Used in steamed meat dishes, this shrimp sauce is usually accompanied with fresh ginger slivers to balance the fishy flavor. Granted, the taste is exotic, but it is worth trying. Should be refrigerated in an airtight jar.

Sweet Bean Sauce

This Northern sauce is the counterpart of the Cantonese hoisin sauce. Made from soy beans, rice, tomato paste, water, sugar, maltose, salt, red pepper, garlic, sesame seed, and natural spices, sweet bean sauce is somewhat milder and less sweet than the hoisin sauce. The two sauces are interchangeable.

SOY SAUCES

There are basically two major kinds of soy sauces used in Chinese cooking for flavoring: *dark soy* and *light soy,* with shades in between. There is a great deal of confusion on the labels of soy sauces because some brands do not specify in English whether they are light soy or dark soy. The best way to identify which is by two Chinese ideograms. If you see the ideogram 生 somewhere near the center of the label, you have located a bottle of light soy. If you make out this character 老 on the label, you have a genuine bottle of dark soy!

A minor kind of soy sauce which is less salty, called thick soy, is used primarily for coloring and secondarily for flavoring.

Light Soy Sauce

This Cantonese soy sauce adds less color when used and has a more subtle flavor than the dark variety. If you want a dish to retain its natural coloring and flavor, you would use light soy for the dish. For example, light soy is preferred in most seafood dishes in order to preserve their delicate flavors and colors. If light soy is unavailable, dark soy will do as a substitute. In general, light soy contains approximately 1,300 mg. sodium per tablespoon. However, if you use Gold Orchid light soy, the sodium content goes down to approximately 1,000 mg. per tablespoon.

Dark Soy Sauce

This soy has more of the reddish-brown coloring and flavor that you associate with soy sauce. All-purpose soy sauce is considered to be in this category. Dark soy is excellent for red-cooked (stewed) and spicy meat and vegetable dishes. There is a wide variation of sodium content between brands. The brands which contain a consistently lower sodium level, approximately 1,000 mg. per tablespoon, are Kimlan, Kikkoman, and Yamasa All Purpose Soy Sauce. If a lower sodium level soy sauce is desired, then Kimlan Saltish Soy Sauce or Kikkoman Milder Soy Sauce, which both contain approximately 620 mg. of sodium per tablespoon, would be suitable. These two are referred to in the recipes as lower sodium soy sauce.

Thick Soy Sauce

Although it is a concentrated version of regular soy sauce, thick soy contains less salt. Made of molasses, salt, and soy bean extracts, it is valued for its rich reddish-brown coloring and strong soy saucy flavor. The sodium content is approximately 750 mg. per tablespoon. Half a teaspoon will impart strong coloring and flavor to many dishes.

生抽

老抽

珠油

鎮江醋 浙醋 竹筍 腐竹 圓竹 芽菜 粉絲

VINEGARS

Chinkiang Vinegar (Chinese Brown Vinegar)

Chinese vinegars are rice-based and are generally not as sour as their Western counterparts. This particular vinegar is mixed with spices to give it a fragrant herbal bouquet. Chinkiang vinegar is used frequently in Eastern and Northern Chinese regional dishes.

Chinese Red Vinegar

This vinegar has a very light taste. Again, it is not as sour as ordinary vinegar. A dash does wonders to eliminate strong odors in meat and sea-food dishes. Chinese red vinegar has a delightfully sweetish taste for a vinegar.

FOODSTUFFS USED IN CHINESE COOKING

Bamboo Shoots These crunchy ivory-colored shoots are commonly available in cans and come in chunks, slices, matchsticks, or diced. Bamboo shoots are used as a complement in a dish to add color, variation, lightness, and texture. The taste is very mild.

Bean Curd Skin This yellowish, thin, flat sheet is the skin which forms on the surface of a cooling pan of boiled soy milk. The skin is then dried and packaged. Bean curd skin has to be soaked to soften before cooking (see Preparation Techniques). It has a slight nutty flavor. Store in a tightly closed bag; should keep for a few months before turning rancid.

Bean Curd Stick It is made the same way as bean curd skin, except it is rolled up and comes packaged as a folded stick. Must be soaked longer than bean curd skin prior to cooking.

Bean Sprouts There are two varieties of bean sprouts. The less common one is sprouted from soy beans and has large heads. The most common variety is sprouted from tiny green mung beans. All fresh bean sprouts have yellow heads and white translucent shoots of about 2 to 3 inches. They require a very short cooking time. When stir-fried, they have a juicy crunchy texture and a refreshingly subtle flavor.

Bean Threads Made from mung beans, these translucent noodle-like threads will take on the taste and aroma of any seasonings added to them. Bean threads come from the store dry and hard. They need to be soaked or blanched before cooking. When softened, bean threads have a resilient, smooth consistency.

Bitter Melon A very unusual vegetable, this bright green bumpy cucumber-sized melon has a bitter taste to the unfamiliar palate. Chinese say the taste has to be acquired. Afficionados say the taste is refreshingly golden.

Bok Choy This green leafy vegetable with long white stalks is very popular among Chinese. Somewhat resembling Swiss chard in taste, bok choy is sweeter, juicier, and milder. The texture is crisp when not overcooked. The best type of bok choy, called choy sum, is the smaller stalk with little yellow flower blossoms in the center of the top.

Chinese Broccoli With a color resembling collard greens, this leafy vegetable has a crunchy, slightly mustardy flavor. Usually stir-fried, Chinese broccoli is a favorite vegetable among Chinese people.

Fuzzy Melon A fuzzy-looking green melon that has a pleasant mild flavor, this vegetable is usually stewed or steamed. Except for the skin, which is removed with a peeler, the whole melon is edible, including the tender seeds. When cooked, fuzzy melon has a tender and silky smooth texture.

Law Bak (Daikon) (Chinese White Turnip) A white turnip that may be shaped like an eggplant or a cylinder of 1 inch to 2½ inches, this root vegetable has a slight sharp taste but milder than that of the common red radish. The skin is removed with a peeler before cooking. The texture of law bak resembles that of radish.

Napa or Chinese Cabbage (Celery Cabbage) With light yellow leaves and white stalks, this tightly wrapped leafy vegetable is milder and has a more delicate flavor than the common cabbage. When cooked, Napa cabbage is soft and moist.

Snow Peas The name "snow peas" encompasses not only the peas but also the tender green pods as well. These crispy peas (and pods) are subtly sweet and delicate in taste. Their fresh color and crisp texture lightens heavy meat dishes.

苦瓜 白菜 芥蘭 節瓜 蘿蔔 蕹菜 雪豆

豆
腐

水
豆
腐

馬
蹄

冬
瓜

Tofu, Regular or Firm Made from soy milk, tofu is an important source of protein in the Chinese diet. It has a pleasing white color and the ability to absorb the flavors of sauces and condiments added to it. Tofu may be fried, stuffed, and broiled.

Tofu, Soft Similar to regular tofu, this tofu has a greater water content. Soft tofu is valued for its custard-like silky smooth texture. It is usually cooked by gentle stir-frying and steaming. Soft tofu is much too fragile and watery for stuffing or broiling.

Water Chestnut This is the bulb part of a plant grown in watery fields. It has a thin leather-like dark brown skin and succulent, crunchy white flesh. It is commonly available in cans. Fresh water chestnuts sometimes are available in Chinese grocery stores.

Winter Melon This melon is as big as a pumpkin and has a hard, waxy green skin. It is sold by the slice in Chinese groceries. Only the cooked firm white flesh is eaten. The skin, center pulpy part, and the seeds are discarded. The taste is subtle and mild.

Chinese Preparation Techniques

FIRST THINGS FIRST

Before you start cooking a dish, please sit down and read through the recipe completely. The recipe format presupposes that all the ingredients are prepared and at hand so that the cooking may proceed efficiently without any last-minute frantic search for a missing item.

- Be sure to allow about 20 minutes (longer if specified) for any ingredients that require presoaking.
- Cut the meat and vegetables ahead of time.
- Measure and mix separately the marinades, sauces, and cornstarch mixture. Set within easy reach.
- Have the proper pots, pans, and utensils ready.

LIQUID PREPARATIONS

Marinades

Primarily, marinades tenderize, add or enhance flavor, and improve meat texture. Sometimes they also act to help eliminate strong tastes and odors. Wine and vinegar are tenderizing agents. Flavoring agents are soy sauce, ginger, garlic, green onion (scallion), sesame oil, sugar, and white pepper. The texture-improving agents are cornstarch and egg white. Ginger and Chinese red vinegar may be used effectively to neutralize strong tastes and odors, particularly in fish and seafood. These agents may be used in various combinations. Meats and seafood may be marinated for 15 minutes to an hour, depending on convenience or usage.

Sauces

Sauces are used for flavor enhancement and coloring of the various ingredients in a dish. Chinese sauces could be bland, fragrant, hot, or contrasting, such as hot and sour or sweet and sour. Basic condiments for making sauces are soy sauces (light and dark), oyster sauce, Chinese red vinegar, Chinese brown vinegar (Chinkiang), white vinegar, wine, sugar, and various bean-based sauces.

Cornstarch Mixtures

Cornstarch mixture is used as a thickener to give body to the sauce. The Chinese prefer cornstarch to flour because of its translucent and superior thickening properties. The cornstarch mixture should not be stirred in as one of the first cooking steps because the mixture would congeal and slow the cooking process. Cornstarch mixture is usually put into the frying pan as one of the last cooking steps before the dish goes to the table. Because cornstarch has a tendency to settle, it is necessary to suspend the mixture immediately before you stir it into the pan. Continue to stir the contents in the pan until the liquid thickens or the cornstarch may congeal into little glassy lumps.

SOLID PREPARATIONS

Cutting Up the Ingredients

In Chinese cooking, the size and shape of the ingredients are very important to the appearance, texture, and cooking time of each dish. Cutting plays a vital role in the preparation of a Chinese meal. If the different components of a dish are cut improperly, some of the ingredients may be overdone while others remain raw.

It is essential that you use a sharp knife. The best kind to use is a Chinese cleaver. It comes in two or more thicknesses. The thicker ones can chop through small bones and gristle but are relatively heavy. The thinnest one is used for cutting meat and vegetables only. We recommend the latter because it is less fatiguing to use, and the recipes in this book do not call for chopping through bones. If you prefer, you can always get a thicker one later on to complete your knife collection. The broadness of the Chinese cleaver is great for smashing, scooping, and transferring ingredients from the chopping board.

Explanation of some cutting terms:

Chop	Similar to grind. Could be coarse or fine chop.
Cube	Cut in large cubes, approximately ¾ to 1 inch.
Dice	Cut in little cubes, approximately ¼ to ½ inch.

Matchstick	Cut in elongated rectangular shapes approximately ⅛ inch square by 1½ inches long.
Mince	Same as fine chop.
Roll-Cut	Usually for cutting tubular vegetables. Place vegetable horizontally in front of you and make a diagonal cut. With the knife in the same diagonal position, rotate the vegetable half a turn and cut again. Each cut piece should resemble a triangular wedge. With practice, all the pieces will be about the same size.
Shred	Cut in elongated shapes, approximately 1/16 inch square by 1 inch long.
Slice	Cut in thin (⅛ inch or less), broad slices across the grain of the meat with the knife blade slanting away from you. For example, the chunk of meat you are cutting may have a cross section of only 1½ inches wide by ½ inch high. By slicing slantwise, you will be able to turn out slices with cross sections of 1½ inches wide by ¾ inch high.

DRY INGREDIENTS

Items such as dried shrimp, dried mushrooms, and dried bean curd skins and sticks need to be soaked until soft before they are usable. First, we would recommend that you rinse them once or twice before soaking in order to get rid of any surface impurities. Then soak in warm water until soft.

Dried Shrimp Softens easily within 10 to 20 minutes. After being drained, the shrimps are usually chopped coarsely and stir-fried in oil first to bring out the fragrance. Then the major components of the dish are put in.

Dried Mushrooms, Mook Yee, and Lily Buds Need to be soaked for about 20 minutes. From time to time squeeze them to facilitate the softening process. Once softened, all parts of the mook yee and lily buds are used. However, only the caps of the mushrooms need to be softened because the stems are cut off and discarded. When ready, the mushrooms are squeezed to get rid of any excess water. Then prepare the mushrooms, mook yee, and lily buds as directed by the recipe.

Dried Bean Curd Skins and Sticks These take a relatively long time to soften, especially the sticks. The skins may be soaked in hot water for about 1 hour, making sure that they are completely immersed. If they are not soft, then continue to soak a little longer. The bean curd sticks are U-shaped in appearance. Break them in half and soak in water overnight. Turn the immersed sticks occasionally to help the softening process.

Tofu (Soybean Cake)

Because of its substantial protein content and ability to take on the taste and flavor of any condiment, tofu enjoys great popularity among Chinese and Westerners alike. Unlike high-priced steaks, tofu is affordable by both rich and poor. Tofu is cholesterol-free and when eaten with grains, such as rice, its protein quality is like that of meat.

Tofu comes in two styles: soft and firm. Soft tofu is great for most tofu dishes. Its creamy color and silky smoothness is irresistible. Firm tofu is used for dishes that call for pressed or stuffed tofu. Firm tofu may be substituted for soft tofu but not vice versa.

When a recipe calls for pan-fried or stir-fried, the tofu must be drained and then dried with paper towels or a dish towel. If this is not done, the tofu will not brown at all. As tofu comes already cooked, the cooking time for any dish need not be long. If tofu is overcooked, its delectable smoothness will turn coarse and excess amounts of liquid will ooze from the tofu and into the sauce. What a shame that would be!

6

Chinese Cooking Techniques

Chinese cuisine employs a variety of cooking methods to attain its pleasing results. A number of the techniques are similar to those of Western cooking and require no special comments. Some are unique to Chinese cookery or are important to the recipes in this book. We think it is appropriate to discuss some general principles of Chinese cooking before going into the specific techniques.

GENERAL PRINCIPLES

A basic principle of Chinese cooking is to prepare food to the peak of its flavor, texture, and color. Green vegetables should never be cooked until they are limp, dull, and yellow; nor are meats cooked to a stringy toughness. Therefore, a maxim of Chinese food preparation is never to overcook! Undercooking is also undesirable for obvious reasons. Preparing a dish just right does require practice and experience. But cheer up, it does not require as much as you might think!

Another principle is that components of most Chinese dishes are cut into bite size before cooking for easy eating with chopsticks. This preparation also economizes on cooking fuel, as cooking time is shortened because heat penetrates the small pieces quickly.

A further principle of Chinese cuisine is that food should be served immediately after cooking, or as soon as practical. Keeping Chinese food warm in an oven or on a steam table for a long period of time will destroy the intended results of the cooking method. Vegetables will lose their crispness, brilliant colors, and valuable vitamins and meats will taste as unappealing as they look. Chinese food is meant to be enjoyed at the peak

49

of succulence, taste, and aroma. This means that the delectable morsels are to be consumed as soon as they are prepared. Of course, if you are preparing more than one dish, some warming in the oven may be necessary. The main point is to avoid unnecessary delays.

A final and very important principle is that the cooking of the various components of a dish must be timed carefully. All the ingredients are not tossed into the pan to be stir-fried at the same time. Rather, there is a vital sequence in which an ingredient is put into the frying pan. Here is an example of a common sequence in stir-frying:

- Heat oil until hazy. Add ginger, garlic, or other specified condiments.

- Meat is stir-fried until it is approximately 80 percent done and then removed from the pan. This prevents the meat from becoming over-cooked with a resulting dry and stringy texture.

- Vegetables are stir-fried until almost done but still crisp.

- Meat is then returned to the pan and stir-fried until completely cooked. This usually takes less than a minute.

- Sauce is poured in and allowed to bubble.

- The cornstarch mixture is suspended, poured into the frying pan, and stirred continuously until the sauce thickens.

- Contents are immediately removed to a serving platter, ready to be enjoyed.

Now for some specific techniques:

Clay Pot Cooking

A Chinese clay pot is preferred. Because of its special heat-proof properties, it can be used directly on any stovetop or in an oven. The heat on the pot should be low initially and gradually increased over a 5-minute period so that the pot has time to adjust to the cooking temperature. Before placing the pot on the stovetop, make sure there is liquid in it. Otherwise, the clay pot will crack from the heat. Also, a hot clay pot should never be placed on a wet or cold surface or splashed with cold water. You might end up with a cracked pot. Alternatives to the Chinese clay pot are Corning Ware, thick metal and enamel pots, or cast-iron Dutch ovens. Ingredients are often braised in a frying pan before being combined in the pot for slow cooking.

Stir-Frying

Stir-frying is the best-known Chinese cooking method to Americans. The Cantonese, natives of South China, first brought this cooking technique and the delights of Chinese cuisine with them when they came to America in the 1800s.

Stir-frying requires that the cook constantly stir, turn, and toss the ingredients in the pan. The temperature needs to be as high as it is safe for the pan and the cooking time as short as necessary to cook the ingredients. For example, stir-frying for a minute or two is considered adequate cooking time for most vegetables and meats. In some of our recipes you are instructed to stir-fry the meat for a very short time and then remove it from the pan. You may notice that the meat is not done. Don't panic! A few steps later in the instructions, the meat will be returned to the pan for further cooking.

The aim of stir-frying is to cook the vegetables and meat quickly in order to seal in the juices and flavors. If the cooking temperature is not sufficiently high, the ingredients will absorb the oil, rather than be sealed by it. The natural juices will also leak out from the meat. Generally, little water, if any, is added until the very end to make gravy. An exception to this is when "hard" vegetables, such as cauliflower or broccoli, are stir-fried. Some water is added in the cooking process to soften them to a palatable yet crisp texture.

Requisites for successful stir-frying:

- Pan should be heated as hot as permitted by the manufacturer.

- Before ingredients are put in for stir-frying, the oil should be heated until it just begins to smoke — this is referred as being "hazy" in the recipes.

- Ingredients should be cut approximately the same size and shape.

- Ingredients must be fresh, as stir-frying brings out the natural flavors. If the components are old and stale, the cooked flavors and aroma will be likewise.

- Use water only when called for and in the small amounts specified.

- Cooking time should be as short as necessary. A major sin of novices is to overcook.

Dry-Frying

Dry-frying and stir-frying are similar in that both require much stirring, turning, and tossing. However, the duration of cooking time for dry-frying is considerably longer than for stir-frying. Also, dry-frying requires no addition of water during cooking. This technique coats the main ingredients with the condiments and gives the meat and vegetable a pleasant chewy texture.

Steaming

Steaming is cooking with moist heat. In contrast to boiling or stewing, the food is not immersed in liquid but is placed in a dish which is elevated above the boiling water, where the heat from the steam cooks the food. The best type of cookware used for this technique is a Chinese aluminum steamer. Resembling an over-sized double boiler, the steamer comes with three sections and a cover. The lowest section is a pot to contain the boiling water. The two upper sections have perforated bottoms to allow the steam to flow up and the droplets of water to run down. Food to be steamed is placed in the two upper sections. If you are steaming only one dish, then use one upper section only.

A second alternative is to purchase a bamboo steamer to be used in conjunction with a wok. You will have to match the size of the steamer to the wok or vice versa. Make sure that the bamboo steamer is at least 3 inches smaller in diameter than the wok and will sit securely in it.

A third and most economical alternative is to purchase a 2- or 3-inch-high steaming rack from a Chinese market. This rack is to be used in conjunction with a deep pot or round Dutch oven. Fill the pot with boiling water until the level is about 1 inch below the top of the rack. The dish containing the ingredients to be steamed is then placed on the rack and the pot is covered.

The purpose of steaming is to cook food gently in order to enhance the natural flavors. The resulting benefits of steaming are that the natural juices stay with the food, the flavor is subtle, and the texture is soft and tender to the palate.

Requisites for successful steaming:

- Diameter of the steaming dish should be small enough to allow steam to rise and circulate freely over the food to be cooked. There should be at least an inch of space between the steaming dish and the side of the steamer.

- Dish containing the ingredients to be steamed should sit at least 1 inch above the surface of the boiling water.

- Heat-proof steaming dish should be deep enough to hold not only the food but also the additional liquid resulting from steam condensation (about ¼ cup or less).

- Water should be maintained at a rolling boil even before the food is placed into the steamer.

- Steamer, or pot, should always be covered while steaming. To maintain desired temperature, avoid unnecessary peeking.

- From time to time, check to ensure that there is sufficient water in the pot. Add boiling water as needed.

Red-Cooking

Red-cooking is similar to Western braising in that the meat is first browned before liquid is added to simmer it. The coloring of the ingredients comes from simmering with soy sauce and other spices.

The aim of red-cooking is to tenderize and to allow the spices and flavors of the surrounding liquid to permeate the meat and vegetables.

Mock Deep-Frying

This method is to simulate the results of deep-frying without the accompanying oiliness and high calorie content. The meat to be "deep-fried" is first coated with cornstarch, then broiled to a crispy brown. Cornstarch is preferred over wheat flour because it gives a crisper coating.

For best results, if you are using an electric oven, place the meat on a rack about 7 inches from the broiling element and leave the door slightly ajar. To broil meat in a gas oven, position the rack at its lowest level away from the flames.

7

Recipes

HOW TO USE THE RECIPES

Each of the recipes yields four servings. If you wish to serve more or fewer people, the amounts of the ingredients may be adjusted proportionally. However, the cooking time will vary.

The recipe format is divided into two main sections. The first contains the *Ingredients*, and the second contains the *Instructions*. The *Steps* for the *Ingredients* section correspond to the *Steps* for the *Instructions* section. For example, *Step 1* under *Ingredients* may list specific amounts of soy sauce, oil, and cornstarch. *Step 1* under *Instructions* will tell you what to do with them.

To obtain satisfying results, you must read through the entire recipe and have all the condiments combined and ingredients cut and ready *before* the pan or wok is on the fire.

PLEASE NOTE! Certain items in the *Ingredients* section may need to be soaked ahead of time (see Preparation Techniques).

Information on calories, sodium, and cholesterol content per serving are at the bottom of each recipe. *Further Modifications in Sodium* are included for those who desire or need to reduce sodium intake to an even lower level.

Good luck and have a delicious, hearty great time cooking and eating!

CHICKEN

CHICKEN STIR-FRIED WITH SWEET BEAN SAUCE

Steps	Ingredients
1	3 chicken breast halves (Bone, skin, and cut into ½-inch squares.)
	½ tablespoon dark soy sauce
	2 teaspoons wine
2	1 egg white, very lightly beaten
	1 teaspoon cornstarch
3	½ tablespoon oil
	1 medium green bell pepper (Seed, rib, and cut into ½-inch squares.)
	½ cup bamboo shoots, thinly sliced into ½-inch squares
4	½ tablespoon oil
	1 tablespoon sweet bean sauce
	½ teaspoon sesame oil

Steps	Instructions
1	Mix the chicken pieces with the soy sauce and wine.
2	Add the egg white and cornstarch and mix thoroughly with the chicken pieces. Let stand for 15 minutes.
3	Heat the oil in a pan over high heat until hazy. Put in the green peppers and bamboo shoots and stir-fry for 2 minutes. Take out and set within easy reach.
4	Heat the oil in a pan over high heat until hazy. Put in the chicken and stir-fry briskly for 2 minutes, separating the pieces for even browning. Add the sweet bean sauce and sesame oil and continue stir-frying for 30 seconds. Return the green bell peppers and bamboo shoots to the pan and stir for 20 to 30 seconds. Serve hot.

Yields 4 Servings   *Per Serving:* 166 calories, 329 mg. sodium, 51 mg. cholesterol

Further Modifications in Sodium: Reduce sodium to *236 mg. per serving* by decreasing the sweet bean sauce to 2 teaspoons and substituting lower sodium soy sauce for the regular dark soy sauce.

CHICKEN WITH CASHEW NUTS

Steps	Ingredients
1	1 teaspoon wine ½ teaspoon cornstarch ½ egg white, slightly beaten 1 teaspoon sesame oil pinch of white pepper
2	3 chicken breast halves (Bone, skin, and cut into ¾-inch cubes.)
3	1 tablespoon dark soy sauce 1 teaspoon wine 1 teaspoon Chinese red vinegar 1 teaspoon sugar
4	1 teaspoon cornstarch 2 tablespoons water
5	1 teaspoon oil 3 ounces raw cashew nuts
6	4 cups boiling water
7	1 tablespoon oil 2 slices ginger, minced 1 clove garlic, minced 1 medium green bell pepper (Seed, rib, and cut into ¾-inch squares.) 6 water chestnuts, sliced 1 stalk green onion (scallion), minced

Steps	Instructions
1	Combine the ingredients to form the *Marinade*.
2	Mix the chicken into the *Marinade* and let stand for 15 minutes.
3	Combine ingredients to form *Sauce*. Set within easy reach.
4	Combine ingredients to form *Cornstarch Mixture*. Set within easy reach.
5	Heat the 1 teaspoon of oil in a pan over medium-high heat until hazy. Put in the cashew nuts and stir-fry continuously until nicely browned. Remove from pan and cool so the nuts will be crisp.
6	Put marinated chicken into the boiling water. When chicken turns white, drain and let cool. Pat dry with paper towels. Set within easy reach.
7	Heat the 1 tablespoon of oil in a pan over high heat until hazy. Put in the ginger and garlic and stir-fry briskly for 15 to 20 seconds. Put in chicken and pepper and stir-fry for 30 to 40 seconds. Add water chestnuts and onions. Return the cashews to pan. Add the *Sauce* and stir-fry briskly for 30 seconds. Suspend the *Cornstarch Mixture*, pour it into pan and stir until the sauce thickens. Serve hot.

Yields 4 Servings   *Per Serving:* 299 calories, 335 mg. sodium, 51 mg. cholesterol

Further Modifications in Sodium: Reduce sodium to *236 mg. per serving* by substituting lower sodium soy sauce for the regular dark soy sauce.

CHICKEN STIR-FRIED WITH MUSHROOMS
(Moo Goo Gai Pan)

毛菇雞片

Steps	Ingredients
1	1 teaspoon dark soy sauce ½ tablespoon wine 1 teaspoon cornstarch
2	3 chicken breast halves (Bone, skin, and cut into ¾-inch squares.) 1 teaspoon sesame oil
3	2 teaspoons dark soy sauce ½ teaspoon sugar 1 tablespoon wine ¼ teaspoon white pepper 2 tablespoons water
4	1 teaspoon cornstarch 2 tablespoons water
5	1 tablespoon oil 1 slice ginger, approximately 1 inch in diameter by ⅛ inch thick, smashed with the side of a cleaver 2 small stalks green onions (scallions), cut into 2-inch lengths 4 water chestnuts, sliced thinly 2 ounces snow peas (16 pieces) (Remove tips and strings and cut into thirds diagonally.) 4 ounces fresh button mushrooms, sliced thinly

Steps	Instructions
1	Combine ingredients to form the *Marinade*.
2	Mix the chicken with the Marinade and stir in the sesame oil. Let stand for 20 minutes.
3	Combine ingredients to form the *Sauce*. Set within easy reach.
4	Combine ingredients to form the *Cornstarch Mixture*. Set within easy reach.
5	Heat the oil in a pan over high heat until hazy. Put in the ginger and brown on both sides. Discard ginger. Put in chicken and stir-fry briskly for 1 minute. Add onions, water chestnuts, snow peas, and mushrooms and stir-fry for 30 seconds. Pour in the *Sauce* and stir-fry for 30 seconds. Suspend *Cornstarch Mixture*, pour into pan, and stir until thickened. Serve hot.

Yields 4 Servings   *Per Serving:* 173 calories, 311 mg. sodium, 51 mg. cholesterol

Further Modifications in Sodium: Reduce sodium to *212 mg. per serving* by substituting lower sodium soy sauce for regular dark soy sauce.

CANTONESE CHICKEN SALAD

Steps	Ingredients
1	3 chicken breast halves water
2	1 tablespoon hoisin sauce 1 teaspoon five spice powder 1 tablespoon lemon juice ½ tablespoon sesame oil 1 tablespoon sugar ½ tablespoon hot mustard powder, such as Colman's ½ teaspoon white pepper ½ tablespoon oil 1 tablespoon Chinese red vinegar ½ tablespoon dark soy sauce
3	1 to 2 stalks green onions (scallions), cut into 1-inch lengths, then shredded 1 small head lettuce, shredded
4	juice of ½ lemon 1 tablespoon toasted sesame seeds

Steps	Instructions
1	Bring a pot of water to a boil. Add the chicken, being sure the water just covers the chicken. When water begins to boil again, simmer covered for approximately 20 minutes or until the chicken is cooked. Allow chicken to cool, then cut it into matchstick-size pieces.
2	Combine ingredients to form the *Sauce*. Mix with shredded chicken and let stand at least 20 minutes.
3	Mix green onions with lettuce and arrange on serving platter. Place the chicken on top.
4	When ready to serve, add squeezed lemon juice, mix, and sprinkle sesame seeds on top.

Yields 4 Servings   Per Serving: 188 calories, 346 mg. sodium, 51 mg. cholesterol

Further Modifications in Sodium: Reduce sodium to *254 mg. per serving* by decreasing the hoisin sauce to 2 teaspoons and by substituting lower sodium soy sauce for the regular dark soy sauce.

CURRIED CHICKEN

咖
哩
雞

Steps	Ingredients
1	3 chicken breast halves (Bone, skin, and cut into 4 pieces crosswise.)
	½ cup flour
2	½ tablespoon oil
	½ tablespoon oil
	1 small yellow onion (Cut in half, then cut each half into 6 chunks.)
	1 small green bell pepper (Seed, rib, and cut into ½-inch squares.)
	3 tablespoons Madras-type curry powder
	1 cup water or homemade chicken stock without salt*
3	1¼ cups water or homemade chicken stock without salt*
	1 tablespoon dark soy sauce
	2 medium potatoes, cut into 1½-inch cubes
	1 medium apple, cut into 8 chunks

Steps	Instructions
1	Put the flour in a large plastic bag. Divide chicken pieces into two portions. Put each portion separately into the bag and shake to coat pieces. Discard the remaining flour.
2	Heat the ½ tablespoon oil in a pan over high heat until hazy. Put in the chicken pieces and brown both sides well. Take out and set aside.

Heat the remaining ½ tablespoon oil in a pan over high heat until hazy. Put in the onions and green bell pepper and stir-fry for 1½ minutes. Add the curry powder and stir for 30 seconds. |
| 3 | Transfer contents of pan to a clean pot. Add the chicken pieces and 1¼ cups of water. Put in the soy sauce, potatoes, and apple. Bring to a boil; then immediately reduce heat to low and simmer covered for 45 minutes. Stir occasionally to prevent food from sticking to bottom of pot. Serve hot. |

Yields 4 Servings   Per Serving: 244 calories, 318 mg. sodium, 51 mg. cholesterol

Further Modifications in Sodium: Reduce sodium to *219 mg. per serving* by substituting lower sodium soy sauce for the regular dark soy sauce.

*Homemade chicken stock without salt may be made by boiling the bones from 3 chicken breast halves with 3 cups water, 2 slices ginger, 1 stalk green onion (scallion), and 1 tablespoon wine.

LEMON CHICKEN

檸檬雞

Steps	Ingredients
1	½ small head lettuce, shredded
2	1 tablespoon wine
	1 egg white
	½ tablespoon cornstarch
	¼ teaspoon white pepper
	1 teaspoon sesame oil
3	3 chicken breast halves (Bone, skin, and cut into 1-inch squares.)
4	1 tablespoon light soy sauce
	1 teaspoon wine
	3 tablespoons fresh lemon juice
	1½ tablespoons sugar
5	1 tablespoon oil
	lemon wedges

Steps	Instructions
1	Arrange the lettuce on a serving platter and set aside.
2	Combine the ingredients to form the *Marinade* (avoid overbeating the egg white).
3	Put the chicken pieces into the *Marinade* and let stand for 20 minutes.
4	Combine the ingredients to form the *Sauce*. Set within easy reach.
5	Heat the oil in a pan over high heat until hazy. Add the chicken pieces and stir-fry for 2 minutes, or until the chicken is almost done and well browned on both sides. Pour in the *Sauce* and stir-fry until bubbly. Place the chicken and sauce on top of lettuce. Garnish with lemon.

Yields 4 Servings   *Per Serving: 175 calories, 396 mg. sodium, 51 mg. cholesterol*

Further Modifications in Sodium: Reduce sodium to *222 mg. per serving* by substituting lower sodium soy sauce for the regular light soy sauce.

LYCHEE CHICKEN

荔
枝
雞

Steps	Ingredients
1	1 teaspoon light soy sauce ½ tablespoon wine pinch of white pepper
2	3 chicken breast halves (Carefully bone and skin, leaving the filets intact.)
3	2 teaspoons dark soy sauce 2 tablespoons homemade chicken stock without salt or water 2 tablespoons lychee syrup 2 tablespoons water
4	1 teaspoon cornstarch 1 tablespoon water
5	2½ tablespoons cornstarch 1 tablespoon sesame oil
6	1 20-ounce can lychees (Drain well, reserving 2 tablespoons of the syrup for the *Sauce*.)

Steps	Instructions
1	Combine ingredients to form the *Marinade*.
2	Add chicken filets to the *Marinade* and let stand 15 minutes.
3	In a medium saucepan, combine the ingredients to form the *Sauce*. Set aside.
4	Combine the ingredients to form the *Cornstarch Mixture*. Set aside.
5	Spread the cornstarch on a plate. Dredge both sides of the chicken in cornstarch. Place on a broiling rack 6 to 7 inches from heating elements. Broil 3 to 4 minutes. Brush with sesame oil and continue broiling for 2 to 3 minutes. Turn chicken pieces and repeat. Remove and slice into pieces 1½ inch long by ½ inch wide. Put on platter and keep warm in oven.
6	Heat the *Sauce* until bubbly. Suspend the *Cornstarch Mixture*, pour into pan and stir until thickened. Add lychees and chicken pieces. Serve when hot.

Yields 4 Servings   *Per Serving:* 221 calories, 359 mg. sodium, 51 mg. cholesterol

Further Modifications in Sodium: Reduce sodium to *235 mg. per serving* by substituting lower sodium soy sauce for the regular light and dark soy sauce.

CHICKEN STIR-FRIED WITH GREEN BELL PEPPER

青椒雞絲

Steps	Ingredients
1	½ tablespoon light soy sauce
	2 teaspoons wine
	1 teaspoon cornstarch
	pinch of white pepper
	1 egg white
2	3 chicken breast halves (Bone, skin, and cut into matchstick-size strips.)
3	1 teaspoon light soy sauce
	1 teaspoon cornstarch
	2 tablespoons water
4	1 tablespoon oil
	1 teaspoon oil
	1½ to 2 small green bell peppers (Seed, rib, and cut into matchstick-size strips.)
	1 teaspoon sesame oil

Steps	Instructions
1	Combine the ingredients to form the *Marinade*.
2	Put the chicken into the *Marinade*, stir thoroughly, and let stand for 15 minutes. Stir occasionally.
3	Combine the ingredients to form the *Sauce*. Set within easy reach.
4	Heat the tablespoon oil in a pan over high heat until hazy. Put in the chicken and stir-fry briskly, separating the pieces for even browning. When lightly brown, take out and set within easy reach.

Heat the teaspoon oil in the pan until hazy. Put in the pepper and stir-fry for 1 minute. Return the chicken to the pan. Suspend the *Sauce* and pour it into the pan. Stir until the sauce is thickened. Sprinkle in the sesame oil. Serve hot.

Yields 4 Servings   Per Serving: 174 calories, 347 mg. sodium, 51 mg. cholesterol

Further Modifications in Sodium: Reduce sodium to *202 mg. per serving* by substituting lower sodium soy sauce for the regular light soy sauce.

凉拌雞絲

CHICKEN SALAD WITH SESAME PASTE

Steps	Ingredients
1	5 cups water
	3 chicken breast halves
	2 stalks green onion (scallions), cut into 1-inch lengths
2	1 teaspoon light soy sauce
	1 tablespoon water
3	2 cups shredded lettuce
	1 medium carrot, grated
	1 cucumber, thinly sliced
4	3 tablespoons sesame paste
	1½ tablespoons sesame oil
	1 tablespoon wine
	1 teaspoon sugar
	2 teaspoons light soy sauce
	½ tablespoon red chili oil
5	2 teaspoons sugar
	2 tablespoons water
	juice of ½ lemon
	2 tablespoons sesame seeds, toasted

Steps	Instructions
1	Bring the water to a boil in a medium saucepan. Put the chicken in and boil for 10 minutes. Add green onions and continue boiling for another 5 minutes. Remove chicken, bone, and remove the skin. Shred chicken meat.
2	Combine the light soy sauce and water. Sprinkle over the chicken and mix.
3	Arrange the lettuce, carrots, and cucumber on a serving platter. Place the chicken pieces on top.
4	Combine the ingredients to form the *Sauce*. Pour sauce over the chicken salad 5 minutes before serving.
5	Combine the sugar, water, and lemon juice and pour over salad. Toss the salad and top with sesame seeds. Serve.

Yields 4 Servings   *Per Serving:* 294 calories, 396 mg. sodium, 51 mg. cholesterol

Further Modifications in Sodium: Reduce sodium to *222 mg. per serving* by substituting lower sodium soy sauce for the regular light soy sauce.

CHICKEN STIR-FRIED WITH SNOW PEAS

Steps	Ingredients
1	1 teaspoon cornstarch
	¼ teaspoon sugar
	½ egg white, lightly beaten
	1 teaspoon light soy sauce
	½ teaspoon sesame oil
2	3 chicken breast halves (Bone, skin, and cut into matchstick-size pieces).
3	2 teaspoons light soy sauce
	½ cup homemade chicken stock without salt or water
	2 teaspoons cornstarch
4	1 tablespoon oil
	½ tablespoon oil
	1 ounce wood fungus (Soak, stem, and cut into ½-inch wide strips.)
	6 ounces snow peas, tips and strings removed

Steps	Instructions
1	Combine ingredients to form the *Marinade*.
2	Mix the chicken into the *Marinade*. Let stand for 30 minutes.
3	Combine ingredients to form the *Sauce*. Set within easy reach.
4	Heat the tablespoon oil in a pan over high heat until hazy. Put the chicken in and stir-fry briskly for 1 to 1½ minutes. Take out and set within easy reach. Heat the ½ tablespoon oil in the pan over high heat until hazy. Put in wood fungus and stir-fry for 1 minute. Put in snow peas and continue to stir-fry for 1 minute. Return chicken to pan and stir-fry for 30 seconds. Pour in *Sauce*. Continue stirring until Sauce thickens. Serve hot.

Yields 4 Servings   Per Serving: 201 calories, 396 mg. sodium, 51 mg. cholesterol

Further Modifications in Sodium: Reduce sodium to *222 mg. per serving* by subsituting lower sodium soy sauce for the regular light soy sauce.

宫
保
雞
丁

KUNG PAO CHICKEN

Steps	Ingredients

1
1 teaspoon wine
1 tablespoon cornstarch
1 teaspoon dark soy sauce
pinch of white pepper

2
3 chicken breast halves (Bone, skin, and cut into ½-inch cubes.)

3
½ tablespoon dark soy sauce
1 tablespoon wine
2 teaspoons sugar
½ teaspoon hot bean sauce or regular bean sauce without chili to reduce "hotness"
1 teaspoon cornstarch
1 teaspoon Chinkiang vinegar (Chinese brown vinegar)

4
1 tablespoon oil
½ tablespoon oil
2 to 6 whole dry red peppers
1 clove garlic, smashed with the side of a cleaver
1 teaspoon minced ginger
1 medium green bell pepper (Seed, rib, and cut into ½-inch squares.)
5 Chinese dried mushrooms (Soak, stem, squeeze out excess water, and quarter.)
½ cup bamboo shoots, diced into ¼-inch cubes

Steps	Instructions
1	Combine ingredients to form the *Marinade*.
2	Add chicken to the *Marinade* and let stand for 10 minutes.
3	Combine ingredients to form the *Sauce*. Set within easy reach.
4	Heat 1 tablespoon oil in a pan over high heat until hazy. Add chicken pieces and stir-fry briskly, separating the chicken pieces. Cook for 1½ minutes, or until the chicken is 80 percent done. Remove from the pan and set within easy reach.

Heat the remaining ½ tablespoon oil in the pan until hazy. Stir-fry the dry red peppers for 5 to 10 seconds and take out. Put in the garlic and ginger and stir-fry for 10 seconds. Add green pepper and mushrooms to the pan and stir-fry for 5 seconds. Add bamboo shoots and stir-fry for 5 seconds longer. Return chicken to pan and stir-fry for approximately 10 to 15 seconds. Suspend the *Sauce* and stir it into the pan for 10 to 15 seconds, or until thickened. Serve hot.

Yields 4 Servings   *Per Serving:* 187 calories, 331 mg. sodium, 51 mg. cholesterol

Further Modifications in Sodium: Reduce sodium to *249 mg. per serving* by substituting lower sodium soy sauce for the regular dark soy sauce.

SWEET AND SOUR COLD CHICKEN

甜
酸
凍
雞

Steps	Ingredients
1	5 cups water
	1 slice ginger, approximately 1 inch in diameter by ⅛ inch thick, smashed with the side of a cleaver.
	1 stalk green onion (scallion)
	3 chicken breast halves, skinned (do not bone)
2	2 tablespoons sugar
	2 tablespoons white vinegar
	1 tablespoon dark soy sauce
	½ tablespoon wine
	1 stalk green onion (scallion), minced
3	1 tablespoon oil
	2 slices ginger, finely minced
	2 cloves garlic, finely minced
	¼ to ½ teaspoon red chili pepper flakes

Steps	Instructions
1	Bring 5 cups of water to a boil. Put in ginger and green onion and boil for 5 minutes. Add the chicken, being sure water completely covers the chicken. Cover the pot, turn heat to low, and simmer for 15 to 20 minutes. Do not overcook. Remove chicken and rinse it with cold water until meat is cool. Bone and cut the chicken into ¾-inch squares. Arrange it on a serving platter, cover and refrigerate.
2	Combine ingredients to form the *Sauce*. Set within easy reach.
3	Heat the oil in a pan over high heat until hazy. Add the ginger, garlic, and red chili peppers and stir-fry for 3 to 5 seconds. Pour in the *Sauce* and stir until somewhat thickened. Pour the sauce into a bowl, cool, and refrigerate. To serve, pour the *Sauce* over chicken pieces.

Yields 4 Servings   *Per Serving:* 162 calories, 308 mg. sodium, 51 mg. cholesterol

Further Modifications in Sodium: Reduce sodium to *209 mg. per serving* by substituting lower sodium soy sauce for the regular dark soy sauce.

SESAME CHICKEN

芝麻雞

Steps	Ingredients
1	1 tablespoon dark soy sauce
	1 tablespoon wine
	1 teaspoon sugar
	1 teaspoon white vinegar
	2 slices ginger, approximately 1 inch in diameter by ⅛ inch thick, cut into thin strips
	½ teaspoon white pepper
2	16 chicken drumettes (the meatiest joint — or bicep — of the wing), skinned
3	½ cup sesame seeds

Steps	Instructions
1	Combine ingredients to form the *Marinade*.
2	Put the drumettes into *Marinade* and let stand for 15 to 20 minutes.
3	Remove the ginger if desired. Dredge each drumette in sesame seeds and place on a broiling rack with a pan underneath to catch drippings.
	Broil 6 to 7 inches from heating elements for 12 minutes, turning occasionally for even browning. Can be served hot or cold.

Yields 4 Servings   *Per Serving:* 190 calories, 307 mg. sodium, 51 mg. cholesterol

Further Modifications in Sodium: Reduce sodium to *208 mg. per serving* by substituting lower sodium soy sauce for the regular dark soy sauce.

茄
汁
芝
麻
雞

TOMATO-SESAME CHICKEN

Steps	Ingredients
1	½ head lettuce, shredded
2	½ tablespoon dark soy sauce
	1 tablespoon wine
	3 chicken breast halves (Bone, skin, and cut into 1-inch squares.)
3	3 tablespoons tomato paste without salt
	1½ tablespoons white vinegar
	½ tablespoon dark soy sauce
	¼ teaspoon white pepper
	1½ tablespoons sugar
4	1 tablespoon oil
	4 slices ginger, approximately 1 inch in diameter by ⅛ inch thick, smashed with the side of a cleaver
	¼ cup water or homemade chicken stock without salt
5	3 tablespoons toasted sesame seeds
	1 teaspoon sesame oil

Steps	Instructions
1	Arrange the lettuce on a serving platter. Set aside.
2	Combine the soy sauce and wine and mix with chicken pieces. Let stand for 20 minutes.
3	Combine ingredients to form the *Sauce.* Set within easy reach.
4	Heat the oil in a pan over high heat until hazy. Add the ginger and brown. Put in the chicken pieces and brown lightly on both sides. Add the *Sauce* and stir-fry for 2 minutes. Pour in the ¼ cup water and turn heat to medium-low, cover, and simmer for 8 minutes. Add a small amount of water if sauce becomes too thick.
5	Stir in the sesame seeds and oil and continue to simmer chicken for another 5 minutes. Remove from pan and place on top of the lettuce.

Yields 4 Servings   Per Serving: 215 calories, 318 mg. sodium, 51 mg. cholesterol

Further Modifications in Sodium: Reduce sodium to *219 mg. per serving* by substituting lower sodium soy sauce for the regular dark soy sauce.

SHERRY CHICKEN

醉
雞

Steps	Ingredients
1	3 slices ginger, approximately 1 inch in diameter by ⅛ inch thick
	2 small stalks green onions (scallions), cut into 2-inch lengths
	3 cups water
2	3 chicken breast halves
3	⅓ cup dry sherry
4	1 tablespoon light soy sauce
	½ tablespoon Chinese red vinegar
	½ teaspoon sugar
	1 tablespoon dry sherry reserved from sherry used as marinade for chicken

Steps	Instructions
1	Put the ginger and green onions into a medium-sized saucepan and add the 3 cups water. Bring to a boil.
2	Put the chicken into boiling water. Be sure chicken is completely covered by water. Bring to a boil again, cover, and immediately reduce heat to low, allowing chicken to simmer for 10 to 12 minutes. Turn off heat, and let the chicken sit for an additional 10 minutes in the covered pot. Remove chicken and let cool. (The liquid may be reserved for stock.) Bone and skin the chicken and put it into a container with a lid.
3	Pour the dry sherry over the chicken, cover, and refrigerate overnight. The chicken should be basted with sherry occasionally.
4	Combine ingredients to form the *Sauce.* Remove chicken from container, cut it into pieces 1½ by 2 by ¾ inch and arrange on a platter. Sprinkle with the *Sauce* and serve cold.

Yields 4 Servings   *Per Serving:* 121 calories, 396 mg. sodium, 51 mg. cholesterol

Further Modifications in Sodium: Reduce sodium to *222 mg. per serving* by substituting lower sodium soy sauce for the regular light soy sauce.

紅燒栗子雞

BRAISED CHICKEN WITH CHESTNUTS

Steps	Ingredients
1	½ pound chestnuts in shells (Slit one end of each chestnut with a knife.)
	1 pot of water
2	1 tablespoon dark soy sauce
	1 teaspoon sugar
	1 tablespoon wine
3	1 teaspoon cornstarch
	1 tablespoon water
4	1 tablespoon oil
	2 slices ginger, approximately 1 inch in diameter by ⅛ inch thick, smashed with the side of a cleaver
	1 stalk green onion (scallion), cut into 2-inch lengths
	3 chicken breast halves (Bone, skin, and cut into 1-inch squares.)
	½ cup water or homemade chicken stock without salt

Steps	Instructions
1	Boil the chestnuts in a pot of water for 10 minutes. Drain and cool. Then remove the shells and skins. Set aside.
2	Combine ingredients to form the *Sauce*. Set within easy reach.
3	Combine ingredients to form the *Cornstarch Mixture*. Set within easy reach.
4	Heat the oil in a pan over high heat until hazy. Put in the ginger and green onion and brown for 15 seconds. Add chicken pieces and stir-fry for 1 minute. Pour in the *Sauce* and stir for 1 minute. Add the ½ cup water and chestnuts. When the liquid begins to boil, immediately turn the heat to low, cover, and simmer for 10 to 15 minutes. Suspend the *Cornstarch Mixture*, pour it into pan and stir until thickened. Serve hot.

Yields 4 Servings   *Per Serving:* 229 calories, 310 mg. sodium, 51 mg. cholesterol

Further Modifications in Sodium: Reduce sodium to *211 mg. per serving* by substituting lower sodium soy sauce for the regular dark soy sauce.

STEWED CHICKEN

Steps	Ingredients
1	3 chicken breast halves (Bone, skin, and cut into 1-inch squares.)
	1 large stalk green onion (scallion), cut into 2-inch lengths
	1 tablespoon wine
	1 tablespoon light soy sauce
	⅛ teaspoon white pepper
	½ teaspoon sugar
	¼ cup sliced bamboo shoots
	6 Chinese dried mushrooms (Soak, stem, squeeze out excess water, and quarter.)
	1½ cups homemade chicken stock without salt
2	2 tablespoons + 1 teaspoon cornstarch
	3 tablespoons water

Steps	Instructions
1	Combine ingredients in a 1-quart pot with tight-fitting lid. Bring to a boil, then turn to simmer, cover, and cook for 20 to 30 minutes.
2	Combine ingredients to form the *Cornstarch Mixture.* Bring the soup to a boil and slowly pour in the *Cornstarch Mixture,* stirring until thickened. Serve hot.

Yields 4 Servings   *Per Serving:* 145 calories, 382 mg. sodium, 51 mg. cholesterol

Further Modifications in Sodium: Reduce sodium to *208 mg. per serving* by substituting lower sodium soy sauce for the regular light soy sauce.

嗜嗜雞

焗
雞
塊

BAKED/BROILED CHICKEN

Steps	Ingredients
1	1 tablespoon dark soy sauce 1 tablespoon wine 1 tablespoon Chinese red vinegar ½ tablespoon sugar ¼ teaspoon black pepper 3 slices ginger, approximately 1 inch in diameter by ⅛ inch thick, cut into thin shreds
2	3 chicken breast halves (Bone, skin, and cut in half horizontally.)
3	½ cup flour
4	1 tablespoon sesame oil remaining *Marinade*

Steps	Instructions
1	Combine the ingredients to form the *Marinade*.
2	Mix the chicken with the *Marinade*, coating all sides. Then let stand for 30 minutes.
3	Preheat the oven to 375 degrees. Put the flour into a large plastic bag. Add chicken pieces and shake vigorously to coat each piece well.
4	Combine the sesame oil with the remaining *Marinade*. Place a rack on top of a cookie sheet. Arrange the chicken pieces on rack. Bake chicken for 8 to 10 minutes. Baste with *Marinade* and bake for an additional 5 minutes on the same side. Turn chicken and repeat. Turn oven to broil and brown the chicken well on both sides. Serve hot.

Yields 4 Servings   *Per Serving:* 177 calories, 334 mg. sodium, 51 mg. cholesterol

Further Modifications in Sodium: Reduce sodium to *235 mg. per serving* by substituting lower sodium soy sauce for the regular dark soy sauce.

RED-COOKED CHICKEN

紅燒雞

Steps	Ingredients
1	1 pod star anise
	½ teaspoon thick soy sauce
	1 tablespoon dark soy sauce
	1 tablespoon Chinese red vinegar
	1 tablespoon sugar
	1 teaspoon sesame oil
	1 cup homemade chicken stock without salt or water
2	1 tablespoon oil
	4 chicken breast halves (Bone, skin, and cut into 4 pieces crosswise.)
	4 slices ginger, approximately 1 inch in diameter by ⅛ inch thick, smashed with the side of a cleaver
	3 stalks green onions (scallions), cut into 2-inch lengths
	3 cloves garlic, smashed with the side of a cleaver

Steps	Instructions
1	Combine ingredients to form the *Sauce*. Set within easy reach.
2	Heat the oil in a pan over high heat until hazy. Brown the chicken pieces with the ginger, green onions, and garlic. Reduce the heat to medium-high; add the *Sauce*. Cover and cook for 20 minutes. Stir occasionally for even browning of the chicken. Uncover and continue cooking until liquid has partially evaporated (approximately 10 minutes). Serve.

Yields 4 Servings   *Per Serving:* 197 calories, 388 mg. sodium, 68 mg. cholesterol

Further Modifications in Sodium: Reduce sodium to *289 mg. per serving* by substituting lower sodium soy sauce for the regular dark soy sauce.

CLAY POT CHICKEN

沙
鍋
雞

Steps	Ingredients
1	2 tablespoons wine
	¼ teaspoon sesame oil
	pinch of white pepper
	2 teaspoons cornstarch
	1 tablespoon chee hou sauce
	1 teaspoon sugar
2	4 chicken breast halves (Bone, skin, and cut each half breast into 4 pieces crosswise.)
3	6 large outer leaves of lettuce
	1 cup sliced raw carrots
	2 tablespoons water
4	1 tablespoon oil
	½ tablespoon oil
	3 slices ginger, each approximately 1 inch in diameter by ⅛ inch thick, smashed with side of cleaver
	1 large clove garlic, minced
	1 medium yellow onion. (Cut in half, then cut each half into 6 chunks.)
	2 tablespoons wine
	½ cup water or homemade chicken stock without salt
	1 teaspoon dark soy sauce

Steps	Instructions
1	Combine ingredients to form the *Marinade*.
2	Mix the chicken pieces with the *Marinade* and let stand for 20 minutes.
3	Line the bottom of a clay pot or small casserole dish with the lettuce leaves. Spread the carrots on top, then sprinkle the 2 tablespoons water on top.
4	Preheat oven to 350 degrees. Heat the 1 tablespoon oil in a pan over high heat until hazy. Put in the chicken and stir-fry for 2 minutes. Take the chicken out and set aside. (Chicken does not need to be completely cooked at this point.) Heat the ½ tablespoon oil in a pan until hazy. Put in the ginger, garlic, and onions and brown slightly. Return the chicken to the pan and add the wine, water, and soy sauce. Stir. Transfer contents of pan into the clay pot or casserole dish. Bake in preheated oven for 15 minutes. Serve steaming hot.

Yields 4 Servings   *Per Serving:* 237 calories, 316 mg. sodium, 68 mg. cholesterol.

Further Modifications in Sodium: Reduce sodium to *214 mg. per serving* by decreasing the chee hou sauce to ½ tablespoon and substituting lower sodium soy sauce for the regular dark soy sauce.

STEAMED CHICKEN WITH MUSHROOMS

Steps	Ingredients
1	1 teaspoon cornstarch
	1 tablespoon light soy sauce
	1 teaspoon wine
	½ teaspoon sugar
2	3 chicken breast halves (Bone, skin, and cut into bite-size pieces no more than $\frac{1}{16}$-inch thick.)
3	½ cup bamboo shoots, thinly sliced into ½-inch squares
	5 Chinese dried mushrooms (Soak, squeeze out excess water, stem, and cut into ⅛-inch-wide strips.)
	4 slices ginger, approximately 1 inch in diameter by ⅛ inch thick
4	½ teaspoon sesame oil

Steps	Instructions
1	In a medium-size heat-proof dish, combine the ingredients to form the *Marinade*.
2	Mix the chicken into the *Marinade* and let stand for 15 minutes.
3	Mix the bamboo shoots with the chicken pieces. Place the mushrooms on top of the chicken. Arrange the ginger slices on top of chicken and mushrooms. Steam covered for 15 minutes or until chicken is white and firm.
4	Remove from the steamer and discard ginger. Sprinkle sesame oil on top of the chicken. Serve hot.

Yields 4 Servings   *Per Serving:* 118 calories, 382 mg. sodium, 51 mg. cholesterol

Further Modifications in Sodium: Reduce sodium to *208 mg. per serving* by substituting lower sodium soy sauce for the regular light soy sauce.

SEAFOOD

浸
魚
片

POACHED FILET OF FISH

Steps	Ingredients
1	3 cups water
	2 slices ginger, approximately 1 inch in diameter by ⅛ inch thick, smashed with the side of a cleaver
	2 stalks green onion (scallions), cut into 2-inch lengths
	1 pound fish filets, cut into 1½-inch squares
2	1 tablespoon wine
	2½ teaspoons light soy sauce
	1 teaspoon sugar
	½ teaspoon sesame oil
3	1 tablespoon oil
	½ tablespoon minced ginger
	2 stalks green onions (scallions), finely minced

Steps	Instructions
1	Put the ginger and green onions into a pot containing the 3 cups of water. Bring the water to a boil and boil for 3 minutes. Gently add the fish slices. When water begins to boil again, remove the fish slices immediately and set on a platter. Keep warm.
2	Combine ingredients to form the *Sauce*. Set within easy reach.
3	Heat oil in a pan over high heat until hazy. Put in ginger and fry for 10 seconds. Put in green onions and stir-fry another 10 seconds. Pour in *Sauce* and heat until bubbly. Then pour the sauce over the fish slices and serve hot.

Yields 4 Servings   *Per Serving:* 143 calories, 351 mg. sodium, 57 mg. cholesterol

Further Modifications in Sodium: Reduce sodium to *206 mg. per serving* by substituting lower sodium soy sauce for the regular light soy sauce.

清
蒸
紅
魚

STEAMED SALMON

Steps	Ingredients
1	½ tablespoon dark soy sauce ½ tablespoon wine ½ teaspoon sugar ⅛ teaspoon black pepper
2	1 pound salmon steaks, wiped dry
3	½ teaspoon cornstarch 1 tablespoon water
4	white sections of 2 stalks of green onions (scallions), cut into 2-inch lengths and shredded lengthwise 3 slices ginger, approximately 1 inch in diameter by ⅛ inch thick, thinly sliced into strips
5	2 tablespoons drippings from steaming dish ½ tablespoon dark soy sauce 1 teaspoon sesame oil
6	green section of 1 stalk of green onion (scallion), cut into ½-inch pieces

Steps	Instructions
1	Combine ingredients to form the *Marinade*.
2	Coat both sides of fish well with all of the *Marinade*. Let stand for 15 minutes.
3	Combine ingredients to form the *Cornstarch Mixture*. Set within easy reach.
4	Place the fish steaks in a heat-proof dish. Lay the white sections of the onion underneath and on top of the fish. Place ginger on top of salmon. Steam fish for 6 minutes over boiling water. Do not overcook.
5	Put the 2 tablespoons of drippings from the steaming dish in a small saucepan. Add the dark soy sauce and sesame oil. Continue heating until bubbly. Suspend *Cornstarch Mixture*, add it to the pan, and stir until thickened. Pour sauce over fish steaks.
6	Sprinkle the green sections of onion over the fish. Serve hot.

Yields 4 Servings   *Per Serving:* 140 calories, 314 mg. sodium, 35 mg. cholesterol

Further Modifications in Sodium: Reduce sodium to *215 mg. per serving* by substituting lower sodium soy sauce for the regular dark soy sauce.

STEAMED WHOLE FISH

Steps	Ingredients
1	2½ pounds fresh whole rock cod fish (or substitute sea bass, pike or similar fish) (Scale, clean, and dry well on paper towels. Head may be removed.)
2	white sections of 3 stalks of green onions (scallions), cut into 1½-inch lengths
	4 slices ginger, approximately 1 inch in diameter by ⅟₁₆ inch thick, cut into fine slivers
	2½ ounces well-trimmed boneless pork, cut into matchstick-size pieces
	1 teaspoon light soy sauce
	⅛ teaspoon white pepper
	½ tablespoon sesame oil mixed with ½ tablespoon cooking oil
3	green sections of 3 stalks of green onions (scallions), cut into 1½-inch lengths
	2 teaspoons light soy sauce mixed with ½ tablespoon wine

Steps	Instructions
1	Make 3 diagonal cuts at the thickest part of the fish (near the back).
2	Arrange half of the white sections of the green onions on a heat-proof steaming plate. Put the fish on top. Top the fish with the ginger, remaining half of the white sections of green onions, pork, 1 teaspoon light soy sauce, white pepper, and oil mixture. Bring the water in the steaming pot to a rolling boil. Put the plate of fish in, cover, and steam over high heat for 8 minutes or until just done. Do not overcook.
3	Take fish out and spread the green section of the green onions over the cooked fish. Sprinkle the soy sauce and wine mixture on top. Serve immediately.

Yields 4 Servings   *Per Serving:* 139 calories, 396 mg. sodium, 56 mg. cholesterol

Further Modifications in Sodium: Reduce sodium to *222 mg. per serving* by substituting lower sodium soy sauce for the regular light soy sauce.

煎檸檬魚

PAN-FRIED FISH WITH LEMON SAUCE

Steps	Ingredients

1
- 1 teaspoon light soy sauce
- 1 teaspoon wine
- ¼ teaspoon white pepper
- 1 slice ginger, approximately 1 inch in diameter by ⅛ inch thick, finely minced

2
- 1 pound rock cod filet or any firm white fish (Rinse and dry with paper towels.)

3
- ½ tablespoon light soy sauce
- 2 tablespoons sugar
- juice from ½ fresh medium lemon
- 1 tablespoon water

4
- ½ teaspoon cornstarch
- 2 tablespoons water

5
- ½ egg white, lightly beaten
- 2 tablespoons cornstarch, spread on a dinner plate

6
- 1 tablespoon oil
- 2 slices ginger, peeled and smashed with the side of a cleaver
- 2 cloves garlic smashed with the side of a cleaver
- ½ tablespoon oil
- ½ fresh lemon, cut into thin slices

Steps	Instructions
1	Combine ingredients to form the *Marinade*.
2	Put fish filets into the *Marinade* and let stand for 15 minutes. Be sure filets are well coated with marinade.
3	Combine ingredients to form the *Sauce*. Set within easy reach.
4	Combine ingredients to form the *Cornstarch Mixture*. Set within reach.
5	Add the lightly beaten egg white into the marinated fish, mix for even coating, and then let stand for 5 minutes. Dredge each filet on both sides with the cornstarch.
6	Heat the oil in a pan over medium-high heat. Put in the ginger and garlic and brown, then discard. Put in the fish filets and pan-fry for 2½ minutes, or until lightly browned. Add the remaining ½ tablespoon oil to the pan and brown the other side of the fish for 2½ minutes. Remove to a serving platter. Top fish filets with lemon slices. Keep warm. Bring the *Sauce* to a boil in a small pan. Suspend the *Cornstarch Mixture;* stir it into the sauce until thickened. Pour over the fish and serve immediately.

Yields 4 Servings   *Per Serving:* 185 calories, 357 mg. sodium, 57 mg. cholesterol

Further Modifications in Sodium: Reduce sodium to *212 mg. per serving* by substituting lower sodium soy sauce for the regular light soy sauce.

魚
片
炒
芽
菜

FISH SLICES WITH BEAN SPROUTS

Steps	Ingredients
1	½ tablespoon light soy sauce 1 tablespoon wine ¼ teaspoon black pepper 1 tablespoon cornstarch 1 egg white
2	1 pound rock cod filet or any firm white fish (Wash and cut into strips 1 inch wide by 1½ inches long by ¼ inch thick.)
3	½ tablespoon dark soy sauce ½ teaspoon sugar ½ teaspoon sesame oil 2 tablespoons water 1 teaspoon cornstarch
4	1 tablespoon oil 1 clove garlic, minced 1 teaspoon minced ginger
5	½ tablespoon oil 12 ounces bean sprouts, washed and drained well

Steps	Instructions
1	Combine ingredients to form the *Marinade.*
2	Put fish filet slices into the *Marinade* and mix until well coated. Let stand for 30 to 45 minutes.
3	Combine ingredients to form the *Sauce.* Set within easy reach.
4	Heat the oil in a pan over high heat until hazy. Put in the garlic and ginger and brown. Add the fish slices and evenly brown both sides for 10 to 20 seconds each. Gently remove to a platter.
5	Add the remaining ½ tablespoon oil to the pan and heat until hazy. Put in bean sprouts and stir-fry for 1 minute. Take out and arrange on a serving platter. Return fish to hot pan and stir-fry for 10 seconds, or until piping hot. Suspend the *Sauce* and pour it into the pan. Heat until bubbly. Arrange fish and sauce on top of bean sprouts and serve hot.

Yields 4 Servings   Per Serving: 197 calories, 384 mg. sodium, 57 mg. cholesterol

Further Modifications in Sodium: Reduce sodium to *247 mg. per serving* by substituting lower sodium soy sauce for the regular dark soy sauce and light soy sauce.

STEAMED FILET OF SOLE
WITH BLACK BEAN SAUCE

豆
豉
蒸
魚

Steps	Ingredients
1	1 pound sole filet
	1 slice ginger, approximately 1 inch in diameter by ⅛ inch thick, smashed with the side of a cleaver
	3 slices ginger, approximately 1 inch in diameter by ⅛ inch thick, cut into very thin strips
	1 teaspoon sesame oil
2	1 tablespoon black beans, rinsed and mashed with 1 teaspoon water
	2 cloves garlic, finely minced
	1 teaspoon oil
3	2 teaspoons dark soy sauce
	1 teaspoon sesame oil

Steps	Instructions
1	Place fish filets in a heat-proof dish for steaming. Rub the filets with the smashed slice of ginger. Top the filets with the ginger strips and sesame oil.
2	Combine ingredients to form the *Sauce.* Spread evenly on top of the filets.
3	Bring water in a steamer to a boil, put in the dish of filets and steam for approximately 8 minutes. Avoid overcooking. When cooked, remove the dish and top the fish with the soy sauce and sesame oil. Serve hot. (If desired, ginger slices may be removed before serving.)

Yields 4 Servings   *Per Serving:* 126 calories, 322 mg. sodium, 57 mg. cholesterol

Further Modifications in Sodium: Reduce sodium to *256 mg. per serving* by substituting lower sodium soy sauce for the regular dark soy sauce.

PAN-FRIED FISH PATTIES

Steps	Ingredients
1	1 pound fish filet (cod, perch or similar fish), finely minced
	2 slices of ginger approximately 1 inch in diameter by ⅛ inch thick, finely minced
	white sections of 3 green onions (scallions), finely minced
	8 water chestnuts, finely minced
	½ tablespoon light soy sauce
	⅛ teaspoon white pepper
	2 tablespoons water
2	4 teaspoons cornstarch
	½ teaspoon sesame oil
	2 egg whites, lightly beaten
3	2 teaspoons oil
	2 teaspoons oil
4	½ teaspoon cornstarch
	1½ tablespoons water
5	1 teaspoon light soy sauce
	1 teaspoon wine
	½ teaspoon sugar
	3 tablespoons water
	4 Chinese dried mushrooms (soak, squeeze dry, stem, and slice into thin strips.)

Steps	Instructions
1	Combine ingredients in a blender and mix for 5 minutes or until pasty. If mixing by hand, slowly add the water to the remaining ingredients and mix vigorously until a paste forms.
2	Put in the cornstarch 1 teaspoon at a time while stirring. Add the sesame oil and egg white. Mix thoroughly until smooth and pasty. Remove and form 4 patties.
3	Heat 2 teaspoons oil in a pan over medium-high heat until hazy. Pan-fry half of the fish patties until lightly browned on both sides. Remove and place on a serving platter. Heat the remaining 2 teaspoons oil in a pan over medium-high heat. Put in the other 2 fish patties and fry as above. Remove and keep patties warm.
4	Combine ingredients to form the *Cornstarch Mixture*. Set within easy reach.
5	Combine the ingredients in a small saucepan and bring to a boil. Suspend the *Cornstarch Mixture* and add to saucepan, stirring until the mixture thickens. Pour over the fish patties and serve immediately.

Yields 4 Servings   *Per Serving:* 170 calories, 377 mg. sodium, 57 mg. cholesterol

Further Modifications in Sodium: Reduce sodium to *232 mg. per serving* by substituting lower sodium soy sauce for the regular light soy sauce.

TOMATO SAUCE FISH SLICES

茄
汁
魚
片

Steps	Ingredients
1	1 pound fish filets (rock cod, red snapper or similar fish), cut in strips 1 inch wide by 1½ inches long by ¼ inch thick
	½ teaspoon light soy sauce
	¼ teaspoon white pepper
2	1 egg white, lightly beaten
	1 tablespoon cornstarch
3	2 tablespoons wine
	2 tablespoons tomato paste
	2 tablespoons sugar
	3 tablespoons white vinegar
	2 tablespoons water
	2 teaspoons cornstarch
	½ teaspoon Worcestershire sauce
	2 teaspoons light soy sauce
	1 teaspoon sesame oil
4	1 tablespoon oil
	1 teaspoon minced ginger
	1 teaspoon minced garlic
5	½ tablespoon oil
	½ medium onion, cut into ½-inch squares
	½ cup bamboo shoots or water chestnuts, sliced

Steps	Instructions
1	Dry fish slices with paper towels. Then mix the fish with the light soy sauce and white pepper. Let stand for 15 minutes.
2	Mix the fish slices with the egg white and cornstarch until well coated. Let stand for 30 minutes.
3	Combine the ingredients to form the *Sauce*. Set within easy reach.
4	Heat the 1 tablespoon oil in a pan over high heat until hazy. Put in the ginger and garlic and brown lightly. Put in the fish and stir-fry, being sure to separate the pieces for even browning. Stir-fry for 1 minute. Remove and set within easy reach.
5	Heat the ½ tablespoon oil in a pan over high heat until hazy. Put in the onions and stir-fry for 30 to 45 seconds. Add the bamboo shoots or water chestnuts and stir for 10 seconds. Pour in the *Sauce* and stir until bubbly. Put in the fish and stir-fry gently for 10 seconds. Serve hot.

Yields 4 Servings   *Per Serving:* 211 calories, 375 mg. sodium, 57 mg. cholesterol

Further Modifications in Sodium: Reduce sodium to *230 mg. per serving* by substituting lower sodium soy sauce for the regular light soy sauce.

PAN-FRIED OYSTERS WITH COCKTAIL SAUCE

煎
生
蠔

Steps	Ingredients
1	1 tablespoon tomato paste without salt
	½ tablespoon dark soy sauce
	½ tablespoon white vinegar
	½ tablespoon sugar
	1 tablespoon water or homemade stock without salt
	½ teaspoon sesame oil
2	8 ounces oysters (10-ounce jar), rinsed and drained
	1 egg white
	2 slices ginger, approximately 1 inch in diameter by ⅛ inch thick, smashed with the side of a cleaver and minced.
	½ tablespoon dark soy sauce
	½ teaspoon Chinese brown vinegar
	1 teaspoon wine
	pinch of white pepper
3	3 tablespoons cornstarch
4	1 tablespoon oil

Steps	Instructions
1	Combine ingredients to form the *Cocktail Sauce* and put into a small serving bowl.
2	Dry oysters with paper towel. Combine remaining ingredients in a medium-sized bowl, add the oysters and let stand for 10 to 15 minutes.
3	Spread the cornstarch on a plate. Dredge the oysters to coat all sides well.
4	Heat the oil in a pan over high heat until hazy. Add oysters and brown well, turn and brown the other side. Serve immediately with the *Cocktail Sauce*.

Yields 4 Servings   *Per Serving:* 126 calories, 343 mg. sodium, 28 mg. cholesterol

Further Modifications in Sodium: Reduce sodium to *244 mg. per serving* by substituting lower sodium soy sauce for the regular dark soy sauce.

GREEN ONION AND GINGER OYSTERS

薑
蔥
蠔

Steps	Ingredients
1	1 teaspoon wine
	1 tablespoon dark soy sauce
	½ tablespoon Chinese red vinegar
	1 teaspoon sugar
	pinch of white pepper
2	1 teaspoon cornstarch
	2 tablespoons water
3	1½ tablespoons oil
	4 slices ginger, approximately 1 inch in diameter by ⅛ inch thick, smashed with the side of a cleaver
	1 large stalk green onion (scallion), cut into 2-inch lengths
	8 ounces oysters (10-ounce jar), rinsed and drained well on paper towels

Steps	Instructions
1	Combine ingredients to form the *Sauce.* Set within easy reach.
2	Combine ingredients to form the *Cornstarch Mixture.* Set within easy reach.
3	Heat the oil in a pan over high heat until hazy. Add the ginger and brown. Add onions and stir-fry for 30 seconds. Put in the oysters and stir-fry for 2 minutes. Pour in the *Sauce* and stir for 1 minute. Suspend the *Cornstarch Mixture,* pour it into the pan, and stir until the sauce is thickened. Serve hot.

Yields 4 Servings   *Per Serving:* 111 calories, 339 mg. sodium, 28 mg. cholesterol

Further Modifications in Sodium: Reduce sodium to *240 mg. per serving* by substituting lower sodium soy sauce for the regular dark soy sauce.

BEEF AND LAMB

蒙古牛肉

MONGOLIAN BEEF

Steps	Ingredients
1	1 tablespoon wine
	1 teaspoon cornstarch
	1 teaspoon water
	½ teaspoon sesame oil
2	12 ounces well-trimmed flank steak (Cut across the grain slantwise into thin slices 1½ inches long by ⅛ inch thick.)
3	2 tablespoons hoisin sauce
	1 teaspoon sugar
	2 teaspoons water
4	1 tablespoon oil
	2 slices ginger, minced
	2 cloves garlic, minced
	½ teaspoon flaked red chili pepper
	4 stalks green onions (scallions), cut into 2-inch lengths

Steps	Instructions
1	Combine ingredients to form the *Marinade*.
2	Mix the beef into the *Marinade*. Let stand for 20 minutes.
3	Combine ingredients to form the *Sauce*.
4	Heat the oil in a pan over high heat until hazy. Lightly brown the ginger and garlic. Put in flaked red chili pepper and stir for 3 to 5 seconds. Put in beef and stir-fry briskly for 1 minute, separating the pieces from each other. Put in *Sauce* and green onions and continue to stir-fry for about 1 minute, or until done. Serve hot.

Yields 4 Servings   *Per Serving:* 197 calories, 316 mg. sodium, 58 mg. cholesterol

Further Modifications in Sodium: Reduce sodium to *191 mg. per serving* by decreasing the hoisin sauce to 1 tablespoon.

92

BEEF WITH SATAY SAUCE

沙爹牛肉

Steps	Ingredients
1	¼ teaspoon sugar
	1 teaspoon dark soy sauce
	1 teaspoon wine
	2 teaspoons water
	1 teaspoon cornstarch
2	12 ounces well-trimmed flank steak (Slice across the grain slantwise into 1½-inch-long by ⅛-inch-thick strips.)
3	½ teaspoon sugar
	½ teaspoon cornstarch
	½ tablespoon dark soy sauce
	⅓ cup water
	pinch of white pepper
4	2 teaspoons oil
	2 cloves garlic, finely minced
5	2 teaspoons oil
	2 cloves of shallot, thinly sliced
	½ medium yellow onion, cut into 8 equal chunks
	1 medium green bell pepper (Seed, rib, and cut into ½-inch squares.)
	3 ounces snow peas (approximately 24) (Remove tips and strings.)
	5 teaspoons satay sauce

Steps	Instructions
1	Combine ingredients to form the *Marinade*.
2	Mix the beef into the *Marinade* and let stand for 15 minutes.
3	Combine ingredients to form the *Sauce*. Set within easy reach.
4	Heat the oil in a pan over high heat until hazy. Brown the garlic. Put in the beef and stir-fry briskly for 1 minute. Remove and set within easy reach. Wipe the pan.
5	Heat the oil in a pan over high heat until hazy. Put in the shallots, onion, and green bell peppers and stir-fry for 1 minute. Add snow peas and satay sauce and stir-fry for 1 minute. Return the beef to the pan and continue to stir-fry for 45 seconds. Pour in the *Sauce* and stir until bubbly. Serve hot.

Yields 4 Servings   *Per Serving:* 214 calories, 380 mg. sodium, 58 mg. cholesterol

Further Modifications in Sodium: Reduce sodium to *292 mg. per serving* by substituting lower sodium soy sauce for the regular dark soy sauce and decreasing the satay sauce to 1 tablespoon.

TOMATO BEEF

蕃
茄
牛
肉

Steps	Ingredients
1	1 tablespoon wine
	1 teaspoon Chinese red vinegar
	1 tablespoon cornstarch
	½ teaspoon sesame oil
2	12 ounces well-trimmed flank steak (Slice thinly slantwise into 1½-inch-long by ⅛-inch-thick slices.)
3	¼ teaspoon black pepper
	1 tablespoon dark soy sauce
	1 tablespoon sugar
	1 tablespoon unsalted tomato paste
	2 tablespoons water or homemade chicken stock without salt
4	2 teaspoons cornstarch
	2 tablespoons water
5	1 tablespoon oil
	½ tablespoon oil
	1 medium yellow onion (Cut in half, then cut each half into 6 equal chunks.)
	1 medium green bell pepper (Seed, rib, and cut into ¾-inch squares.)
	3 small or 2 large tomatoes, cut into 6 wedges

Steps	Instructions
1	Combine ingredients to form the *Marinade*.
2	Add beef to the *Marinade* and let stand for 10 to 15 minutes.
3	Combine ingredients to form the *Sauce*. Set within easy reach.
4	Combine ingredients to form the *Cornstarch Mixture*. Set within easy reach.
5	Heat the 1 tablespoon oil in a pan over high heat until hazy. Add the beef and stir-fry for 1 minute. Remove from the pan and set within easy reach. Heat the ½ tablespoon oil in pan until hazy. Add the onions and stir-fry for 30 seconds. Add green peppers and continue to stir for 30 seconds. Return beef to pan and stir-fry for 30 seconds. Add tomatoes. Pour in the *Sauce* and stir until bubbly. Suspend *Cornstarch Mixture* and stir into pan until thickened. Serve hot.

Yields 4 Servings   *Per Serving:* 246 calories, 336 mg. sodium, 58 mg. cholesterol

Further Modifications in Sodium: Reduce sodium to *237 mg. per serving* by substituting lower sodium soy sauce for the regular dark soy sauce.

CURRIED BEEF

Steps	Ingredients
1	12 ounces well-trimmed flank steak (Slice across the grain slantwise into strips 1½ inches long by ⅛ inch thick.)
	1 tablespoon wine
2	⅓ cup water
	½ tablespoon sugar
	1 tablespoon dark soy sauce
3	½ tablespoon cornstarch
	2 tablespoons water
4	½ tablespoon oil
	1 medium yellow onion (Cut in half, then cut each half into 6 equal chunks.)
	1 tablespoon oil
	2 slices ginger, approximately 1 inch in diameter by ⅛ inch thick, finely minced
	2 tablespoons Madras-type curry powder

Steps	Instructions
1	Mix the beef with the wine and let stand for 15 minutes.
2	Combine ingredients to form the *Sauce.* Set within easy reach.
3	Combine ingredients to form the *Cornstarch Mixture.* Set within easy reach.
4	Heat the ½ tablespoon oil in a pan over high heat until hazy. Add the yellow onion and stir-fry for 2 minutes. Add 1 tablespoon oil to the pan and heat until hazy. Put in the ginger and curry powder and stir-fry for 15 to 20 seconds. Put in the beef, stir-fry for 1½ minutes. Pour in the *Sauce* and stir for 1 minute, or until bubbly. Suspend the *Cornstarch Mixture* and pour it into the pan. Stir until thickened. Serve hot.

Yields 4 Servings   *Per Serving:* 197 calories, 319 mg. sodium, 58 mg. cholesterol

Further Modifications in Sodium: Reduce sodium to *220 mg. per serving* by substituting lower sodium soy sauce for the regular dark soy sauce.

咖哩牛肉

BEEF STIR-FRIED WITH ALMONDS

Steps	Ingredients
1	½ tablespoon wine
	1 teaspoon sesame oil
	½ tablespoon cornstarch
	⅛ teaspoon black pepper
2	12 ounces well-trimmed flank steak (Cut slantwise into slices 1 inch long by ⅛ inch thick.)
3	1 tablespoon dark soy sauce
	½ tablespoon wine
	1 teaspoon sugar
	½ tablespoon water
	½ teaspoon Chinese red vinegar
4	1 teaspoon cornstarch
	2 tablespoons water
5	1 teaspoon oil
	2 ounces raw almonds (approximately 40 almonds)
6	½ tablespoon oil
	½ tablespoon oil
	1 slice ginger, approximately 1 inch in diameter by ⅛ inch thick, smashed with the side of a cleaver
	2 cloves garlic, smashed with the side of a cleaver
	2 outer celery stalks, cut diagonally into ⅜-inch-thick slices
	½ cup bamboo shoots cut thinly into 1-inch long by ½-inch wide slices
	1 stalk green onion (scallion), cut into 1-inch sections.

Steps	Instructions
1	Combine the ingredients to form the *Marinade*.
2	Mix the beef into the *Marinade* and let stand for 20 minutes.
3	Combine the ingredients to form the *Sauce*. Set within easy reach.
4	Combine the ingredients to form the *Cornstarch Mixture*. Set within easy reach.
5	Heat the 1 teaspoon oil in a pan over medium-high heat and brown the almonds for approximately 2 to 3 minutes, stirring constantly. Remove onto a plate and let cool.
6	Heat ½ tablespoon oil in a pan over high heat until hazy. Put in the beef and stir-fry briskly for 1½ minutes. Remove and set aside. Heat the remaining ½ tablespoon oil in a pan over high heat until hazy. Put in the ginger and garlic and brown. Add the celery and stir-fry for 1 minute. Add bamboo shoots and stir-fry for 15 seconds. Return the beef to the pan and stir-fry for 1 minute. Put in the almonds and green onions. Pour in the *Sauce* and stir until bubbly. Suspend the *Cornstarch Mixture* and stir into pan until thickened. Serve hot.

Yields 4 Servings   *Per Serving:* 289 calories, 343 mg. sodium, 58 mg. cholesterol

Further Modifications in Sodium: Reduce sodium to *244 mg. per serving* by substituting lower sodium soy sauce for the regular dark soy sauce.

蠔
油
牛
肉

OYSTER SAUCE BEEF

Steps	Ingredients
1	½ tablespoon wine
	1 teaspoon dark soy sauce
	⅛ teaspoon white pepper
	½ teaspoon sesame oil
	1 teaspoon cornstarch
2	12 ounces well-trimmed flank steak (Slice thinly across the grain into 2-inch-long by ⅛-inch-thick strips.)
3	1 tablespoon oyster sauce
	½ teaspoon sugar
	2 tablespoons water
4	2 teaspoons cornstarch
	1 tablespoon water
5	1 tablespoon oil
	2 cloves garlic, finely minced
	1 stalk green onion (scallion), cut into 2-inch lengths
	3 slices ginger, approximately 1 inch in diameter by ⅛ inch thick, smashed with the side of a cleaver
	2 ounces snow peas (approximately 16 to 18) (Remove the tips and strings and cut in half diagonally.)

Steps	Instructions
1	Combine ingredients to form the *Marinade*.
2	Add beef to the *Marinade* and let stand for 30 minutes.
3	Combine the ingredients to form the *Sauce*. Set within easy reach.
4	Combine the ingredients to form the *Cornstarch Mixture*. Set within easy reach.
5	Heat the oil in a pan over high heat until hazy. Add the garlic, green onions, and ginger and brown. Put in the beef and stir-fry briskly for 30 seconds, separating the pieces for even browning. Put in snow peas and continue stir-frying for 30 seconds. Stir in the *Sauce* and heat until bubbly. Suspend the *Cornstarch Mixture* and stir it into the pan. When the sauce thickens, serve hot.

Yields 4 Servings   *Per Serving:* 184 calories, 399 mg. sodium, 61 mg. cholesterol

Further Modifications in Sodium: Reduce sodium to *283 mg. per serving* by decreasing the oyster sauce to 2 teaspoons and substituting lower sodium soy sauce for the regular dark soy sauce.

DRY-FRIED BEEF, SZECHWAN STYLE

Steps	Ingredients
1	½ tablespoon dark soy sauce
	½ tablespoon white wine or sherry
	1 teaspoon minced ginger
2	12 ounces well-trimmed flank steak (Slice thinly *along the grain* into 1½-inch-long matchstick-size strips.)
3	½ tablespoon oil
	1 teaspoon sugar
4	½ tablespoon oil
	½ teaspoon dried red pepper flakes (adjust for desired "hotness")
	1 medium carrot, cut into matchstick-size pieces
	2 stalks celery, cut into matchstick-size pieces
	½ tablespoon dark soy sauce
	1 teaspoon sesame oil

Steps	Instructions
1	Combine ingredients to form the *Marinade.*
2	Mix the beef into the *Marinade* and let stand for 20 minutes.
3	Heat the oil in a pan over high heat until hazy. Put in the beef and stir-fry briskly for 5 to 6 minutes, or until the beef is well browned and very little liquid remains. Sprinkle sugar over meat and stir until dissolved. Remove the meat from the pan and set within easy reach.
4	Heat the oil in a pan until hazy. Add the red pepper flakes, carrots, and celery. Stir-fry for 1 minute. Sprinkle in ½ tablespoon dark soy sauce. Return beef to the pan and stir-fry for 30 seconds. Sprinkle the sesame oil over the beef and stir-fry for 10 seconds. Serve hot.

Yields 4 Servings   *Per Serving:* 182 calories, 348 mg. sodium, 58 mg. cholesterol

Further Modifications in Sodium: Reduce sodium to *249 mg. per serving* by substituting lower sodium soy sauce for the regular dark soy sauce.

咖哩蕃茄牛肉

CURRY-TOMATO BEEF

Steps	Ingredients
1	2 teaspoons dark soy sauce
	2 teaspoons wine
	1 teaspoon cornstarch
	1 tablespoon water
	½ teaspoon sesame oil
2	12 ounces well-trimmed flank steak (Slice across the grain slantwise into 1½-inch-long by ⅛-inch-thick slices.)
3	1 tablespoon sugar
	1 tablespoon Madras-type curry powder
	1 teaspoon dark soy sauce
	3 tablespoons water
4	1 tablespoon cornstarch
	3 tablespoons water
5	1 tablespoon oil
	½ tablespoon oil
	1 medium green bell pepper (Seed, rib, and cut into ¾-inch squares.)
	1 medium yellow onion (Cut in half, then cut each half into 6 equal chunks.)
	2 medium tomatoes, each cut into 6 wedges

Steps	Instructions
1	Combine ingredients to form the *Marinade.*
2	Mix the beef with the *Marinade* and let stand for 20 minutes.
3	Combine ingredients to form *Sauce.* Set within easy reach.
4	Combine ingredients to form the *Cornstarch Mixture.* Set within easy reach.
5	Heat the 1 tablespoon oil in a pan over high heat until hazy. Put in the beef and stir-fry briskly for 1½ minutes, or until 80 percent done. Remove and set within easy reach. Add remaining ½ tablespoon oil to the pan and heat until hazy. Put in the green bell pepper and onions and stir-fry for 1½ minutes. Return beef to pan and stir-fry for 30 seconds. Put in tomatoes and gently stir-fry for 30 seconds. Pour in *Sauce* and stir-fry until bubbly. Suspend the *Cornstarch Mixture* and stir into the pan until the sauce thickens. Serve hot.

Yields 4 Servings   *Per Serving:* 234 calories, 326 mg. sodium, 58 mg. cholesterol

Further Modifications in Sodium: Reduce sodium to *227 mg. per serving* by substituting lower sodium soy sauce for the regular dark soy sauce.

GINGER BEEF

Steps	Ingredients
1	1 tablespoon wine
	1 teaspoon wine vinegar
	½ teaspoon cornstarch
	1 teaspoon water
2	12 ounces well-trimmed flank steak (Slice across the grain slantwise into 1½-inch-long by ⅛-inch-thick slices.)
3	1 tablespoon dark soy sauce
	¼ cup water
	1 teaspoon sesame oil
	1 teaspoon sugar
	1 tablespoon wine
4	½ tablespoon cornstarch
	1 tablespoon water
5	1 tablespoon oil
	2 cloves garlic, smashed with the side of a cleaver
	¼ cup sliced ginger, smashed with the side of a cleaver
	3 stalks green onions (scallions), cut into 1½-inch lengths

Steps	Instructions
1	Combine ingredients to form the *Marinade*.
2	Mix the beef into the *Marinade* and let stand for 20 minutes.
3	Combine ingredients to form the *Sauce*. Set within easy reach.
4	Combine ingredients to form the *Cornstarch Mixture*. Set within easy reach.
5	Heat the oil in a pan over high heat until hazy. Add the garlic and brown. Put in the beef, ginger, and green onions and stir-fry briskly for 1 minute. Pour in the *Sauce* and continue stir-frying until the liquid bubbles. Suspend the *Cornstarch Mixture* and add to the pan. Stir until thickened. Serve hot.

Yields 4 Servings   *Per Serving:* 197 calories, 326 mg. sodium, 58 mg. cholesterol

Further Modifications in Sodium: Reduce sodium to *227 mg. per serving* by substituting lower sodium soy sauce for the regular dark soy sauce.

生薑炒牛肉

冬
菇
炒
牛
肉

BEEF STIR-FRIED WITH DRIED MUSHROOMS

Steps	Ingredients
1	½ teaspoon five spice powder
	1 tablespoon wine
	½ teaspoon ginger, finely minced
	1 clove garlic, finely minced
	1 teaspoon sesame oil
	½ teaspoon oil
2	12 ounces well-trimmed flank steak (Slice across the grain slantwise into 1½-inch-long by ⅛-inch-thick slices.)
3	1 tablespoon dark soy sauce
	2 teaspoons sugar
	⅛ teaspoon white pepper
4	2 teaspoons cornstarch
	1 tablespoon water
5	1 tablespoon oil
	9 medium Chinese dried mushrooms (Soak, stem, squeeze out excess water, and cut into strips ⅛ inch wide.)
	1 small yellow onion (Cut in half, then cut each half into 8 equal chunks.)
	1 stalk green onion (scallion) (Cut into 2-inch lengths and shred lengthwise.)

Steps	Instructions
1	Combine ingredients to form the *Marinade*.
2	Put the beef into the *Marinade* and let stand for 20 minutes.
3	Combine the ingredients to form the *Sauce*. Set within easy reach.
4	Combine the ingredients to form the *Cornstarch Mixture*. Set within easy reach.
5	Heat the oil in a pan over high heat until hazy. Put in the mushrooms and yellow onion. Stir-fry for 1 minute. Add the beef to the pan and stir-fry briskly for 1 minute. Pour in the *Sauce* and heat until bubbly. Suspend the *Cornstarch Mixture* and stir into the pan until thickened. Garnish with green onions and serve.

Yields 4 Servings   *Per Serving:* 204 calories, 317 mg. sodium, 58 mg. cholesterol

Further Modifications in Sodium: Reduce sodium to *218 mg. per serving* by substituting lower sodium soy sauce for the regular dark soy sauce.

PEPPER BEEF WITH BLACK BEAN SAUCE

豉椒牛肉

Steps	Ingredients
1	1 teaspoon sugar
	½ tablespoon dark soy sauce
	4 tablespoons water
	1 teaspoon cornstarch
	2 teaspoons wine
2	12 ounces well-trimmed flank steak (Slice across the grain into 1½-inch-long by ⅛-inch-thick strips.)
3	1 tablespoon oil
	½ tablespoon oil
	2 cloves garlic, smashed with the side of a cleaver
	1 tablespoon minced ginger
	1 medium green bell pepper (Seed, rib, and cut into ¾-inch square pieces.)
	1 medium yellow onion (Cut in half, then cut each half into 6 equal chunks.)
	2 tablespoons fermented black beans, rinsed then mashed with 1 tablespoon water

Steps	Instructions
1	Combine ingredients to form the *Marinade*.
2	Mix the beef into the *Marinade* and let stand for 15 minutes.
3	Heat the 1 tablespoon oil in a pan over high heat until hazy. Put in the beef and stir-fry briskly for 45 seconds, or until 80 percent done. Remove and set within easy reach. Heat the ½ tablespoon oil in the pan until hazy. Brown the garlic and ginger. Discard the garlic. Add the green bell pepper and onion and stir-fry for 1 minute. Return the beef with its accompanying juices to the pan, stir-fry for 30 seconds. Serve piping hot.

Yields 4 Servings   *Per Serving:* 207 calories, 348 mg. sodium, 58 mg. cholesterol

Further Modifications in Sodium: Reduce sodium to *224 mg. per serving* by decreasing the black beans to 1 tablespoon and substituting lower sodium soy sauce for the regular dark soy sauce.

紅
燒
牛
肉

SZECHWAN BEEF STEW

Steps		Ingredients
1	12	ounces boneless beef shank, well trimmed and cut into 1-inch cubes
	1¼	cups homemade stock without salt or water
2	1	tablespoon wine
	3	stalks green onions (scallions), cut into 4-inch lengths
	3	slices ginger, 1 inch in diameter by ⅛ inch thick, smashed
	1	whole pod star anise
3	½	tablespoon oil
	3	cloves garlic, smashed
	1	teaspoon Szechwan peppercorns
	¼	teaspoon flaked red peppers (if hot dish is desired)
	2	teaspoons hot bean sauce
	2	tablespoons homemade stock without salt or water
4	3	medium carrots, roll-cut into 1-inch chunks, or use 1½ carrots and 1½ cups law bak (daikon)
	½	tablespoon dark soy sauce
	1	tablespoon sesame oil
5	1	tablespoon cornstarch
	⅓	cup homemade stock without salt or water

Steps	Instructions
1	Put the meat into a pot and add the stock or water. Bring to a boil watching carefully as foaming may occur. Skim off the foam and replace any liquid lost.
2	Add the wine, green onion, ginger, and star anise to the meat. Cover the pot and simmer over low heat for approximately 45 minutes, stirring occasionally.
3	Heat the oil in a pan over high heat until hazy. Add the garlic, peppercorns, and flaked red peppers (optional) and brown. Add the hot bean sauce and stir for 10 seconds. Put in 2 tablespoons homemade stock and stir until bubbly. Line a strainer with cheesecloth and pour the contents through the strainer into the pot of beef. Tie up the cheesecloth with the garlic and peppercorn residue and put it into the pot with the beef.
4	Add carrots, soy sauce, and oil to pot and continue simmering for an additional 45 minutes. Stir often to coat the contents.
5	Combine cornstarch with the cooled homemade stock and add to pot, stirring constantly until the sauce is thickened. Discard ginger, star anise, and cheesecloth sack. Serve immediately.

Yields 4 Servings   *Per Serving:* 235 calories, 383 mg. sodium, 58 mg. cholesterol

Further Modifications in Sodium: Reduce sodium to *334 mg. per serving* by substituting lower sodium sauce for the regular dark soy sauce.

BEEF STIR-FRIED WITH SHOESTRING POTATOES

牛
肉
炒
薯
仔
絲

Steps	Ingredients
1	1 teaspoon Worcestershire sauce
	1 tablespoon dark soy sauce
	½ teaspoon cornstarch
	1 teaspoon wine
	⅛ teaspoon sesame oil
	⅛ teaspoon sugar
	pinch of white pepper
2	12 ounces well-trimmed flank steak (Cut lengthwise *along* the grain into matchstick-size pieces.)
3	½ tablespoon oil
	1 medium potato, peeled (Cut into matchstick-size pieces, rinse well under water, and dry on paper towels.)
	pinch of white pepper
4	2 teaspoons oil
	1 stalk green onion (scallion) (Cut into 1½-inch lengths and shred.)

Steps	Instructions
1	Combine ingredients to form the *Marinade.*
2	Mix the beef into the *Marinade* and let stand for 15 minutes.
3	Heat the oil in a pan over high heat until hazy. Put in the potatoes and sprinkle in the pepper. Stir-fry until the potatoes are browned. Remove from pan and set within easy reach.
4	Heat the remaining 2 teaspoons oil in the pan until hazy. Put in the beef with accompanying juices and the green onions. Stir-fry until the beef is lightly browned. Add the potatoes and stir-fry for 1 minute. Serve hot.

Yields 4 Servings   *Per Serving:* 189 calories, 333 mg. sodium, 58 mg. cholesterol

Further Modifications in Sodium: Reduce sodium to *234 mg. per serving* by substituting lower sodium soy sauce for the regular dark soy sauce.

STEAMED BEEF PATTY

蒸
牛
肉
餅

Steps	Ingredients
1	⅛ teaspoon black pepper
	½ teaspoon sesame oil
	1 tablespoon light soy sauce
	1½ teaspoons cornstarch
	1 teaspoon wine
2	12 ounces well-trimmed beef, ground
	12 water chestnuts, chopped coarsely
	4 Chinese dried mushrooms (Soak, stem, squeeze out excess water, and chop.)
	½ egg white, slightly beaten
3	1 slice ginger, approximately 1 inch in diameter by ⅛ inch thick, sliced into thin strips
4	1 teaspoon sesame oil

Steps	Instructions
1	Combine ingredients to form the *Sauce* in a heat-proof dish.
2	Combine the beef, water chestnuts, Chinese mushrooms, and egg white into the *Sauce*. Spread the beef mixture in the dish, pressing to form a patty ⅜ inch thick.
3	Place the ginger strips on top of beef patty. Place the dish in steamer and steam for 12 minutes covered.
4	Remove the dish from the steamer. Discard ginger strips. Sprinkle with sesame oil. Serve hot.

Yields 4 Servings   *Per Serving:* 157 calories, 398 mg. sodium, 58 mg. cholesterol

Further Modifications in Sodium: Reduce sodium to *224 mg. per serving* by substituting lower sodium soy sauce for the regular light soy sauce.

LAMB STIR-FRIED WITH GREEN ONIONS

Steps	Ingredients
1	½ tablespoon oil
	2 teaspoons dark soy sauce
	1 tablespoon wine
	½ teaspoon Szechwan peppercorn powder*
2	12 ounces boneless leg of lamb meat, well trimmed and cut into very thin slices across the grain
	4 stalks green onions (scallions) (Cut into 1½-inch lengths, then shred lengthwise.)
3	1 teaspoon dark soy sauce
	1 tablespoon Chinese brown vinegar
	1 tablespoon sesame oil
4	1 tablespoon oil
	3 cloves garlic, very thinly sliced

Steps	Instructions
1	Combine the ingredients to form the *Marinade*.
2	Put the lamb into the *Marinade* and let stand for 30 minutes. Then add the green onions.
3	Combine the ingredients to form the *Sauce*. Set within easy reach.
4	Heat the oil in a pan over high heat until hazy. Add the garlic and stir-fry until browned. Put the lamb and green onions in and stir-fry for 1 minute. Pour in the *Sauce* and continue stir-frying until bubbly. Serve hot.

Yields 4 Servings   *Per Serving:* 212 calories, 343 mg. sodium, 60 mg. cholesterol

Further Modifications in Sodium: Reduce sodium to *244 mg. per serving* by substituting lower sodium soy sauce for the regular dark soy sauce.

To prepare powder: Place 1 tablespoon whole Szechwan peppercorns in a small pan over medium heat. Stir constantly until peppercorns turn dark brown in color. Take out and put into a small bowl. Crush into a fine powder by using the pommel of a cleaver. Discard any uncrushed pieces. Measure out the ½ teaspoon powder and store remainder for future use.

LAMB WITH SWEET BEAN SAUCE

Steps	Ingredients
1	1 tablespoon sweet bean sauce
	½ tablespoon dark soy sauce
	1 teaspoon sugar
	2 tablespoons water
2	12 ounces well-trimmed boneless lamb, thinly sliced
	3 cups boiling water
3	1 tablespoon oil
	3 cloves garlic, smashed with the side of a cleaver
	1 stalk green onion (scallion), cut into ⅛-inch sections

Steps	Instructions
1	Combine ingredients to form the *Sauce*. Set within easy reach.
2	Put the sliced lamb into the boiling water for 1 minute, then remove and drain well.
3	Heat the oil in a pan over high heat until hazy. Brown the garlic and green onion. Put in the lamb and stir-fry briskly for 30 seconds. Pour in the *Sauce* and continue stir-frying for 30 seconds. Serve hot.

Yields 4 Servings   *Per Serving:* 161 calories, 319 mg. sodium, 60 mg. cholesterol

Further Modifications in Sodium: Reduce sodium to *270 mg. per serving* by substituting lower sodium soy sauce for the regular dark soy sauce.

醬爆羊肉

切
羊
肉

COLD CUT LAMB

Steps	Ingredients
1	1 tablespoon wine
	½ teaspoon white pepper
	12 ounces well-trimmed boneless leg of lamb, in one piece
2	1 dried red chili pepper
	1 stalk green onion (scallion), shredded
	1 clove garlic, minced
3	1 small cucumber, peeled and thinly sliced into 7-inch-long strips
4	1 tablespoon dark soy sauce
	1 tablespoon sugar
	½ tablespoon oil
	½ tablespoon sesame oil
	⅓ cup water

Steps	Instructions
1	Combine wine and white pepper and rub the mixture over the lamb. Then place the meat in a medium saucepan.
2	Add the chili pepper, green onion, and garlic to the pan. Fill the pan with water until meat is covered. Bring to a boil, reduce the heat to medium, cover, and cook for 45 minutes. The meat should be soft but firm. Remove meat from pan when cooked and let it cool. Then slice across the grain as thinly as possible. Arrange on a serving platter. Refrigerate until ready to use.
3	Arrange the cucumber slices on the serving platter with the lamb.
4	Combine ingredients to form the *Sauce*. Pour the sauce over the lamb and cucumber at least 1 hour before serving.

Yields 4 Servings   Per Serving: 169 calories, 317 mg. sodium, 60 mg. cholesterol

Further Modifications in Sodium: Reduce sodium to *218 mg. per serving* by substituting lower sodium soy sauce for the regular dark soy sauce.

PORK

薑
蔥
肉

BOY SCOUT PORK

Steps	Ingredients
1	1 tablespoon Chinese red vinegar
	1 tablespoon dark soy sauce
	2 tablespoons brown sugar
	1 teaspoon sesame oil
2	12 ounces well-trimmed boneless pork loin, cut into matchstick-size pieces.
3	1 tablespoon oil
	2 slices ginger, approximately 1 inch in diameter by ⅛ inch thick, smashed with the side of a cleaver
	2 cloves garlic, smashed with the side of a cleaver
	1 large stalk green onion (scallion), cut into 1½-inch lengths
	½ cup bamboo shoots, cut into matchstick size
	1 tablespoon water

Steps	Instructions
1	Combine ingredients to form the *Marinade*.
2	Put pork in the *Marinade* and let stand 15 minutes.
3	Heat the oil in a pan over high heat until hazy. Brown the ginger, garlic, and green onion for 1 minute. Put in pork and stir-fry until most of liquid has evaporated (3 to 5 minutes). Put in bamboo shoots. Reduce heat to medium-high and add 1 tablespoon water. Continue cooking until the liquid thickens. Serve hot.

Yields 4 Servings   *Per Serving:* 214 calories, 316 mg. sodium, 53 mg. cholesterol

Further Modifications in Sodium: Reduce sodium to *180 mg. per serving* by substituting lower sodium soy sauce for the regular dark soy sauce.

咕
嚕
肉

SWEET AND SOUR PORK CANTONESE

Steps	Ingredients

Steps **Ingredients**

1
    1 tablespoon wine
    ½ tablespoon dark soy sauce
    ⅛ teaspoon white pepper

2
  12 ounces well-trimmed boneless pork butt (Lightly tenderize with a mallet and cut into 1-inch cubes.)

3
    2 tablespoons tomato paste without salt
    2 tablespoons white vinegar
    2 tablespoons sugar
    ½ tablespoon dark soy sauce
    1 teaspoon sesame oil
    2 tablespoons water
    2 tablespoons pineapple juice

4
  2½ tablespoons cornstarch (Spread on a 10- to 12-inch plate.)
    2 teaspoons sesame oil

5
    ½ tablespoon oil
    3 slices ginger, approximately 1 inch in diameter by ⅛ inch thick, smashed with the side of a cleaver
    1 small green bell pepper (Seed, rib, and cut into ¾-inch squares.)
    1 small yellow onion (Cut in half, then cut each half into 8 equal chunks.)
    1 8-ounce can unsweetened pineapple chunks packed in juice (Drain well, reserving 2 tablespoons juice for the sauce.)

Steps	Instructions
1	Combine ingredients to form the *Marinade*.
2	Mix the pork into the *Marinade* and let stand for at least 20 minutes.
3	Combine ingredients to form *Sauce*. Set within easy reach.
4	Dredge pieces of pork in cornstarch so all sides are well coated. Broil pork on a rack which has been placed over a cookie sheet. Put the rack approximately 7 to 8 inches away from the heating element. Broil for 5 minutes, then baste with the sesame oil. Continue to broil the same side for an additional 5 minutes. Then turn the pieces over and repeat. Remove the pork when nicely browned and keep warm.
5	Heat the oil in a pan over high heat until hazy. Put in the ginger and brown on both sides. Put in the green pepper and onion and stir-fry briskly for 1½ minutes. Pour in the *Sauce* and return the pork to the pan. Add the pineapple chunks and stir for 10 seconds or until bubbly. Serve hot.

Yields 4 Servings   *Per Serving:* 304 calories, 321 mg. sodium, 53 mg. cholesterol

Further Modifications in Sodium: Reduce sodium to *222 mg. per serving* by substituting lower sodium soy sauce for the regular dark soy sauce.

魚
香
肉
絲

FRAGRANT PORK

Steps	Ingredients
1	½ tablespoon cornstarch
	½ teaspoon sesame oil
2	12 ounces well-trimmed boneless pork loin, cut into matchstick-size pieces
3	1 medium stalk green onion (scallion), minced
	½ tablespoon dark soy sauce
	1 tablespoon Chinese brown vinegar
	1 teaspoon hot bean sauce
	1 tablespoon wine
	1 teaspoon sugar
	½ teaspoon sesame oil
4	1 tablespoon oil
	½ tablespoon oil
	½ tablespoon minced ginger
	1 teaspoon minced garlic
	½ cup bamboo shoots or water chestnuts, cut into fine strips
	4 medium wood fungus (Soak for 15 minutes, cut out and discard any tough parts, and cut the wood fungus into fine strips.)

Steps	Instructions
1	Combine the ingredients to form the *Marinade*.
2	Mix the pork into the *Marinade* and let stand for 15 minutes.
3	Combine the ingredients to form the *Sauce*. Set within easy reach.
4	Heat the 1 tablespoon oil in a pan over high heat until hazy. Put in the pork and stir-fry briskly for 1½ minutes. Remove from the pan and set within easy reach. (The pork does not need to be completely cooked at this point.)

Heat the pan with the remaining ½ tablespoon oil until hazy. Put in the ginger and garlic and brown. Put in the bamboo shoots or water chestnuts and wood fungus. Stir briskly for 30 seconds. Return the pork to the pan and stir-fry for 30 seconds. Add the *Sauce* and continue stir-frying until bubbly. Serve hot.

Yields 4 Servings   *Per Serving:* 227 calories, 276 mg. sodium, 53 mg. cholesterol

Further Modifications in Sodium: Reduce sodium to *227 mg. per serving* by substituting lower sodium soy sauce for the regular dark soy sauce.

TWICE-COOKED PORK

回
鍋
肉

Steps	Ingredients
1	5 cups water 1 cup ice cubes
2	5 cups water 12 ounces well-trimmed boneless pork loin (Slice into thin strips 1½ inches wide by 1½ inches long.)
3	½ tablespoon hot bean sauce ½ tablespoon dark soy sauce 1 teaspoon sugar 1 teaspoon sesame oil 1 teaspoon wine
4	½ tablespoon oil 6 Chinese dried mushrooms (Soak, squeeze out excess water, stem, and quarter.) ½ cup bamboo shoots, thinly sliced into 1-inch squares 1 small green bell pepper (Seed, rib, and cut into 1-inch squares.)
5	½ tablespoon oil 2 tablespoons water

Steps	Instructions
1	Put the water and ice cubes in a bowl and set aside.
2	Bring the 5 cups water to a boil in a medium-sized saucepan. Put in the pork slices and stir to separate. When the meat is barely cooked, pour the pork into a colander and immediately rinse with cold running water. Then plunge the meat into the bowl of ice water. Add more ice cubes from time to time.*
3	Combine ingredients to form the *Sauce*. Set within easy reach.
4	Heat the oil in a pan over high heat until hazy. Put in the pork and mushrooms and stir-fry for 2 minutes. Add the bamboo shoots and green peppers and stir-fry for 1 minute. Remove and set aside.
5	Heat the oil in a pan until hazy. Pour in the *Sauce* and stir well. Add the water and stir until bubbly. Return the pork mixture to the pan and stir-fry briskly until the ingredients are piping hot. Serve hot.

Yields 4 Servings   *Per Serving:* 203 calories, 294 mg. sodium, 53 mg. cholesterol

Further Modifications in Sodium: Reduce sodium to *203 mg. per serving* by decreasing the hot bean sauce to 1 teaspoon and substituting lower sodium soy sauce for the regular dark soy sauce.

*Ice water firms up the meat and gives it more body.

BOILED PORK WITH HOT PEPPER SAUCE

蒜
泥
白
肉

Steps	Ingredients
1	12 ounces well-trimmed boneless pork butt, in one piece
	water
2	1 tablespoon water
	2 teaspoons sweet bean sauce
	2 teaspoons dark soy sauce
	1 teaspoon Chinese brown vinegar
	½ teaspoon hot chili oil
3	1 teaspoon oil
	2 to 3 cloves garlic, finely minced
4	1 cup cold water
	1 teaspoon white vinegar
	1 teaspoon sugar
	½ medium cucumber, peeled and thinly sliced lengthwise
5	1 tablespoon sesame seeds

Steps	Instructions
1	Put the whole piece of pork into a pot. Add enough water to cover the pork. Bring the water to a boil, then simmer, covered, for approximately 30 minutes. Do not overcook. When the meat is cooked, take it out and allow it to cool. If prepared earlier, refrigerate.
2	Combine ingredients to form the *Sauce*. Set within easy reach.
3	Heat the 1 teaspoon oil in a pan over medium-high heat. Add the garlic and stir until lightly browned. Add the *Sauce* and stir until bubbly. Set aside to cool.
4	Combine the cold water with the vinegar and sugar. Add the cucumber slices to the vinegar mixture and soak, refrigerated, for 30 minutes or more.
5	Slice the pork as thinly as possible across the grain. Arrange the slices on a serving platter. Decorate with the drained, chilled cucumber slices. When ready to serve, pour the *Sauce* over the pork slices and sprinkle with sesame seeds.

Yields 4 Servings   *Per Serving:* 188 calories, 324 mg. sodium, 53 mg. cholesterol

Further Modifications in Sodium: Reduce sodium to *258 mg. per serving* by substituting lower sodium soy sauce for the regular dark soy sauce.

PORK WITH SWEET BEAN SAUCE

Steps	Ingredients
1	½ tablespoon wine 1 teaspoon dark soy sauce ⅛ teaspoon white pepper 1 teaspoon cornstarch
2	12 ounces well-trimmed boneless pork loin, cut into matchstick-size pieces 1 teaspoon sesame oil
3	1½ tablespoons sweet bean sauce 4 cloves garlic, finely minced (Use less, if desired.) 1 tablespoon water
4	1 tablespoon oil ½ tablespoon oil ½ medium green bell pepper (Seed, rib, and cut into matchstick-size pieces.) 6 water chestnuts (Cut into ⅟₁₆-inch-thick slices, then cut into thirds lengthwise.)

Steps	Instructions
1	Combine ingredients to form the *Marinade*.
2	Mix the pork in the *Marinade*, then add the sesame oil. Let stand for 15 minutes.
3	Combine ingredients to form the *Sauce*. Set within easy reach.
4	Heat the 1 tablespoon oil in a pan over high heat until hazy. Put in the pork and stir-fry for 1½ minutes. Remove the pork and set aside. Heat the ½ tablespoon oil in the pan until hazy. Put in the green bell pepper and stir-fry for 1 minute. Add the water chestnuts and continue stir-frying for 10 seconds. Stir in the *Sauce* and heat until it is bubbly. Return the pork and accompanying juices to the pan and stir-fry for 1 minute. Serve hot.

Yields 4 Servings   *Per Serving:* 224 calories, 321 mg. sodium, 53 mg. cholesterol

Further Modifications in Sodium: Reduce sodium to *224 mg. per serving* by decreasing the sweet bean sauce to 1 tablespoon and substituting lower sodium soy sauce for the regular dark soy sauce.

花生炆肉

STEWED PORK WITH PEANUTS AND FRESH MUSHROOMS

Steps	Ingredients
1	1 cup water
	½ cup raw peanuts, skinned
2	12 ounces well-trimmed boneless pork butt, cut into 1-inch cubes
	1 tablespoon dark soy sauce
	½ tablespoon sugar
	1 teaspoon Chinese brown vinegar
	pinch of white pepper
	1 tablespoon wine
3	1 cup fresh button mushrooms

Steps	Instructions
1	Put the water in a pot and add the peanuts. Cover and bring to a boil. Then reduce the heat to low and simmer for 20 minutes.
2	Add the ingredients listed in step 2 to the pot. Bring the contents to a boil again and reduce the heat to low. Cover and simmer for an additional 20 minutes. Stir frequently to ensure even cooking.
3	Add the mushrooms, cover, and cook for 2 minutes. Serve hot.

Yields 4 Servings   _Per Serving:_ 257 calories, 321 mg. sodium, 53 mg. cholesterol

Further Modifications in Sodium: Reduce sodium to _222 mg. per serving_ by substituting lower sodium soy sauce for the regular dark soy sauce.

南乳爆肉絲

PORK WITH RED FERMENTED BEAN CAKE

Steps	Ingredients
1	1 egg white, lightly beaten
	12 ounces well-trimmed boneless pork loin, cut into matchstick-size pieces
2	1½ tablespoons mashed red fermented bean cake
	1 tablespoon wine
	1 teaspoon sugar
	1 teaspoon cornstarch
	2 tablespoons water
3	1½ tablespoons oil
	1 stalk green onion (scallion), cut into 2-inch lengths

Steps	Instructions
1	Mix the egg white with the pork and stir thoroughly. Let stand for 10 minutes.
2	Combine the ingredients to form the *Sauce*. Set within easy reach.
3	Heat the oil in a pan over high heat until hazy. Put in the pork and stir-fry, separating the pieces for even browning. Stir for 2 minutes, or until the pork turns white. Pour in the *Sauce* and continue stir-frying until bubbly and thickened. Put in green onion and stir for 10 seconds. Serve hot.

Yields 4 Servings   *Per Serving:* 204 calories, 298 mg. sodium, 53 mg. cholesterol

Further Modifications in Sodium: Reduce sodium to *215 mg. per serving* by decreasing the red fermented bean cake to 1 tablespoon.

SWEET AND SOUR PORK, NORTHERN STYLE

糖
醋
肉

Steps	Ingredients	
1	2	tablespoons Chinese brown vinegar
	2	tablespoons sugar
	½	tablespoons wine
	1	tablespoon dark soy sauce
		pinch of white pepper
2	1	tablespoon oil
	2	slices ginger, each 1 inch in diameter by ⅛ inch thick, smashed with the side of a cleaver
	2	cloves garlic, smashed with the side of a cleaver
	12	ounces well-trimmed boneless pork loin (Cut into thin slices 2 inches long by ¾ inch wide by ⅛ inch thick.)

Steps	Instructions
1	Combine ingredients to form the *Sauce*. Set within easy reach.
2	Heat the oil in a pan over high heat until hazy. Add the ginger and garlic and brown. Put in the pork slices and stir-fry until the pork is cooked and half the sauce has evaporated. Serve hot.

Yields 4 Servings   *Per Serving:* 203 calories, 343 mg. sodium, 53 mg. cholesterol

Further Modifications in Sodium: Reduce sodium to *244 mg. per serving* by substituting lower sodium soy sauce for the regular dark soy sauce.

腐
竹
炆
豬
肉

PORK WITH DRIED BEAN CURD STICKS IN FERMENTED BEAN CAKE SAUCE

Steps	Ingredients
1	½ tablespoon oil
	2 slices ginger, approximately 1 inch in diameter by ⅛ inch thick, smashed with the side of a cleaver
	2 cloves garlic, smashed with the side of a cleaver
	10 ounces well-trimmed boneless pork butt, cut into 1-inch cubes
2	1½ cups homemade stock without salt or water
	2 U-shaped dried bean curd sticks (Presoak for 2 hours, or until soft, and cut into 2-inch lengths.)
	6 Chinese dried mushrooms (Soak, squeeze out excess water, stem, and quarter.)
	1 cup sliced bamboo shoots
	½ small yellow onion, cut into 6 equal chunks
3	1 tablespoon wine
	1 tablespoon fermented bean cake, mashed
	½ tablespoon dark soy sauce
	½ tablespoon sugar
	½ teaspoon sesame oil
	1 stalk green onion (scallion), cut crosswise into ⅛-inch sections

Steps	Instructions
1	Heat the oil in a pan over high heat until hazy. Brown the ginger and garlic. Add the pork and brown on all sides. Remove from the pan and set aside.
2	In a medium-sized saucepan, bring the homemade stock or water to a boil. Put in the pork with the ginger and garlic, bean curd sticks, mushrooms, bamboo shoots, and onion. When the liquid begins to boil again, turn the heat to low and simmer for 30 minutes.
3	Combine the ingredients to form the *Sauce* and add the sauce all at once to the pot. Stir. Cover and simmer for 45 minutes to 1 hour, or until the pork is tender. Stir occasionally. Serve hot.

Yields 4 Servings   *Per Serving:* 234 calories, 339 mg. sodium, 44 mg. cholesterol

Further Modifications in Sodium: Reduce sodium to *290 mg. per serving* by substituting lower sodium soy sauce for the regular dark soy sauce.

PORK WITH FERMENTED BEAN CAKE

Steps	Ingredients
1	½ tablespoon dark soy sauce
	2 tablespoons wine
	1 tablespoon sugar
	1 tablespoon fermented bean curd
2	½ teaspoon cornstarch
	2 tablespoons water
3	1 tablespoon oil
	2 cloves garlic, smashed with the side of a cleaver
	12 ounces well-trimmed boneless pork loin (Slice across the grain into 1-inch-long by ¾-inch-wide by ⅛-inch-thick slices.)
	½ medium yellow onion, cut into 8 equal chunks

Steps	Instructions
1	Combine ingredients to form the *Sauce*. Set within easy reach.
2	Combine ingredients to form the *Cornstarch Mixture*. Set within easy reach.
3	Heat the oil in a pan over high heat until hazy. Brown the garlic and discard. Put in the pork and stir-fry briskly for 1 minute. Add the onion and continue stir-frying for 2 minutes. Pour in the *Sauce* and stir until it is bubbly. Suspend the *Cornstarch Mixture* and stir it into the pan until the sauce has thickened. Serve hot.

Yields 4 Servings   *Per Serving:* 197 calories, 314 mg. sodium, 53 mg. cholesterol

Further Modifications in Sodium: Reduce sodium to *215 mg. per serving* by decreasing the fermented bean cure to 2 teaspoons and substituting lower sodium soy sauce for the regular dark soy sauce.

鹹
蝦
蒸
豬
肉

STEAMED PORK WITH SHRIMP PASTE

Steps	Ingredients
1	½ teaspoon cornstarch
	2 teaspoons wine
	1 tablespoon shrimp paste
	1 teaspoon sesame oil
2	12 ounces well-trimmed boneless pork loin (Sliced across the grain into 1½-inch-long by 1-inch-wide by ⅛-inch-thick slices.)
3	4 slices ginger, approximately 1 inch in diameter by ⅛ inch thick, cut into thin strips

Steps	Instructions
1	Combine ingredients to form the *Marinade*.
2	Mix the pork slices into the *Marinade* and let stand for 15 minutes. Spread the meat mixture in a heat-proof dish.
3	Top the pork with ginger strips. Place in a steamer and cook for 30 minutes. Serve hot.

Yields 4 Servings   *Per Serving:* 158 calories, 359 mg. sodium, 57 mg. cholesterol

Further Modifications in Sodium: Reduce sodium to *199 mg. per serving* by decreasing the shrimp paste to ½ tablespoon.

TOFU

豆腐肉粒

TOFU STIR-FRIED WITH GROUND PORK

Steps	Ingredients
1	½ tablespoon sugar
	1 tablespoon dark soy sauce
	½ tablespoon wine
	1 tablespoon water
2	2 teaspoons cornstarch
	3 tablespoons water
3	1 tablespoon oil
	1 teaspoon minced ginger
	white section of 1 stalk of green onion (scallion), minced
	6 ounces well-trimmed boneless pork, ground
	1 tub (14 to 16 ounces) soft tofu, cut into ¾-inch squares
	½ teaspoon red pepper flakes
	green section of 1 stalk of green onion, cut into 1½-inch lengths

Steps	Instructions
1	Combine the ingredients to form the *Sauce*. Set within easy reach.
2	Combine the ingredients to form the *Cornstarch Mixture*. Set within easy reach.
3	Heat the oil in a pan over high heat until hazy. Add the ginger and white sections of green onion and brown lightly. Put in the pork and stir-fry for 45 seconds, separating the pieces for even browning. Add the tofu and gently stir-fry for 1 minute. Turn down heat to medium-high. Pour in the *Sauce* and sprinkle in the red pepper flakes. Stir, cover, and cook for 45 seconds. Suspend the *Cornstarch Mixture* and stir it into the pan until the sauce is thickened. Serve hot, garnished with the green sections of onion.

Yields 4 Servings   *Per Serving:* 205 calories, 288 mg. sodium, 27 mg. cholesterol

Further Modifications in Sodium: Reduce sodium to *189 mg. per serving* by substituting lower sodium soy sauce for the regular dark soy sauce.

TOFU AND PORK WITH OYSTER SAUCE

蠔
油
豆
腐
肉

Steps	Ingredients
1	1 teaspoon light soy sauce
	1 teaspoon sugar
	1 tablespoon wine
	¼ teaspoon white pepper
2	⅓ cup water
	1 tablespoon cornstarch
	2 teaspoons oyster sauce
3	1 tablespoon oil
	2 cloves garlic
	16 ounces soft tofu (Cut into 1-inch cubes, drain, and dry on paper towels.)
4	½ tablespoon oil
	6 ounces well-trimmed boneless pork loin, sliced thinly across the grain
	8 Chinese dried mushrooms (Soak, squeeze out excess water, stem, and quarter.)
	½ cup water
	1 stalk green onion, cut into 2-inch lengths

Steps	Instructions
1	Combine the ingredients to form the *Sauce*. Set within easy reach.
2	Combine the ingredients to form the *Cornstarch Mixture*. Set within easy reach.
3	Heat the 1 tablespoon oil in a pan over high heat until hazy. Brown and discard the garlic. Put in the tofu and stir-fry gently until lightly brown on both sides. Remove from the pan and set within easy reach.
4	Heat the ½ tablespoon oil in a pan over high heat until hazy. Put in the pork and stir-fry until lightly browned. Pour in the *Sauce* and stir for 5 to 10 seconds. Add the mushrooms and return the tofu to the pan. Stir-fry for 10 seconds. Pour in the water and gently stir until the liquid is bubbly. Suspend the *Cornstarch Mixture* and add to pan, gently stir until the sauce thickens. Serve hot, garnished with the green onions.

Yields 4 Servings   *Per Serving:* 230 calories, 313 mg. sodium, 27 mg. cholesterol

Further Modifications in Sodium: Reduce sodium to *255 mg. per serving* by substituting lower sodium soy sauce for the regular light soy sauce.

MA PO TOFU

Steps	Ingredients
1	1 tub (14 to 16 ounces) soft tofu, drained, cut into ½-inch cubes
	4½ cups water
2	½ tablespoon hot bean sauce
	2 teaspoons dark soy sauce
	½ teaspoon sugar
	½ teaspoon sesame oil
	1 tablespoon wine
3	1 teaspoon cornstarch
	¼ cup water
4	1 tablespoon oil
	1 clove garlic, minced
	1 stalk green onion (scallion), minced
	5 ounces well-trimmed boneless pork, ground or coarsely chopped
	⅓ cup water

Steps	Instructions
1	Heat the 4½ cups water in a medium-sized saucepan until boiling. Put in the diced tofu and when the water returns to boil, cook for 30 seconds. Remove the tofu and drain in a colander.
2	Combine the ingredients to form the *Sauce*. Set within easy reach.
3	Combine the ingredients to form the *Cornstarch Mixture*. Set within easy reach.
4	Heat the oil in a pan over high heat until hazy. Put in the garlic and brown. Add the green onion and pork and stir-fry briskly for 1 minute. Pour in the *Sauce* and stir until bubbly. Put the tofu in and pour in the ⅓ cup water. When mixture is hot and bubbly, suspend the *Cornstarch Mixture* and stir it into pan. Cook until the sauce has thickened. Serve hot.

Yields 4 Servings   *Per Serving:* 195 calories, 324 mg. sodium, 22 mg. cholesterol

Further Modifications in Sodium: Reduce sodium to *216 mg. per serving* by decreasing the hot bean sauce to 1 teaspoon and substituting lower sodium soy sauce for the regular dark soy sauce.

麻
婆
豆
腐

宫保豆腐

KUNG PAO TOFU

Steps	Ingredients
1	1 tablespoon wine
	½ teaspoon cornstarch
2	5 ounces well-trimmed boneless pork, thinly sliced
3	½ tablespoon dark soy sauce
	1 teaspoon sugar
	¼ cup water
	½ teaspoon sesame oil
4	1 teaspoon cornstarch
	2 tablespoons water
5	1 tablespoon oil
	1 tub (approximately 14 ounces) soft tofu (Cut into ¾-inch cubes and dry on paper towels for 30 minutes.)
	½ tablespoon oil
	4 Chinese dried mushrooms (Soak, squeeze out excess water, stem, and cut into thin strips.)
	½ tablespoon hot bean sauce
	2 stalks green onions (scallions), cut into 2-inch lengths

Steps	Instructions
1	Combine ingredients to form the *Marinade*.
2	Put meat into the *Marinade* and let stand for 15 minutes.
3	Combine ingredients to form the *Sauce*. Set within easy reach.
4	Combine ingredients to form the *Cornstarch Mixture*. Set within easy reach.
5	Heat the 1 tablespoon oil in a pan over high heat until hazy. Add the tofu and fry gently until the tofu is slightly brown on both sides. Remove and set aside. Heat the remaining ½ tablespoon oil until hazy. Put in the pork and stir-fry briskly for 30 seconds. Add the mushrooms and continue stir-frying for 30 seconds. Put in the hot bean sauce and stir-fry for 30 seconds. Return the tofu to the pan and stir gently until hot. Pour in the *Sauce* and stir until the liquid is bubbly. Suspend the *Cornstarch Mixture*, then add it to the pan. Stir until thickened. Serve immediately, garnished with green onions.

Yields 4 Servings   *Per Serving:* 217 calories, 283 mg. sodium, 22 mg. cholesterol

Further Modifications in Sodium: Reduce sodium to *192 mg. per serving* by decreasing the hot bean sauce to 1 teaspoon and by substituting lower sodium soy sauce for the regular dark soy sauce.

STIR-FRIED PRESSED TOFU

Steps	Ingredients
1	3 squares (approximately 10 to 12 ounces) firm tofu
2	1 tablespoon wine ½ teaspoon cornstarch 1 teaspoon sesame oil
3	5 ounces well-trimmed boneless pork, cut into matchstick-size pieces
4	1 tablespoon dark soy sauce 1½ tablespoons water ½ teaspoon sugar
5	1 teaspoon cornstarch 2 tablespoons water
6	1 tablespoon oil ½ teaspoon hot bean sauce ½ medium green bell pepper (Seed, rib, and cut into matchstick-size pieces.) ½ cup bamboo shoots, cut into matchstick-size pieces

Steps	Instructions
1	Line a plate with 3 paper towels. Place the tofu on top and cover with additional paper towels. Press with 10-pound weight (use a pot filled with 4 quarts of water). Refrigerate overnight. When adequately pressed, cut into ¼-inch cubes.
2	Combine ingredients to form the *Marinade*.
3	Mix the pork into the *Marinade* and let stand for 15 minutes.
4	Combine ingredients to form the *Sauce*. Set within easy reach.
5	Combine ingredients to form the *Cornstarch Mixture*. Set within easy reach.
6	Heat the oil in a pan over high heat until hazy. Put in the hot bean sauce. Stir for 3 seconds. Put in the pork and stir-fry briskly for 1 minute. Add green pepper and bamboo shoots and continue stir-frying for 30 seconds. Put in tofu and stir gently for 1 minute. Pour in the *Sauce* and heat until bubbly. Suspend the *Cornstarch Mixture* and stir into the pan. Cook until the sauce is thickened. Serve hot.

Yields 4 Servings   *Per Serving:* 191 calories, 325 mg. sodium, 22 mg. cholesterol

Further Modifications in Sodium: Reduce sodium to *226 mg. per serving* by substituting lower sodium soy sauce for the regular dark soy sauce.

釀
豆
腐

STUFFED TOFU

Steps	Ingredients
1	1 tub (14 to 16 ounces) firm tofu
2	6 ounces white fish fillet, such as sole, cod, bass, or similar fish, chopped well
	1 tablespoon dried shrimp (Soak for 20 minutes, drain, and chop fine.)
	½ tablespoon minced green onion (scallion)
	½ tablespoon light soy sauce
	pinch of white pepper
	½ teaspoon sesame oil
	½ teaspoon cornstarch mixed with 1 teaspoon water
3	1 tablespoon chee hou sauce
	1 teaspoon sesame oil
	1 teaspoon wine
	pinch of white pepper
	½ cup water
4	¼ teaspoon cornstarch
	1 teaspoon water
5	1 tablespoon oil
	1 slice ginger, approximately 1 inch in diameter by ⅛ inch thick, smashed with the side of a cleaver
	1 clove garlic, smashed with the side of a cleaver

Steps	Instructions
1	Cut tofu block into 4 equal slices crosswise. Lay the slices side by side and press them between paper towels. Place a 5-pound weight on top of the tofu slices, using a heavy chopping board on top of the tofu slices and a pot of water on top of the chopping board. Press for 1 hour.
2	Combine the ingredients to form the *Stuffing Mixture*. To prepare the stuffed tofu, cut each tofu slice diagonally to yield 8 triangular pieces. Carefully hollow out tofu without breaking the sides. Gently fill each tofu triangle with the *Stuffing Mixture*.
3	Combine the ingredients to form the *Sauce*. Set within easy reach.
4	Combine the ingredients to form the *Cornstarch Mixture*. Set within easy reach.
5	Heat the oil in a pan over medium-high heat until hazy. Brown the ginger and garlic and discard. Put in the stuffed tofu and brown lightly on both sides for a total of 4 minutes. Pour in the *Sauce*, stir gently, cover, and simmer for 5 minutes. Turn the tofu over and simmer an additional 5 minutes. Remove tofu to a serving platter, cover, and keep warm. Bring the *Sauce* in the pan to a boil, suspend the *Cornstarch Mixture*, and stir into the pan until the sauce is thickened. Pour the sauce over the stuffed tofu and served hot.

Yields 4 Servings　　*Per Serving:* 174 calories, 355 mg. sodium, 24 mg. cholesterol

Further Modifications in Sodium: Reduce sodium to *268 mg. per serving* by substituting lower sodium soy sauce for the regular light soy sauce.

TOFU BEEF WITH CHEE HOU SAUCE

柱
侯
豆
腐

Steps	Ingredients
1	1 teaspoon dark soy sauce
	1 tablespoon wine
	½ teaspoon cornstarch
	½ teaspoon sesame oil
	pinch of white pepper
2	6 ounces well-trimmed flank steak (Cut slantwise across the grain into thin slices 1½ inches long by ⅛ inch thick.)
3	1 teaspoon cornstarch
	1 tablespoon water
4	½ tablespoon oil
	2 slices ginger, approximately 1 inch in diameter by ⅛ inch thick, minced
	2 cloves garlic, minced
	3 tablespoons homemade stock without salt
	12 ounces soft tofu, cut in ½-inch cubes
	1½ tablespoons chee hou sauce
	1 stalk green onion (scallion), cut into 1-inch lengths

Steps	Instructions
1	Combine ingredients to form the *Marinade*.
2	Mix the beef into the *Marinade*. Let stand for 20 minutes.
3	Combine ingredients to form *Cornstarch Mixture*. Set within easy reach.
4	Heat the oil in a pan over high heat until hazy. Lightly brown ginger and garlic, then discard. Put in beef and stir-fry briskly for about 1 minute. Remove and set within easy reach. Heat pan again over high heat with 3 tablespoons stock until the stock is bubbly. Put in tofu and stir gently until bubbly. Put in chee hou sauce and stir gently for about 1 minute. Return the beef to pan and continue to stir for about 30 seconds. Suspend the *Cornstarch Mixture*, add it to the pan, and stir until the sauce is thickened. Serve hot, garnished with green onions.

Yields 4 Servings   *Per Serving:* 174 calories, 330 mg. sodium, 29 mg. cholesterol

Further Modifications in Sodium: Reduce sodium to *228 mg. per serving* by substituting lower sodium soy sauce for the regular dark soy sauce.

STEAMED BEAN CURD ROLLS

Steps	Ingredients
1	4 ounces well-trimmed boneless pork, ground
	1 green onion (scallion), minced
	1 slice ginger, approximately 1 inch in diameter by ⅛ inch thick, minced
	3 Chinese dried mushrooms (Soak, squeeze out excess water, stem, and cut into thin strips.)
	½ cup bamboo shoots, cut into matchstick-size pieces
	1 tablespoon light soy sauce
2	4 dried bean curd sheets (Soak until soft, rinse twice, and drain.)
3	1 teaspoon sesame oil

Steps	Instructions
1	Combine the ingredients in a small bowl.
2	Put one fourth of the ingredients on 1 sheet of bean curd. Roll up starting at the short end, being sure to tuck in the edges as you go. Repeat with remaining 3 sheets of bean curd. Place in a steaming dish and steam for 25 minutes. Remove and cut each roll into 3 to 4 pieces.
3	Sprinkle the sesame oil on the rolls and serve hot.

Yields 4 Servings   *Per Serving:* 180 calories, 374 mg. sodium, 18 mg. cholesterol

Further Modifications in Sodium: Reduce sodium to *200 mg. per serving* by substituting lower sodium soy sauce for the regular light soy sauce.

FROZEN DRIED TOFU WITH PORK

炒冰豆腐

Steps	Ingredients
1	3 squares (approximately 10 to 12 ounces) firm tofu
2	½ tablespoon wine
	½ teaspoon cornstarch
	½ teaspoon sesame oil
3	5 ounces well-trimmed boneless pork, cut into matchstick-size pieces
4	1 tablespoon dark soy sauce
	2 tablespoons water
	1 teaspoon sugar
	1 teaspoon sesame oil
	⅛ teaspoon white pepper
5	1 tablespoon oil
	½ medium green bell pepper (Seed, rib, and cut into matchstick-size pieces.)

Steps	Instructions
1	Freeze the 3 squares of tofu overnight. Take out and thaw. Gently press out excess water with paper towels. Be careful not to break up the tofu. Cut the tofu into strips ¼ inch thick.
2	Combine the ingredients to form the *Marinade*.
3	Mix the pork into the *Marinade* and let stand for 15 minutes.
4	Combine the ingredients to form the *Sauce*. Set within easy reach.
5	Heat the oil in a pan over high heat until hazy. Put in the pork and stir-fry for 30 seconds. Add the green bell peppers and continue to stir-fry for 1 minute. Gently put in the tofu and carefully stir-fry for 30 seconds. Pour in the *Sauce* and stir until it is bubbly. Serve hot.

Yields 4 Servings   *Per Serving:* 186 calories, 283 mg. sodium, 22 mg. cholesterol

Further Modifications in Sodium: Reduce sodium to *184 mg. per serving* by substituting lower sodium soy sauce for the regular dark soy sauce.

TOFU PORK PATTY

Steps	Ingredients
1	8 ounces well-trimmed boneless pork, ground
	2-inch white section from a stalk of green onion (scallion), finely minced
	¼ teaspoon finely minced ginger
	½ tablespoon light soy sauce
	pinch of white pepper
2	8 ounces soft tofu, whipped with a fork until fairly smooth
	½ teaspoon light soy sauce
3	remaining green section of stalk of green onion (scallion), cut into ⅛-inch sections

Steps	Instructions
1	In an 8-inch-diameter heat-proof dish, mix the ingredients together well. Form a meat patty on the bottom of the dish.
2	Mix the mashed tofu with the light soy sauce. Spread the tofu mixture on top of the meat mixture. Steam the dish over boiling water, covered, over medium-high heat for 15 to 20 minutes. (Add water to the steaming pot if necessary.)
3	Serve hot, garnished with green sections of onion.

Yields 4 Servings   *Per Serving:* 153 calories, 261 mg. sodium, 35 mg. cholesterol

Further Modifications in Sodium: Reduce sodium to *145 mg. per serving* by substituting lower sodium soy sauce for the regular light soy sauce.

豆
腐
肉
餅

VEGETARIAN CHICKEN

素
雞

Steps	Ingredients
1	½ cup homemade stock made without salt or water
	1 tablespoon dark soy sauce
	1 tablespoon sugar
	½ tablespoon sesame oil
	½ tablespoon wine
2	6 Chinese dried mushrooms (Soak, squeeze out excess water, stem, and chop fine.)
	3 tablespoons finely chopped bamboo shoots
	½ teaspoon cornstarch
3	8 full-sized sheets dried bean curd (Soak until soft, rinse twice, and drain.)
	cheesecloth for wrapping
4	½ tablespoon oil
5	2 tablespoons of remaining Sauce
	6 tablespoons of drippings from steaming dish
	1 teaspoon cornstarch

Steps	Instructions
1	Combine the ingredients to form the *Sauce* in a small saucepan. Bring to a boil.
2	Add mushrooms and bamboo shoots to the *Sauce*. Remove from the heat and allow to cool. When lukewarm, stir in the cornstarch until well blended.
3	Lay 1 bean curd sheet on a chopping board. Spoon a small amount of *Sauce* on top and spread evenly. Repeat layering and spooning of sauce until all 8 sheets of bean curd are used. Be sure to retain 2 tablespoons of the sauce for Step 5. Cut the stack of bean curd sheets in half crosswise to yield approximately two 8-by-8-inch squares. Roll each square in thirds, being sure to tuck in edges. Wrap each bean curd roll in cheesecloth. Place the rolls in a heat-proof dish and steam over boiling water for 10 minutes. Remove the rolls from the steaming dish and remove the cheesecloth wrapping. Set within easy reach.
4	Heat the oil in a pan over medium heat. Put in both rolls and brown each side lightly for 1 to 2 minutes. Remove and set on a chopping board. Cut crosswise into 1-inch-wide strips and arrange on a serving platter.
5	Combine the 2 tablespoons remaining *Sauce* with 6 tablespoons drippings from the steaming dish and stir in the 1 teaspoon cornstarch. Bring to a boil, stirring constantly until thickened. Pour over the Vegetarian Chicken and serve hot.

Yields 4 Servings   *Per Serving:* 269 calories, 306 mg. sodium, 0 mg. cholesterol

Further Modifications in Sodium: Reduce sodium to *207 mg. per serving* by substituting lower sodium soy sauce for the regular dark soy sauce.

TOFU WITH FRESH MUSHROOMS
AND DRIED SHRIMP

鮮
菇
燒
豆
腐

Steps	Ingredients
1	1 tablespoon dark soy sauce
	2 teaspoons sugar
	½ teaspoon sesame oil
	4 tablespoons homemade stock without salt or water
2	1 teaspoon cornstarch
	2 tablespoons water
3	½ tablespoon oil
	½ tablespoon oil
	12 ounces soft tofu (Drain, dry on paper towels, cut into 1½-inch squares ½ inch thick.)
	½ tablespoon oil
	3 tablespoons dried shrimp (Rinse, soak, drain, and mince.)
	8 medium fresh button mushrooms, sliced

Steps   Instructions

1   Combine the ingredients to form the *Sauce*. Set within easy reach.

2   Combine the ingredients to form the *Cornstarch Mixture*. Set within easy reach.

3   Heat ½ tablespoon oil in a pan over high heat until hazy. Put in half of the tofu and brown on both sides. Remove. Repeat with the second ½ tablespoon oil and other half of tofu. Heat third ½ tablespoon oil in the pan until hazy. Put in the minced dried shrimp and mushrooms and stir-fry briskly for 20 to 30 seconds. Return the tofu to the pan. Pour in the *Sauce* and stir until bubbly. Suspend the *Cornstarch Mixture* and stir into pan until the sauce is thickened. Serve hot.

Yields 4 Servings   *Per Serving:* 145 calories, 308 mg. sodium, 7 mg. cholesterol

Further Modifications in Sodium: Reduce sodium to *209 mg. per serving* by substituting lower sodium soy sauce for the regular dark soy sauce.

STEAMED TOFU WITH PORK

Steps		Ingredients
1	12	ounces soft tofu, cut into 1½-inch-long by ¾-inch-thick pieces.
2	1	stalk green onion (scallion), minced
	1	slice ginger, approximately 1 inch in diameter by ⅛ inch thick, minced
	½	tablespoon wine
	½	teaspoon sugar
	1	tablespoon light soy sauce
	⅛	teaspoon white pepper
	1	teaspoon sesame oil
3	4	ounces well-trimmed boneless pork, ground or finely chopped

Steps	Instructions
1	Place the tofu pieces in a heat-proof dish. Pour boiling water over the tofu and let stand for 2 minutes. Drain and set aside.
2	Combine the ingredients to form the *Sauce*.
3	Mix the pork into the *Sauce*. Drain the tofu once again, then spread the pork mixture evenly on top of the tofu. Steam the tofu over boiling water for 18 minutes, covered. Serve hot.

Yields 4 Servings   *Per Serving:* 137 calories, 351 mg. sodium, 18 mg. cholesterol

Further Modifications in Sodium: Reduce sodium to *177 mg. per serving* by substituting lower sodium soy sauce for the regular light soy sauce.

豆腐蒸豬肉

BEAN CURD STICKS WITH PORK

Steps	Ingredients
1	1 tablespoon dark soy sauce
	½ tablespoon sugar
	½ tablespoon wine
2	1 tablespoon oil
	6 ounces well-trimmed boneless pork, thinly sliced
	3 ounces dried bean curd sticks (Soak overnight, rinse 3 times, drain and squeeze out excess water, and cut into 2-inch lengths.)
	6 Chinese dried mushrooms (Soak, squeeze out excess water, stem, and quarter.)
	½ cup bamboo shoots, cut into 1-inch-long by ¾-inch-wide strips
	½ cup homemade stock without salt or ½ cup water

Steps	Instructions
1	Combine ingredients to form the *Sauce.* Set within easy reach.
2	Heat the oil in a pan over high heat until hazy. Add the pork and stir-fry for 1½ minutes. Add bean curd sticks and mushrooms and stir-fry for 30 seconds. Put in the bamboo shoots and pour in the homemade stock. Turn heat to low and cover. Simmer for 5 minutes. Stir in the *Sauce* and serve hot.

Yields 4 Servings   *Per Serving:* 231 calories, 306 mg. sodium, 27 mg. cholesterol

Further Modifications in Sodium: Reduce sodium to *207 mg. per serving* by substituting lower sodium soy sauce for the regular dark soy sauce.

TOFU WITH TOMATOES

蕃茄炒豆腐

Steps	Ingredients
1	1 tablespoon dark soy sauce
	1 teaspoon Chinese red vinegar
	2 teaspoons sugar
	2 tablespoons water
2	½ teaspoon cornstarch
	1 tablespoon water
3	1 tablespoon oil
	12 ounces soft tofu, cut into ¾-inch cubes
	½ medium green bell pepper, cut into thin slivers
	2 small tomatoes, cut into thin slices
	1 teaspoon sesame oil

Steps	Instructions
1	Combine ingredients to form the *Sauce*. Set within easy reach.
2	Combine ingredients to form the *Cornstarch Mixture*. Set within easy reach.
3	Heat the 1 tablespoon oil in a pan over high heat until hazy. Put in the tofu and stir-fry gently for 1 minute. Put in the green pepper and tomatoes and continue stirring for 1 minute. Pour in the *Sauce* and stir until bubbly. Suspend the *Cornstarch Mixture* and stir into the pan until the sauce is thickened. Remove from the pan to a serving platter and sprinkle the sesame oil on top. Serve hot.

Yields 4 Servings   *Per Serving:* 135 calories, 270 mg. sodium, 0 mg. cholesterol

Further Modifications in Sodium: Reduce sodium to *171 mg. per serving* by substituting lower sodium soy sauce for the regular dark soy sauce.

VEGETABLES

BOK CHOY STIR-FRIED WITH BEEF

Steps	Ingredients
1	1 tablespoon water
	1 tablespoon white wine or sherry
	1 tablespoon dark soy sauce
	1 tablespoon cornstarch
	½ teaspoon sesame oil
2	8 ounces flank steak, well trimmed (Slice thinly across the grain into 1½-inch-long strips.)
3	2 teaspoons oil
	1 slice ginger, approximately 1 inch in diameter by ⅛ inch thick, smashed with the side of a cleaver
4	½ tablespoon oil
	2 cloves garlic, smashed with the side of a cleaver
	12 ounces bok choy
	2 tablespoons water

Steps	Instructions
1	Combine ingredients to form the *Marinade,* stir well.
2	Add meat to the *Marinade* and let stand for 15 minutes.
3	Heat the oil in a pan over high heat until hazy. Add the ginger and brown. (If desired, remove ginger and discard.) Add the beef and accompanying juices and stir-fry for about 2 minutes. Remove the beef and wipe the pan.
4	Heat the oil in the pan until hazy. Add the garlic and brown. Put in the bok choy and stir-fry for about 3 minutes, or until tender but crisp. Add the water to the bok choy and stir-fry for an additional 2 minutes. Return the beef and accompanying juices to the pan and stir-fry for 1 minute. Serve hot.

Yields 4 Servings   *Per Serving: 157 calories, 321 mg. sodium, 39 mg. cholesterol*

Further Modifications in Sodium: Reduce sodium to *222 mg. per serving* by substituting lower sodium soy sauce for the regular dark soy sauce.

140

STIR-FRIED BROCCOLI

Steps	Ingredients
1	1 tablespoon dark soy sauce
	½ tablespoon wine
	½ teaspoon sugar
	¼ teaspoon sesame oil
2	1 teaspoon cornstarch
	2 tablespoons water
3	1 tablespoon oil
	12 ounces broccoli, cut into 2-inch lengths
	¼ cup homemade stock without salt or water
4	1 tablespoon toasted sesame seeds

Steps	Instructions
1	Combine ingredients to form the *Sauce.* Set within easy reach.
2	Combine ingredients to form the *Cornstarch Mixture.* Set within easy reach.
3	Heat the oil in a pan over high heat until hazy. Add the broccoli and stir-fry for 1 minute. Add the homemade stock or water, cover, and cook for 2 minutes, stirring occasionally. Uncover, add the *Sauce.* and stir-fry until bubbly. Suspend the *Cornstarch Mixture,* add it to the pan, and stir until the sauce is thickened.
4	Arrange on a serving platter, sprinkle with the sesame seeds, and serve hot.

Yields 4 Servings   *Per Serving:* 83 calories, 263 mg. sodium, 0 mg. cholesterol

Further Modifications in Sodium: Reduce sodium to *164 mg. per serving* by substituting lower sodium soy sauce for the regular dark soy sauce.

ASPARAGUS WITH CHICKEN

莉
筍
雞
球

Steps	Ingredients
1	½ teaspoon wine ½ teaspoon cornstarch ½ teaspoon sesame oil
2	2 chicken breast halves (Bone, skin, and cut into 1-inch cubes.)
3	2 teaspoons dark soy sauce 1 teaspoon sugar 1 teaspoon wine
4	1 teaspoon cornstarch 2 tablespoons water
5	2 teaspoons oil 1 tablespoon oil 2 cloves garlic, smashed with the side of a cleaver 1 tablespoon salted black beans (Rinse, drain, and mash coarsely with the pommel of a cleaver.) 1 pound fresh asparagus (Snap off hard root ends, then cut diagonally into ¼-inch-thick slices.) ¼ cup water

Steps	Instructions
1	Combine ingredients to form the *Marinade*.
2	Put the chicken into the *Marinade* and let stand for 15 minutes.
3	Combine ingredients to form the *Sauce*. Set within easy reach.
4	Combine ingredients to form the *Cornstarch Mixture*. Set within easy reach.
5	Heat the 2 teaspoons oil in a pan over high heat until hazy. Put in the chicken and stir-fry briskly for 1 minute or until the chicken turns white. Remove and set aside. Wipe pan. Heat the 1 tablespoon oil in the pan over high heat until hazy. Put in the garlic and mashed black beans and stir-fry for 15 to 20 seconds. Put in the asparagus and stir-fry an additional 15 to 20 seconds. Add the water and continue stirring for 1 minute. Return the chicken to the pan and stir-fry for 1 minute. Pour in the *Sauce* and heat until bubbly. Suspend the *Cornstarch Mixture*, add it to the pan, and stir until the sauce is thickened. Serve hot.

Yields 4 Servings   *Per Serving: 166 calories, 283 mg. sodium, 34 mg. cholesterol*

Further Modifications in Sodium: Reduce sodium to *217 mg. per serving* by substituting lower sodium soy sauce for the regular dark soy sauce.

CABBAGE WITH BEAN THREADS

椰
菜
粉
絲

Steps	Ingredients
1	½ teaspoon wine
	½ teaspoon dark soy sauce
	½ teaspoon cornstarch
2	3 ounces well-trimmed boneless pork, coarsely chopped
3	1 1.7-ounce package mung bean threads, cut into 4-inch lengths
	5 cups boiling water
4	½ tablespoon wine
	1 tablespoon dark soy sauce
	½ teaspoon sugar
	1½ tablespoon water
5	2 teaspoons oil
	1 tablespoon dried shrimp (Soak and chop coarsely.)
	6 Chinese dried mushrooms (Soak, squeeze out excess water, stem, and cut into ⅛-inch strips.)
	2 cups shredded cabbage
	⅔ cup water
6	2 teaspoons oil

Steps	Instructions
1	Combine the ingredients to form the *Marinade*.
2	Put the pork into the *Marinade* and let stand for 10 minutes.
3	Put the bean threads into the pot of boiling water. Let sit for 30 seconds, then pour into a colander and rinse with cold water. Set aside.
4	Combine the ingredients to form the *Sauce*. Set within easy reach.
5	Heat the 2 teaspoons oil in a pan over high heat until hazy. Add the dried shrimp and stir-fry for 5 seconds. Put in the mushrooms and cabbage and stir-fry briskly for 1 minute. Add the ⅔ cup water, stir, cover, and cook for 1 minute. Add the drained bean threads and stir-fry for 1 minute. Put the contents of the pan in a bowl and set within easy reach.
6	Heat the 2 teaspoons oil in a pan over high heat until hazy. Put in the pork and stir-fry briskly for 2 minutes. Pour in the *Sauce* and return the cabbage and bean threads to the pan. Stir until hot.

Yields 4 Servings   *Per Serving:* 145 calories, 333 mg. sodium, 13 mg. cholesterol

Further Modifications in Sodium: Reduce sodium to *218 mg. per serving* by substituting lower sodium soy sauce for the regular dark soy sauce.

STIR-FRIED BEAN SPROUTS

清炒芽菜

Steps	Ingredients
1	1 tablespoon oil
	1 slice ginger, approximately 1 inch in diameter by ⅛ inch thick, smashed with the side of a cleaver
	2 cloves garlic, smashed with the side of a cleaver
	1 pound bean sprouts, rinsed and drained
	1 tablespoon light soy sauce
	pinch of white pepper
	½ teaspoon sesame oil

Steps	Instructions
1	Heat the oil in a pan over high heat until hazy. Put in the ginger and garlic and brown. Add the bean sprouts and stir-fry for 1½ to 2 minutes. Add the soy sauce and white pepper and stir-fry for 30 seconds to 1 minute. Sprinkle with sesame oil and serve hot.

Yields 4 Servings   *Per Serving:* 77 calories, 331 mg. sodium, 0 mg. cholesterol

Further Modifications in Sodium: Reduce sodium to *157 mg. per serving* by substituting lower sodium soy sauce for the regular light soy sauce.

CAULIFLOWER WITH CHICKEN IN BLACK BEAN SAUCE

雞球炒椰菜花

Steps	Ingredients
1	½ tablespoon wine
	½ teaspoon cornstarch
	½ teaspoon sesame oil
2	2 chicken breast halves (Bone, skin, and cut into ¾-inch squares.)
3	2 cloves garlic, finely minced
	2 teaspoons salted black beans, rinsed
	2 teaspoons dark soy sauce
4	1 teaspoon cornstarch
	2 tablespoons water
5	½ tablespoon oil
	1 tablespoon oil
	12 ounces fresh cauliflower (Rinse and separate into small buds.)
	½ teaspoon sugar
	¼ cup water

Steps	Instructions
1	Combine ingredients to form the *Marinade*.
2	Put the chicken into the *Marinade* and let stand for 15 minutes.
3	Combine garlic and black beans in a small bowl and mash with the pommel of the cleaver. Add the soy sauce to form the *Sauce*. Set within easy reach
4	Combine ingredients to form the *Cornstarch Mixture*. Set within easy reach.
5	Heat the ½ tablespoon oil in a pan over high heat until hazy. Put in the chicken and stir-fry briskly for 1½ minutes or until the chicken is 80 percent done. Remove and set within easy reach. Heat the 1 tablespoon oil in the pan until hazy. Add the cauliflower buds and stir-fry for 1 minute. Add the sugar and ¼ cup water and cover. Cook for 3 minutes or until cauliflower is cooked but still crisp, stirring occasionally. Return the chicken to the pan and stir-fry for 1 minute. Put in the *Sauce* and stir-fry for 10 seconds, or until it is bubbly. Suspend the *Cornstarch Mixture* and stir into the pan. When the sauce is thickened, serve hot.

Yields 4 Servings   *Per Serving:* 153 calories, 267 mg. sodium, 34 mg. cholesterol

Further Modifications in Sodium: Reduce sodium to *201 mg. per serving* by substituting lower sodium soy sauce for the regular dark soy sauce.

DRY-FRIED STRING BEANS

Steps	Ingredients
1	1 tablespoon oil
	12 ounces fresh string beans, cut into 1½-inch lengths
	¼ cup water
	1 tablespoon dark soy sauce
	½ tablespoon sesame oil
	½ tablespoon toasted sesame seeds

Steps	Instructions
1	Heat the oil in a pan over high heat until hazy. Add the string beans and stir-fry for 1 minute. Add the water and stir-fry for 2 to 3 minutes, or until cooked but crisp. (Additional water may be added if necessary.) Sprinkle in the soy sauce, sesame oil, and sesame seeds. Stir and serve hot.

Yields 4 Servings   *Per Serving:* 81 calories, 255 mg. sodium, 0 mg. cholesterol

Further Modifications in Sodium: Reduce sodium to *156 mg. per serving* by substituting lower sodium soy sauce for the regular dark soy sauce.

乾燒青豆

COLD BEAN SPROUTS

Steps	Ingredients
1	1 tablespoon light soy sauce
	1 teaspoon sesame oil
	½ teaspoon sugar
	1 teaspoon Chinese red vinegar
2	2 teaspoons oil
	12 ounces bean sprouts, washed and drained well
3	1 teaspoon oil
	2 tablespoons dried shrimp (Soak, drain, and chop coarsely.)

Steps	Instructions
1	Combine ingredients to form the *Sauce*. Set within easy reach.
2	Heat the oil in a pan over high heat until hazy. Put in the bean sprouts and stir-fry briskly for 1½ minutes or until barely cooked. Take out and let cool. Then refrigerate until ready to serve.
3	Heat the oil in a pan over high heat until hazy. Put in the shrimp and stir-fry for 5 to 10 seconds. Take out and let cool. When ready to serve, mix the shrimp and *Sauce* with bean sprouts.

Yields 4 Servings   *Per Serving:* 74 calories, 373 mg. sodium, 5 mg. cholesterol

Further Modifications in Sodium: Reduce sodium to *199 mg. per serving* by substituting lower sodium soy sauce for the regular light soy sauce.

STIR-FRIED CABBAGE

Steps	Ingredients
1	1 tablespoon dark soy sauce
	½ tablespoon sugar
	2 tablespoon water
2	½ teaspoon cornstarch
	2 tablespoons water
3	1 tablespoon oil
	1 small head (approximately 12 to 16 ounces) cabbage (Cut into 8 equal wedges. Then cut each wedge into 4 to 5 equal triangular pieces.)

Steps	Instructions
1	Combine ingredients to form the *Sauce.* Set within easy reach.
2	Combine ingredients to form the *Cornstarch Mixture.* Set within easy reach.
3	Heat the oil in a pan over high heat until hazy. Put in cabbage and stir-fry for 2 minutes. Stir in the *Sauce* and continue stir-frying for 2 minutes, or until only half of the liquid remains. Suspend the *Cornstarch Mixture,* add it to the pan, and stir until the liquid thickens.

Yields 4 Servings   *Per Serving:* 64 calories, 270 mg. sodium, 0 mg. cholesterol

Further Modifications in Sodium: Reduce sodium to *171 mg. per serving* by substituting lower sodium soy sauce for the regular dark soy sauce.

STEAMED CHINESE (NAPA) CABBAGE

Steps	Ingredients
1	1 pound head Chinese cabbage (Remove root and tip. Cut crosswise into 2-inch cylinders. If needed, tie with string to prevent cabbage from coming apart.)
2	2 tablespoons dried shrimp (Soak for 10 minutes, drain, and chop coarsely.) 1 tablespoon light soy sauce pinch of white pepper 1 teaspoon sesame oil

Steps	Instructions
1	Put the cabbage, cut side up, in a heat-proof dish for steaming.
2	Spread the dried shrimp on top of the cabbage rolls. Sprinkle the soy sauce, white pepper, and sesame oil on top of the rolls. Cover and steam for 25 minutes. Serve hot.

Yields 4 Servings   *Per Serving:* 34 calories, 385 mg. sodium, 5 mg. cholesterol

Further Modifications in Sodium: Reduce sodium to *211 mg. per serving* by substituting lower sodium soy sauce for the regular light soy sauce.

螞蟻上樹

BEAN THREADS WITH GROUND PORK

Steps	Ingredients
1	1 teaspoon dark soy sauce
	1 teaspoon wine
	1 teaspoon cornstarch
2	4 ounces well-trimmed boneless pork loin, ground
3	7 cups water
	1 1.7-ounce package dried bean threads, cut into 6- to 8-inch lengths
4	2 teaspoons dark soy sauce
	1 tablespoon wine
	1 teaspoon sugar
5	½ teaspoon cornstarch
	¼ cup water
6	1 tablespoon oil
	1 teaspoon ginger, minced
	2 teaspoons green onion (scallion), minced
	¾ cup water

Steps	Instructions
1	Combine ingredients to form the *Marinade*.
2	Mix the pork into the *Marinade* and let stand for 10 minutes.
3	Bring the water to boil and add the bean threads. When water begins to boil again, pour the threads into a colander and rinse with cold water.
4	Combine ingredients to form the *Sauce*. Set within easy reach.
5	Combine ingredients to form the *Cornstarch Mixture*. Set within easy reach.
6	Heat the oil in a pan over high heat until hazy. Put in the ginger and garlic and brown. Add the pork and stir-fry briskly for 1 minute. Put the bean threads in the pan and turn the heat down to medium. Add the ¾ cup water. When contents are hot, add the *Sauce* and simmer for 6 to 8 minutes. Suspend the *Cornstarch Mixture* and stir it into the pan until the sauce is thickened. Serve hot.

Yields 4 Servings   *Per Serving:* 133 calories, 264 mg. sodium, 18 mg. cholesterol

Further Modifications in Sodium: Reduce sodium to 165 mg. per serving by substituting lower sodium soy sauce for the regular dark soy sauce.

STIR-FRIED MIXED VEGETABLES

Steps	Ingredients
1	1 teaspoon sugar
	1 tablespoon dark soy sauce
	1 tablespoon wine
	1 teaspoon Chinese red vinegar
	6 tablespoons water
	1 teaspoon sesame oil
	¼ teaspoon white pepper
2	½ tablespoon cornstarch
	4 tablespoons water
3	1 tablespoon oil
	12 ounces fresh cauliflower (Rinse and separate into small buds.)
	1 large carrot, cut into matchstick-size pieces
	4 Chinese dried mushrooms (Soak, squeeze out excess water, stem, and cut into strips.)
	4 ounces snow peas (Remove strings and tips and cut into thirds.)
	4 water chestnuts (Slice into 3 to 4 pieces.)

Steps	Instructions
1	Combine ingredients to form the *Sauce.* Set within easy reach.
2	Combine ingredients to form the *Cornstarch Mixture.* Set within easy reach.
3	Heat the oil in a pan over high heat. Put in the cauliflower and stir-fry for 2 to 3 minutes. Add the carrots and mushrooms and stir for 1 minute. Put in the snow peas and water chestnuts and continue stir-frying for 1½ minutes. Pour in the *Sauce,* cover, and cook for 1 to 2 minutes. Suspend the *Cornstarch Mixture,* pour it into the pan and stir until the sauce is thickened. Serve hot.

Yields 4 Servings   *Per Serving:* 103 calories, 283 mg. sodium, 0 mg. cholesterol

Further Modifications in Sodium: Reduce sodium to *184 mg. per serving* by substituting lower sodium soy sauce for the regular dark soy sauce.

魚
香
茄
子

SZECHWANESE EGGPLANT

Steps	Ingredients
1	2 teaspoons wine
	2 teaspoons dark soy sauce
	1 teaspoon sugar
	2 teaspoons Chinese brown vinegar
	1 teaspoon sesame oil
	⅓ cup homemade stock without salt or water
2	1 teaspoon cornstarch
	2 tablespoons water
3	1 tablespoon oil
	10 ounces eggplant (Peel and cut into strips ¼-inch square by 2 inches long. Soak in cold water for 15 minutes and drain.)
4	½ tablespoon oil
	½ tablespoon minced ginger
	½ tablespoon minced garlic
	2 tablespoons minced green onion (scallion)
	1 teaspoon hot bean sauce

Steps	Instructions
1	Combine the ingredients to form the *Sauce*. Set within easy reach.
2	Combine the ingredients to form the *Cornstarch Mixture*. Set within easy reach.
3	Heat the oil in a pan over high heat until hazy. Put in the eggplant and stir-fry for 3½ minutes. Remove and set within reach.
4	Heat the oil in a pan over high heat until hazy. Put in the ginger, garlic, and green onion and stir-fry for 10 seconds. Add the hot bean sauce and continue stir-frying for 20 seconds. Return the eggplant to the pan and pour in the *Sauce*. Stir for 1 to 2 minutes. Suspend the *Cornstarch Mixture*, stir into the pan and cook until the sauce is thickened. Serve hot.

Yields 4 Servings   *Per Serving:* 94 calories, 273 mg. sodium, 0 mg. cholesterol

Further Modifications in Sodium: Reduce sodium to *207 mg. per serving* by substituting lower sodium soy sauce for the regular dark soy sauce.

STIR-FRIED CHINESE (NAPA) CABBAGE

Steps	Ingredients
1	1 tablespoon light soy sauce
	½ teaspoon sugar
	½ teaspoon sesame oil
	⅛ teaspoon white pepper
	1 teaspoon wine
2	1 teaspoon cornstarch
	2 tablespoons water
3	1 tablespoon oil
	1 slice ginger, approximately 1 inch in diameter by ⅛ inch thick, smashed with the side of a cleaver
	12 ounces Chinese cabbage (Cut the leaves in half lengthwise, then crosswise into 2-inch lengths.)
	1 to 2 tablespoons water

Steps	Instructions
1	Combine ingredients to form the *Sauce*. Set within easy reach.
2	Combine ingredients to form the *Cornstarch Mixture*. Set within easy reach.
3	Heat the oil in a pan over high heat until hazy. Brown the ginger and discard. Put in the cabbage and stir-fry briskly for 2 minutes. Pour in the *Sauce* and continue stir-frying for 30 seconds. (Add the water at this point if liquid has evaporated from pan.) Suspend the *Cornstarch Mixture* and add it to the pan. Stir until the sauce is thickened. Serve hot.

Yields 4 Servings   *Per Serving:* 56 calories, 345 mg. sodium, 0 mg. cholesterol

Further Modifications in Sodium: Reduce sodium to *171 mg. per serving* by substituting lower sodium soy sauce for the regular light soy sauce.

LAW BAK WITH PORK

炒蘿蔔

Steps	Ingredients
1	1 tablespoon wine 1 teaspoon cornstarch ½ tablespoon water
2	6 ounces well-trimmed boneless pork loin, cut into matchstick-size pieces
3	1 tablespoon dark soy sauce ¼ teaspoon white pepper ½ teaspoon sugar 1 teaspoon sesame oil ½ cup water
4	½ tablespoon cornstarch 4 tablespoons water
5	½ tablespoon oil ½ tablespoon oil 1 tablespoon minced ginger 1 pound law bak (daikon), cut into 2-inch-long matchstick-size pieces

Steps	Instructions
1	Combine the ingredients to form the *Marinade*.
2	Mix the pork into the *Marinade* and let stand for 15 minutes.
3	Combine the ingredients to form the *Sauce*. Set within easy reach.
4	Combine the ingredients to form the *Cornstarch Mixture*. Set within easy reach.
5	Heat ½ tablespoon oil in a pan over high heat until hazy. Put in the pork and stir-fry for 2½ minutes, or until the pork turns white. Remove and set within easy reach. Heat the remaining ½ tablespoon oil in the pan until hazy. Brown the ginger. Put in the law bak and stir-fry for 3 minutes. Pour in the *Sauce*, cover the pan, and cook for 5 minutes, stirring occasionally for even cooking. (Add a small amount of water if necessary.) Return the pork to the pan and stir-fry until some of the excess liquid evaporates. Suspend the *Cornstarch Mixture* and stir into pan until the sauce is thickened. Serve hot.

Yields 4 Servings   *Per Serving:* 159 calories, 316 mg. sodium, 27 mg. cholesterol

Further Modifications in Sodium: Reduce the sodium to *217 mg. per serving* by substituting lower sodium soy sauce for the regular dark soy sauce.

STEAMED WINTER MELON WITH GROUND PORK

Steps	Ingredients
1	½ teaspoon light soy sauce
	½ teaspoon wine
	½ teaspoon sesame oil
	½ teaspoon cornstarch
	pinch of white pepper
2	6 ounces well-trimmed boneless pork, ground or coarsely chopped
3	2½ teaspoons light soy sauce
	½ teaspoon sugar
	1 teaspoon sesame oil
4	12 ounces winter melon without skin, pulp, or seeds (approximately 1¼ pounds as purchased with skin, pulp and seeds) (Cut into slices 2 inches by 1½ inches, about ⅛ inch thick.)
	3 Chinese dried mushrooms (Soak, squeeze out excess water, stem, and cut into strips about ⅛ inch wide.)

Steps	Instructions
1	Combine the ingredients to form the *Marinade*.
2	Put the pork into the *Marinade* and let stand for 10 minutes.
3	Combine the ingredients to form the *Sauce*. Set within easy reach.
4	Put the winter melon slices into a heat-proof deep dish. Spread the meat over the winter melon. Spread the mushroom strips over the meat. Put the dish into a steamer. Cover and steam over boiling water for 15 minutes. Lift the cover and sprinkle the *Sauce* over the dish. Cover and steam for another 1 minute. Serve hot.

Yields 4 Servings   *Per Serving:* 114 calories, 359 mg. sodium, 27 mg. cholesterol

Further Modifications in Sodium: Reduce sodium to *185 mg. per serving* by substituting lower sodium soy sauce for the regular light soy sauce.

STUFFED FUZZY MELON

釀
節
瓜

Steps	Ingredients
1	8 ounces well-trimmed boneless pork, ground
	2 Chinese dried mushrooms (Soak, squeeze out water, stem, and chop finely.)
	1 tablespoon dried shrimp (Soak and chop finely.)
	1 tablespoon green onion (scallion), finely minced
	¼ cup finely chopped water chestnuts (or bamboo shoots)
	1 teaspoon sugar
	2 teaspoons dark soy sauce
	1 teaspoon sesame oil
	⅛ teaspoon white pepper
2	2 1-pound fuzzy melons (Scrape off fuzzy surface and cut off tips at each end. Cut each melon into 4 equal cylinders. Hollow out the centers and discard.)
	2½ cups water
	1 tablespoon sugar
3	1 teaspoon light soy sauce
	1 teaspoon wine
4	2 teaspoons cornstarch
	4 teaspoons water
	drippings from steaming dish

Steps	Instructions
1	Combine all ingredients and mix well to form the *Meat Filling*. Set aside.
2	Bring the water to boil in a medium-sized saucepan. Add the 1 tablespoon sugar and put melon pieces in. When water returns to boil, cook the melon for 30 seconds, then turn each piece and boil for additional 30 seconds. Remove and let cool.
3	Combine the light soy sauce and wine. Brush along the interior ring of each melon piece, using up all of the mixture. Stuff each melon piece with the *Meat Filling*. Arrange the melon sections on a heat-proof plate and steam over boiling water for 30 minutes, or until done.
4	Carefully remove plate from steamer. Transfer melon pieces to a serving platter. Mix the cornstarch and water in a small saucepan. Add drippings from the steaming dish. Heat over high heat, stirring until mixture thickens. Pour the sauce over the melon sections and serve hot.

Yields 4 Servings   *Per Serving:* 174 calories, 343 mg. sodium, 38 mg. cholesterol

Further Modifications in Sodium: Reduce sodium to *219 mg. per serving* by substituting lower sodium soy sauce for the light and dark soy sauces.

SPINACH WITH FERMENTED BEAN CAKE

Steps	Ingredients
1	1 tablespoon fermented bean cake (furu)
	1 teaspoon sugar
	2 teaspoons dark soy sauce
2	1 teaspoon cornstarch
	1 tablespoon water
3	2 teaspoons oil
	1 pound fresh spinach (Cut off stems 1½ inches from the roots. Rinse well to remove dirt and drain.)

Steps	Instructions
1	Combine ingredients to form the *Sauce.* Set within easy reach.
2	Combine ingredients to form the *Cornstarch Mixture.* Set within easy reach.
3	Heat the oil in a pan over high heat until hazy. Put in the spinach and stir-fry briskly for 30 seconds. Pour in the *Sauce* and continue stir-frying for 10 to 15 seconds, or until bubbly. Suspend the *Cornstarch Mixture,* add to pan, and stir until the sauce is thickened. Serve hot.

Yields 4 Servings   *Per Serving:* 72 calories, 397 mg. sodium, 0 mg. cholesterol

Further Modifications in Sodium: Reduce sodium to *258 mg. per serving* by substituting fresh string beans for the spinach and substituting lower sodium soy sauce for the regular dark soy sauce.

Reduce sodium to *331 mg. per serving* by substituting lower sodium soy sauce for the regular dark soy sauce.

腐乳菠菜

開
洋
白
菜

CHINESE CABBAGE IN MILK SAUCE

Steps	Ingredients
1	1 tablespoon light soy sauce
	1 tablespoon cornstarch
	3 tablespoons low-fat milk
	¼ cup water
	pinch of white pepper
2	1 tablespoon oil
	2 cloves garlic, smashed with the side of a cleaver
	2 slices ginger, approximately 1 inch in diameter by ⅛ inch thick, smashed with the side of a cleaver
	1 tablespoon dried shrimp (Soak for 10 minutes, squeeze dry, and chop coarsely.)
	12 ounces Chinese cabbage (Cut into strips ½ inch wide by 1½ inches long.)
	2 tablespoons water

Steps	Instructions
1	Combine ingredients to form the *Sauce*. Set within easy reach.
2	Heat the oil in a pan over high heat until hazy. Put in the garlic and ginger; brown, then discard. Put in dried shrimp and stir-fry for 5 to 10 seconds. Add cabbage and stir-fry briskly for about 3 minutes. Add the 2 tablespoons water and continue stirring until the liquid is bubbly and cabbage is tender. Suspend the *Sauce*, pour it into the pan, and stir until it is thickened. Serve hot.

Yields 4 Servings   *Per Serving:* 66 calories, 373 mg. sodium, 3 mg. cholesterol

Further Modifications in Sodium: Reduce sodium to *199 mg. per serving* by substituting lower sodium soy sauce for the light soy sauce.

STEAMED FUZZY MELON

Steps	Ingredients
1	1 tablespoon light soy sauce
	½ teaspoon sugar
	½ tablespoon wine
	½ teaspoon sesame oil
	1 tablespoon water
2	1 1-pound fuzzy melon (Pare and slice into less than ⅛-inch-thick cross sections.)
	½ cup bamboo shoots sliced crosswise into thin sections
	½ tablespoon dried shrimp (Soak and chop coarsely.)

Steps	Instructions
1	Combine the ingredients to form the *Sauce*.
2	Place the fuzzy melon sections in a heat-proof deep dish. Add the bamboo shoots and top with the chopped shrimp.
3	Place the dish in a steamer, cover, and steam over boiling water for 20 minutes or until the melon is soft. When soft, sprinkle in the *Sauce* and steam for another 3 to 5 minutes. Serve hot.

Yields 4 Servings   *Per Serving:* 28 calories, 338 mg. sodium, 1 mg. cholesterol

Further Modifications in Sodium: Reduce sodium to *164 mg. per serving* by substituting lower sodium soy sauce for the regular light soy sauce.

BITTER MELON WITH BEEF
IN BLACK BEAN SAUCE

苦
瓜
炒
牛
肉

Steps	Ingredients
1	1 small bitter melon (approximately ½ pound) (Cut in half lengthwise, remove seeds and soft, loose pulp. Slice crosswise into ⅛-inch-thick slices.)
	5 cups water
2	½ tablespoon wine
	½ teaspoon cornstarch
	½ teaspoon sesame oil
3	6 ounces well-trimmed flank steak (Slice across the grain slantwise into thin slices 1 inch long by ⅛ inch thick.)
4	2 teaspoons dark soy sauce
	½ teaspoon sugar
	½ tablespoon wine
5	2 teaspoons cornstarch
	2 tablespoons water
6	½ tablespoon oil
	½ tablespoon oil
	3 cloves garlic, finely minced
	1 tablespoon fermented black beans, rinsed, drained, and mashed with the pommel of a cleaver
	½ cup water

Steps	Instructions
1	Bring the 5 cups water to a boil in a medium-sized saucepan. Put in the melon and boil for 1 minute. Remove the melon and rinse in cold water. Drain and set aside.
2	Combine the ingredients to form the *Marinade*.
3	Mix the beef into the *Marinade* and let stand for 10 minutes.
4	Combine the ingredients to form the *Sauce*. Set within easy reach.
5	Combine the ingredients to form the *Cornstarch Mixture*. Set aside within easy reach.
6	Heat the ½ tablespoon oil in a pan over high heat until hazy. Put in the beef and stir-fry briskly for 1 minute. Remove and set aside. Heat the remaining ½ tablespoon oil in a pan over high heat until hazy. Put in garlic and stir-fry for 2 to 3 seconds. Add black beans and stir an additional 2 to 3 seconds. Add the melon to the pan and stir-fry for 1 minute. Pour in the ½ cup water and continue stir-frying for 2 minutes, or until cooked but still crisp. Return the beef to the pan and stir. Pour in the *Sauce* and stir until it is bubbly. Suspend the *Cornstarch Mixture* and stir into pan until the sauce is thickened. Serve hot.

Yields 4 Servings   *Per Serving:* 122 calories, 276 mg. sodium, 29 mg. cholesterol

Further Modifications in Sodium: Reduce sodium to *210 mg. per serving* by substituting lower sodium soy sauce for the regular dark soy sauce.

DEEM SUM

POT STICKERS
(Kuo Tieh)

Steps		Ingredients
1	8	ounces lean boneless pork, ground or finely chopped
	3	Chinese dried mushrooms (Soak, squeeze out excess water, and chop.)
	5	ounces Chinese cabbage (2 inner leaves) (Rinse and pat dry with paper towels. Cut in slivers lengthwise ⅛ inch wide and crosswise ⅛ inch. Then chop coarsely.)
	1	medium stalk green onion (scallion), minced
	1	slice ginger, minced
	1	tablespoon dark soy sauce
	½	tablespoon sesame oil
	⅛	teaspoon white pepper
2	1	teaspoon cornstarch
	1	tablespoon water
3	1¼	cups all-purpose flour
	⅓	cup boiling water
	2	tablespoons cold water
4	1	tablespoon oil mixture (½ tablespoon cooking oil plus ½ tablespoon sesame oil)
	½	cup water
	1	tablespoon oil mixture (½ tablespoon cooking oil plus ½ tablespoon sesame oil)
	½	cup water

Steps	Instructions
1	Combine ingredients to form the *Filling*. Set aside.
2	Combine ingredients to form the *Sealer*. Set aside.
3	Pour boiling water over the flour and mix until absorbed. Add cold water and continue stirring until the dough forms a ball and leaves sides of bowl. Remove to a floured surface and knead for approximately 5 to 7 minutes, or until smooth. Divide dough into 4 equal portions. Then divide each portion into 6 equal pieces. To form the skins, roll each piece into a ball, flatten with your palm and roll out into 2½- to 3-inch circles. You should have 24 skins. Place approximately 2 teaspoons of *Filling* in the center of the skin. Brush the *Sealer* halfway around the rim of the skin. Bring the edges together to form a half-moon shape dumpling. Pinch and flute the edges. With fluted edges pointing upward, place dumpling on a platter. Press down slightly so each dumpling will sit up.
4	Heat 1 tablespoon oil mixture in a pan over medium-high heat. Put in 12 dumplings with the edges pointing up and brown the bottoms for about 2 minutes. Then pour in ½ cup water, cover pan and cook for 10 minutes. Remove and keep warm. Put in the last 12 dumplings and repeat the cooking with remaining oil and water. Serve immediately.

Yields 24 Dumplings
Per Serving (6 dumplings): 323 calories, 298 mg. sodium, 35 mg. cholesterol

Further Modifications in Sodium: Reduce sodium to *199 mg. per serving* by substituting lower sodium soy sauce for the regular dark soy sauce.

粉果

GROUND PORK DUMPLINGS
(Fun Guoh)

Steps	Ingredients
1	See Shrimp Dumpling (Hah Gau) recipe for preparation of skins (page 178)
2	½ tablespoon light soy sauce 1 teaspoon wine ⅛ teaspoon five spice powder ½ teaspoon sesame oil ½ tablespoon water
3	½ tablespoon cornstarch 1 tablespoon water
4	2 teaspoons oil 1 tablespoon dried shrimp (Soak for 20 minutes, drain, and mince.) 1 tablespoon chopped carrots 3 Chinese dried mushrooms (Soak, squeeze out excess water, stem, and mince.) 5 ounces well-trimmed boneless pork, coarsely ground 4 water chestnuts, chopped 1 tablespoon frozen petite peas 2 small stalks green onions (scallions), minced

Steps	Instructions
1	Prepare skins following the Hah Gau recipe. Set aside.
2	Combine the ingredients to form the *Sauce*. Set within easy reach.
3	Combine the ingredients to form the *Cornstarch Mixture*. Set within easy reach.
4	To prepare the *Filling*, heat the 2 teaspoons oil in a pan over high heat until hazy. Put in the shrimp, carrots, and mushrooms and stir-fry briskly for 30 seconds. Put in pork and stir-fry for 30 seconds. Add water chestnuts and peas. Pour in the *Sauce*, stir, cover the pan, and cook for 20 seconds. Remove the cover, suspend the *Cornstarch Mixture*, and stir into pan until the sauce is thickened. Add onions, stir, and transfer to a serving platter to cool.

To prepare dumplings, spoon a small portion of the *Filling* into the middle of one skin. Fold the skin in half and press the edges firmly to seal. Place the half-moon shaped dumpling on aluminum foil and cover with plastic wrap. Repeat with the remaining skins, using up all the filling. The dumplings may be wrapped and refrigerated for up to 2 hours. Remove the plastic wrap and place the aluminum foil with dumplings in a steamer and steam over boiling water for 5 minutes. Serve hot.

Yields 24 Dumplings
Per Serving (6 dumplings): 248 calories, 212 mg. sodium, 22 mg. cholesterol

Further Modifications in Sodium: Reduce sodium to *125 mg. per serving* by substituting lower sodium soy sauce for the regular light soy sauce.

春
捲

SPRING ROLLS
(Chun Guen)

Steps		Ingredients
1	2	teaspoons light soy sauce
	¼	teaspoon sugar
	½	teaspoon wine
	½	teaspoon sesame oil
2	½	tablespoon cornstarch
	1	tablespoon water
3	½	tablespoon oil
	6	ounces lean boneless pork, cut into shreds
	½	cup bamboo shoots, cut into matchstick-size pieces
	9	water chestnuts, cut into matchstick-size pieces
	2	cups bean sprouts, rinsed and drained
	1½	tablespoons minced green onions (scallions)
4	1	cup all-purpose flour
	¼	cup plus 2 tablespoons cold water
5	½	tablespoon cornstarch
	½	tablespoon water
6	1½	tablespoons oil

Steps	Instructions
1	Combine ingredients to form the *Sauce*. Set within easy reach.
2	Combine ingredients to form the *Cornstarch Mixture*. Set within easy reach.
3	Heat oil in a pan over high heat until hazy. Put in pork and stir-fry briskly for 1 minute. Add bamboo shoots and fry for 30 seconds. Add the water chestnuts, then pour in the *Sauce*, and stir-fry for 10 seconds. Put in the bean sprouts and stir-fry for 30 seconds. Suspend the *Cornstarch Mixture*, pour it into the pan, and stir until it is bubbly. Add onions. Remove and let *Filling* cool.
4	To prepare skins, pour water over the flour and mix until the dough leaves the sides of the bowl. Knead the dough in the bowl for 5 minutes, or until smooth. Cover the dough with a damp cloth and let stand for 30 minutes. Place the dough on a lightly floured surface and divide it into 8 pieces. Roll each piece out into a 7- to 8-inch circle. Dust lightly with flour before stacking circles on top of each other.
5	Combine cornstarch and water to form the *Sealer*. Set within easy reach. Place one skin on a lightly floured surface. Spoon ⅛ of the *Filling* into the center of the skin and spread filling crosswise 1 inch by 4 inches along the center. Roll up jelly roll style, being sure to tuck in the sides. Brush the open edge with the *Sealer*, complete rolling, and place the spring roll on a lightly floured platter, seam side down. Repeat with remaining 7 skins. At this point, you may cover with plastic wrap and refrigerate for 1 to 2 hours, if desired.
6	Heat the 1½ tablespoons oil in a pan over medium-high heat until hazy. Put in the spring rolls and brown both sides. Serve hot.

Yields 4 Servings
Per Serving (2 spring rolls): 290 calories, 252 mg. sodium, 27 mg. cholesterol

Further Modifications in Sodium: Reduce sodium to *136 mg. per serving* by substituting lower sodium soy sauce for the regular light soy sauce.

GREEN ONION PANCAKES

葱油餅

Steps	Ingredients
1	½ teaspoon onion powder
	2 tablespoons green onion (scallion), thinly sliced
	½ tablespoon vegetable shortening or soft margarine
2	1 cup all-purpose flour
	⅓ cup boiling water
	½ tablespoon cold water
3	¾ teaspoon cooking oil plus ¾ teaspoon sesame oil combined
	¾ teaspoon cooking oil plus ¾ teaspoon sesame oil combined
4	½ tablespoon light soy sauce
	½ teaspoon Chinese red vinegar
	1 teaspoon water
	½ teaspoon sugar

Steps	Instructions
1	Combine ingredients to form the *Spreading Mixture*. Set aside.
2	Pour boiling water over the flour and mix until absorbed. Add the cold water and continue stirring until the dough leaves the sides of the bowl. Turn onto a floured surface and knead until smooth (approximately 6 to 8 minutes). Cover with a damp cloth and let stand for 15 minutes.
	Divide the dough into 4 equal pieces. Roll out 1 piece into a 4-inch circle. Brush one fourth of the *Spreading Mixture* on top. Roll up jelly roll fashion. Then starting at one end, fold into thirds, turn seam side down, and press down with palm of your hand. Roll out again into a 4-inch circle. Repeat with other 3 pieces of dough.
3	Heat ½ tablespoon oil mixture in a pan over high heat until hazy. Put in 2 pancakes and brown slightly, then turn the heat down to medium-high and continue browning for 2 minutes. Turn and brown other side. Repeat with the other 2 pancakes using the remaining ½ tablespoon oil mixture.
4	Combine ingredients to form the *Dipping Sauce*. Serve with the hot pancakes.

Yields 4 Servings   *Per Serving:* 154 calories, 168 mg. sodium, 0 mg. cholesterol

Further Modifications in Sodium: Reduce sodium to *81 mg. per serving* by substituting lower sodium soy sauce for the regular light soy sauce.

BEEF DUMPLINGS
(Sui Mai)

燒
賣

Steps	Ingredients
1	8 ounces lean boneless beef, ground
	½ cup coarsely chopped bamboo shoots
	8 water chestnuts, coarsely chopped
	1 slice ginger, approximately 1 inch in diameter by ⅛ inch thick, minced
	1 tablespoon cornstarch
	½ teaspoon (scant) sugar
	¼ teaspoon black pepper
	1 tablespoon dark soy sauce
	½ tablespoon water
2	1¼ cups all-purpose flour
	⅓ cup boiling water
	2 tablespoons cold water

Steps	Instructions
1	Combine ingredients to form the *Filling*. Set aside.
2	Pour boiling water over the flour and mix until absorbed. Add the cold water and continue stirring until dough leaves the sides of the bowl. Remove to a floured surface and knead for 7 to 8 minutes, or until smooth. Cover with a damp cloth and let stand for 15 minutes.

Divide dough into 4 equal pieces. Then divide each piece into an additional 6 equal pieces. To form the skins, roll each piece into a ball, flatten with the palm of your hand and roll out into a 2½-to 3-inch circle. You should have 24 skins. Form a loose fist with the knuckle of the thumb facing upward. Place one skin on top of the thumb and index finger. Put 2 teaspoons *Filling* in the center of the skin. Allow the dumpling to drop slightly into the hollow of the fist so edges begin to gather. Then pinch and gather the edges together so that the dumpling resembles an inverted sunbonnet. Repeat with other skins. Set on a sheet of foil (gathered edges should be facing upward). Steam over boiling water for 15 minutes. Serve hot.

Yields 4 Servings
Per Serving (6 dumplings): 231 calories, 295 mg. sodium, 39 mg. cholesterol

Further Modifications in Sodium: Reduce sodium to *196 mg. per serving* by substituting lower sodium soy sauce for the regular dark soy sauce.

雞
絲
炒
麵

CHICKEN CHOW MEIN

Steps	Ingredients
1	4 cups water
	8 ounces dried (not instant) noodles made without salt
2	1 teaspoon thick soy sauce
	1½ tablespoons water
	½ tablespoon oil
	½ tablespoon sesame oil
	¼ teaspoon white pepper
3	1 tablespoon sugar
	½ cup water
	4 slices ginger, each 1 inch in diameter by ⅛ inch thick, peeled and minced
	1 tablespoon wine
	2 tablespoons American red wine vinegar
	1 tablespoon dark soy sauce
4	1 teaspoon cornstarch
	1 tablespoon wine
	3 tablespoons water
5	½ tablespoon oil
	3 chicken breast halves (Bone, skin, and cut into matchstick-size strips.)
	1½ celery stalks, thinly sliced on the diagonal
	8 Chinese dried mushrooms (Soak, squeeze out excess water, stem, and cut into thin strips.)
	½ cup water chestnuts, cut into thin strips
6	3 medium stalks green onion (scallion) (Cut into 1-inch lengths, then shred lengthwise.)

Steps	Instructions

Steps   Instructions

1   Bring the water to a boil in a pot. Add the noodles and stir to separate the strands. When the water returns to a boil, let noodles cook for 1 minute, then pour into a colander and rinse with cold water. Drain well and transfer noodles to a baking pan.

2   Combine the ingredients and mix into the noodles. Bake at 375 degrees for 10 minutes. Turn the noodles and bake on the other side for 10 minutes. Turn the oven to broil and brown the top of noodles until crispy. Turn off the oven and leave the noodles in oven until ready for use.

3   Combine the ingredients to form the *Sauce*. Set within easy reach.

4   Combine the ingredients to form the *Cornstarch Mixture*. Set within easy reach.

5   Heat the oil in a pan over high heat until hazy. Put in the chicken and stir-fry for 1 minute. Add celery, mushrooms, and water chestnuts and stir-fry for 1 minute. Pour in the *Sauce* and heat until it is bubbly. Suspend the *Cornstarch Mixture* and stir it into the pan until the sauce is thickened. Pour contents of pan over the browned noodles.

6   Garnish with green onions and serve hot.

Yields 4 Servings   *Per Serving:* 391 calories, 395 mg. sodium, 51 mg. cholesterol

Further Modifications in Sodium: Reduce sodium to *296 mg. per serving* by substituting lower sodium soy sauce for the regular dark soy sauce.

VEGETARIAN FRIED RICE

芽
菜
炒
飯

Steps	Ingredients
1	1 egg, beaten with a fork pinch of white pepper
2	1 tablespoon oil 1 slice ginger, approximately 1 inch in diameter by ⅛ inch thick, smashed with the side of a cleaver 1 clove garlic, smashed with the side of a cleaver 4 cups cooked rice, cooled 1 stalk green onion (scallion), cut thinly crosswise ½ tablespoon oil 1 tablespoon light soy sauce 2 cups bean sprouts, washed and drained ¼ teaspoon sesame oil

Steps	Instructions
1	Mix egg with pepper and set within easy reach.
2	Heat the oil in a pan over high heat until hazy. Add the ginger and garlic and brown. Discard them when brown. Put in the rice and stir-fry briskly for 3 minutes. Put in onion and continue stir-frying for 45 seconds. With a spatula, move the rice to the sides of the pan to form a well in the middle of the pan. Put the ½ tablespoon oil in a well for 30 seconds. Then mix egg with the rice mixture. Sprinkle in the soy sauce and mix with the rice for 1 minute. Add bean sprouts and stir with rice mixture for 1 minute. Sprinkle on the sesame oil and stir-fry for 30 seconds. Serve hot.

Yields 4 Servings   *Per Serving:* 316 calories, 343 mg. sodium, 64 mg. cholesterol

Further Modifications in Sodium: Reduce sodium to *169 mg. per serving* by substituting lower soy sauce for the regular light soy sauce.

Further Modifications in Cholesterol: Reduce cholesterol to *0 mg. per serving* by using only the egg white in the recipe.

DISCRETIONARY FOODS

PRAWNS IN TOMATO SAUCE

Steps	Ingredients
1	8 ounces fresh prawns (Shell, devein, and dry well on paper towels.)
	1 teaspoon light soy sauce
2	1½ tablespoons tomato paste without salt
	1 tablespoon Worcestershire sauce
	1 teaspoon sugar
	1 tablespoon water
3	1 tablespoon oil
	1 slice ginger, smashed with the side of a cleaver
	3 ounces snow peas (Rinse, remove tips and strings, and cut diagonally into halves.)
	1 stalk green onion (scallion), cut into 2-inch lengths

Steps	Instructions
1	Mix prawns with soy sauce and let stand for 30 minutes. Then put the prawns on paper towels and dry well. (Drying the prawns ensures a firm, rather than heavy, texture.)
2	Combine ingredients to form the *Sauce*. Set within easy reach.
3	Heat the oil in a pan over high heat until hazy. Put in the ginger and brown. Discard the ginger. Add snow peas and stir-fry for 1 minute. Put in prawns and stir-fry for 1 minute. Add green onion and continue stir-frying for 1 minute, or until the prawns are almost done. Suspend the *Sauce* and stir it into the pan. Stir until bubbly. Serve hot.

Yields 4 Servings   *Per Serving:* 104 calories, 255 mg. sodium, 84 mg. cholesterol

Further Modifications in Sodium: Reduce sodium to *180 mg. per serving* by substituting lower sodium soy sauce for the regular light soy sauce and decreasing the Worcestershire sauce to 2 teaspoons.

CHINESE BROCCOLI STIR-FRIED WITH PRAWNS

芥
蘭
蝦
球

Steps	Ingredients
1	1 teaspoon light soy sauce pinch of white pepper 1 tablespoon wine
2	6 ounces fresh prawns (Shell, devein, and dry well on paper towels.)
3	1 tablespoon wine 1 teaspoon light soy sauce ½ teaspoon sugar
4	1 teaspoon cornstarch 2 tablespoons water
5	1 tablespoon oil 1 slice ginger, approximately 1 inch in diameter by ⅛ inch thick smashed with the side of a cleaver 1 tablespoon chopped green onion (scallion) ½ tablespoon oil 12 ounces Chinese broccoli (or regular broccoli), cut into 2-inch lengths ¼ cup water

Steps	Instructions
1	Combine ingredients to form the *Marinade*.
2	Mix the prawns into the *Marinade* and let stand for 15 minutes. Then thoroughly dry the shrimp on paper towels again.
3	Combine the ingredients to form the *Sauce*. Set within easy reach.
4	Combine the ingredients to form the *Cornstarch Mixture*. Set within easy reach.
5	Heat 1 tablespoon oil in a pan over high heat until hazy. Brown ginger and onion. Discard ginger. Put in prawns and stir-fry for 1 minute. Remove the prawns and set within easy reach. Heat ½ tablespoon oil in the pan until hazy. Put in the broccoli and stir-fry briskly for 1 minute. Add the water, stir, cover, and cook for 2 minutes. Stir occasionally. Return the prawns to the pan and stir-fry briskly for about 30 seconds to 1 minute. Add the *Sauce* and stir-fry briskly for about 30 seconds to 1 minute. Add the *Sauce* and stir-fry until it is bubbly. Suspend the *Cornstarch Mixture*, pour it into the pan, and stir until the sauce is thickened. Serve hot.

Yields 4 Servings   *Per Serving:* 110 calories, 313 mg. sodium, 63 mg. cholesterol

Further Modifications in Sodium: Reduce sodium to *197 mg. per serving* by substituting lower sodium soy sauce for the regular light soy sauce.

CHINESE BROCCOLI WITH CRAB IN WHITE SAUCE

蟹扒芥蘭

Steps	Ingredients
1	2 teaspoons light soy sauce
	1 teaspoon sugar
	1 tablespoon water
	1 teaspoon sesame oil
2	1 egg white, lightly beaten
	⅓ cup water
	2 teaspoons cornstarch
3	1 tablespoon oil
	2 large cloves garlic, smashed with the side of a cleaver
	12 ounces Chinese broccoli (Wash, drain, and cut diagonally into 2-inch lengths.)
	3 tablespoons water
	5 ounces cooked fresh crabmeat, shredded

Steps	Instructions
1	Combine the ingredients to form the *Sauce*. Set within easy reach.
2	Combine the ingredients to form the *Cornstarch Mixture*. Set within easy reach.
3	Heat the 1 tablespoon oil in a pan over high heat until hazy. Brown the garlic and then discard. Put in the broccoli and stir-fry for 1½ minutes. Add the 3 tablespoons of water, cover, and cook for 2 minutes, stirring occasionally. Pour in the *Sauce*, stir, and remove the contents of the pan to a serving platter. Put the crabmeat into the pan. Suspend the *Cornstarch Mixture*, pour it into the pan and stir with the crab until mixture thickens. Arrange the crab on top of the broccoli and serve hot.

Yields 4 Servings   *Per Serving:* 119 calories, 387 mg. sodium, 38 mg. cholesterol

Further Modifications in Sodium: Reduce sodium to *271 mg. per serving* by substituting lower sodium for the regular light soy sauce.

木樨肉

MOO SHU PORK

Steps	Ingredients

1
- 1¼ cups all-purpose flour
- ⅓ cup boiling water
- 2 tablespoons cold water
- 2 tablespoons sesame oil

2
- 2 tablespoons sweet bean sauce
- ½ teaspoon sugar
- 2 tablespoons water

3
- 1 teaspoon oil
- 2 eggs, lightly beaten

4
- 1 tablespoon oil
- 6 ounces well-trimmed boneless pork, cut into matchstick-size pieces
- 4 wood fungus (mook yee) (Soak for 15 minutes, stem, and cut into matchstick-size pieces.)
- ¼ cup lily buds (Soak for 15 minutes and cut each in half.)
- ½ cup bamboo shoots, cut into matchstick-size pieces
- 2 Chinese dried mushrooms (Soak, squeeze out excess water, and cut into matchstick-size pieces.)
- white sections of 2 stalks of green onions (Cut into 1-inch lengths, then sliver.)

Steps   Instructions

1   Pour boiling water over the flour and mix until it is absorbed. Add the cold water and continue stirring until the dough leaves sides of bowl. Turn onto a floured surface and knead until smooth (approximately 6 to 8 minutes). Divide the dough into 8 equal pieces. Roll out each piece into a 6- to 7-inch circle. Brush one side of each pancake with the sesame oil and stack the pancakes in twos with oiled sides together.

 Heat a pan over medium-high heat and place one pair of pancakes in the pan. Brown for 1 to 2 minutes, turn and brown the other side. Repeat with other pancakes. Set aside, keeping pancakes warm and covered with a damp cloth. If softer pancakes are desired, place in a steamer and steam for 3 minutes, or until soft.

2   Combine ingredients to form *Sauce*. Set within easy reach.

3   Heat oil in pan over medium heat. Pour in eggs, scramble, and set aside.

4   Heat the 1 tablespoon oil in pan over high heat until hazy. Put in the pork and stir-fry for 30 seconds. Add wood fungus, lily buds, bamboo shoots, and dried mushrooms and stir-fry for 1 minute. Put in the scrambled eggs. Pour in the *Sauce* and stir-fry for 30 seconds. Remove contents to a serving platter and top with white sections of onions. Serve with warm pancakes.

Yields 8 Pancakes
Per Serving (2 pancakes): 387 calories, 321 mg. sodium, 154 mg. cholesterol

Further Modifications in Sodium: Reduce sodium to *192 mg. per serving* by decreasing the sweet bean sauce to 1 tablespoon.

Further Modifications in Cholesterol: Reduce cholesterol to *27 mg. per serving* by eliminating the egg yolks from the recipe.

LOBSTER CANTONESE

炒
龍
蝦

Steps	Ingredients
1	2 teaspoons dark soy sauce
	1 teaspoon light brown sugar
	½ tablespoon wine
	2 slices ginger, approximately 1 inch in diameter by ⅛ inch thick, finely minced
2	2 teaspoons cornstarch
	2 tablespoons water
3	½ tablespoon oil
	½ medium onion, cut into quarters (Cut each quarter into 4 equal chunks.)
	1 medium green bell pepper (Seed, rib, and cut into ¾-inch squares.)
4	1 tablespoon oil
	1 tablespoon salted black beans, rinsed and mashed
	3 cloves garlic, finely minced
	3 ounces coarsely ground lean pork
5	6½ ounces fresh lobster meat, cut into ¾-inch cubes
	½ cup water
	1 egg white, lightly beaten

Steps	Instructions
1	Combine ingredients to form the *Sauce*. Set within easy reach.
2	Combine ingredients to form the *Cornstarch Mixture*. Set within reach.
3	Heat the oil in a pan over high heat until hazy. Put in the onion and green bell pepper and stir-fry for 1½ minutes. Pour into a platter and set within easy reach.
4	Heat the oil in a pan over high heat until hazy. Put in the black beans and garlic and stir-fry for about 10 seconds. Add pork and stir-fry for 1 minute.
5	Pour in the *Sauce* and add the lobster meat to the pan. Stir-fry for 1 minute. Pour in ½ cup water. Heat until bubbly. Return the onion and pepper to the pan. Suspend the *Cornstarch Mixture*, pour it into the pan, and stir until thickened. Stir in the egg white. Serve hot.

Yields 4 Servings   *Per Serving:* 161 calories, 393 mg. sodium, 58 mg. cholesterol

Further Modifications in Sodium: Reduce sodium to *302 mg. per serving* by substituting lower sodium soy sauce for the regular dark soy sauce and by decreasing the black beans to 2 teaspoons.

SCRAMBLED EGGS WITH TOMATO

蕃
茄
炒
蛋

Steps	Ingredients
1	3 eggs
	1 egg white
	2 teaspoons light soy sauce
	⅛ teaspoon white pepper
2	½ tablespoon oil
	1 medium tomato, cut in half, then into thin wedges
	½ teaspoon sugar
3	1 tablespoon oil

Steps	Instructions
1	Beat the whole eggs with the egg white until well blended. Mix in the soy sauce and pepper. Set within easy reach.
2	Heat the oil in a pan over high heat until hazy. Put in the tomato slices and sugar. Stir-fry briskly for 30 seconds. Take out and set within easy reach.
3	Heat the oil in a pan over high heat until hazy. Pour in the beaten eggs and stir using a folding action. When eggs are half done, add tomato slices and continue to stir-fry until eggs are at desired consistency. Serve hot.

Yields 4 Servings   Per Serving: 122 calories, 275 mg. sodium, 191 mg. cholesterol

Further Modifications in Sodium: Reduce sodium to *159 mg. per serving* by substituting lower sodium soy sauce for the regular light soy sauce.

Further Modifications in Cholesterol: Reduce cholesterol to *64 mg. per serving* by reducing the whole eggs to 1 and increasing the egg whites to 3.

SHRIMP DUMPLINGS
(Hah Gau)

蝦餃

Steps	Ingredients
1	½ tablespoon light soy sauce
	¼ teaspoon sugar
	½ teaspoon wine
	½ teaspoon sesame oil
	½ tablespoon cornstarch
	pinch of white pepper
2	½ pound fresh prawns (Shell, devein, and dry well on paper towels, then chop coarsely.)
	½ cup minced bamboo shoots
	white section of one stalk of green onion (scallion), minced
3	¾ cup wheat starch (deng mein fun)
	¼ cup tapioca flour (sang fun)
	¾ cup boiling water (water must be boiling when poured into flour)
	½ tablespoon oil
4	1 tablespoon oil

Steps	Instructions
1	Combine the ingredients to form the *Marinade*.
2	Mix the shrimp, bamboo shoots, and white section of onion into the *Marinade* and let stand in the refrigerator for 1 hour.
3	To prepare the skins: Place a sifter over a large mixing bowl. Sift the wheat starch and tapioca flour into the bowl. Make a well in the middle of the flour mixture and slowly pour the boiling water in while stirring with chopsticks or a wooden spoon. Continue mixing until the dough forms and leaves the sides of the bowl. Add the ½ tablespoon oil and, with the heel of your hand, knead the dough in the bowl for 4 minutes, or until smooth. Cover and let stand for 20 minutes.
4	Place the 1 tablespoon oil in a small dish. Use a small piece of cheesecloth or paper towel to apply oil to the working surface when needed. Apply oil to the working surface. Roll the dough out into a long cylinder 1 inch in diameter using the palm of your hand and a forward and backward motion. Cut the cylinder into 24 equal pieces. Place one piece of dough on the oiled surface. Dip the cheesecloth into the oil and lightly brush one side of the cleaver with oil. With the palm of your hand, firmly press the cleaver blade down on the piece of dough. Flatten dough into a round skin 2½ inches in diameter. Repeat with rest of the dough, oiling the blade as needed. To form a pouch for the filling, pleat the edge of the skin one-half way around. Fill the pouch, bring the smooth edge to the pleated edge and press together. Place dumpling on a sheet of aluminum foil and cover with plastic wrap. Repeat with the remaining skins. Preferably steam dumpling as soon as made. However, dumpling may be refrigerated up to 2 hours. Place the foil with the dumplings in a steamer and steam over boiling water for 7 minutes. Serve hot.

Yields 4 Servings
Per Serving (6 dumplings): 206 calories, 208 mg. sodium, 42 mg. cholesterol

Further Modifications in Sodium: Reduce sodium to *121 mg. per serving* by substituting lower sodium soy sauce for the regular light soy sauce.

STEAMED EGGS WITH GROUND PORK

肉
粒
蒸
蛋

Steps	Ingredients
1	1 teaspoon wine ½ tablespoon light soy sauce ½ teaspoon cornstarch ½ teaspoon sesame oil
2	3 ounces well-trimmed boneless pork, ground or coarsely chopped
3	1 teaspoon oil 3 eggs, lightly beaten with 6 half-shells of boiled, then cooled water
4	½ tablespoon light soy sauce 1 teaspoon sesame oil 1 teaspoon thinly sliced green onion (scallion)

Steps	Instructions
1	Combine the ingredients to form the *Marinade.*
2	Mix the pork with the *Marinade,* and let stand for 10 minutes.
3	Heat the oil in a pan over high heat until hazy. Add the pork and stir-fry briskly for about 2 minutes. Remove and let cool. Mix the pork with the beaten eggs. Place the egg mixture in a heat-proof dish. Place the dish in a steamer filled with a sufficient amount of water. Be careful that the water level does not touch the bottom of the dish. Cover the steamer and bring the water to a boil over medium-high heat. When water begins to boil, immediately turn heat to low and steam for 15 minutes. (If the heat is too high, the egg mixture will lose its smooth, custard texture.) Turn the heat off and leave cover on until ready to serve. Egg mixture may be kept warm in the steamer for 1 hour.
4	When ready to serve, remove dish from the steamer and sprinkle the soy sauce, sesame oil, and onion on top.

Yields 4 Servings   *Per Serving:* 134 calories, 386 mg. sodium, 205 mg. cholesterol

Further Modifications in Sodium: Reduce sodium to *212 mg. per serving* by substituting lower sodium soy sauce for the regular light soy sauce.

Further Modifications in Cholesterol: Reduce cholesterol to *77 mg. per serving* by using 1 whole egg and 2 egg whites in place of the 3 whole eggs.

STEAMED TOFU AND EGGS

豆腐蒸蛋

Steps	Ingredients
1	water
	8 ounce cube soft tofu
2	2 eggs
	½ teaspoon white pepper
	1 teaspoon light soy sauce
	1 small stalk green onion (scallion), minced
	2 Chinese dried mushrooms (Soak, squeeze out excess water, stem, and chop finely.)
	2 ounces coarsely chopped lean pork
3	½ tablespoon sesame oil
	1 teaspoon light soy sauce

Steps	Instructions
1	Bring a pot of water to boil and add the tofu. Be sure water covers tofu completely. When water begins to boil again, remove the pot from the heat and let the tofu soak for 10 minutes. Remove the tofu and put into a heat-proof serving bowl. Mash the tofu with a fork.
2	Crack the eggs into the tofu and mix thoroughly. Mix the remaining ingredients into the tofu. Steam tofu mixture over medium heat for 10 minutes.
3	Sprinkle with sesame oil and soy sauce. Serve hot.

Yields 4 Servings   *Per Serving:* 131 calories, 261 mg. sodium, 136 mg. cholesterol

Further Modifications in Sodium: Reduce sodium to *145 mg. per serving* by substituting lower sodium soy sauce for the regular light soy sauce.

Further Modifications in Cholesterol: Reduce cholesterol to *73 mg. per serving* by using 1 whole egg and 2 egg whites.

蛋糕

CUSTARD

Steps	Ingredients
1	1 whole egg
	2 egg whites
	1 cup low-fat milk
	1½ tablespoons sugar
	¾ teaspoon vanilla extract
	1 teaspoon lemon juice
2	ground cinnamon
	ground nutmeg

Steps	Instructions
1	Combine ingredients in a small bowl and mix thoroughly. Then distribute evenly among 4 custard cups.
2	Sprinkle each cup of custard with cinnamon and nutmeg. Place the cups in a baking pan containing 1 inch of water. Bake in a 350-degree oven for 40 minutes. Serve hot or cold.

Yields 4 Servings   *Per Serving:* 80 calories, 70 mg. sodium, 68 mg. cholesterol

Further Modifications in Cholesterol: Reduce cholesterol to *1 mg. per serving* by eliminating the whole egg and using 3 egg whites and by substituting non-fat milk for the low-fat milk.

干貝炒芽菜

SCALLOPS WITH BEAN SPROUTS

Steps	Ingredients
1	2 teaspoons light soy sauce
	1 teaspoon Chinese red vinegar
	1 teaspoon sugar
2	8 ounces fresh scallops, cut into ⅜-inch-thick by 1-inch-diameter pieces
	1 tablespoon wine
	pinch of white pepper
3	1½ tablespoons oil
	12 ounces bean sprouts, rinsed and drained
4	1 tablespoon oil
	3 slices ginger, each 1 inch in diameter by ⅛ inch thick, smashed with the side of a cleaver
	1 medium stalk green onion (scallion), cut into 2-inch lengths

Steps	Instructions
1	Combine ingredients to form the *Sauce*. Set within easy reach.
2	Marinate scallops in wine and pepper for 10 to 15 minutes.
3	Heat the oil in a pan over high heat until hazy. Add the bean sprouts and stir-fry for 1 minute. Remove to a platter.
4	Heat the oil in a pan over high heat until hazy. Add the ginger and brown lightly, then discard. Add scallops and stir-fry for 2 minutes. Add green onions and stir-fry for 30 seconds. Pour in the *Sauce* and stir until bubbly. Return the bean sprouts to the pan and stir-fry for 30 seconds. Serve hot.

Yields 4 Servings   *Per Serving:* 132 calories, 375 mg. sodium, 20 mg. cholesterol

Further Modifications in Sodium: Reduce sodium to *259 mg. per serving* by substituting lower sodium soy sauce for the regular light soy sauce.

BEAN SPROUT EGG FOO YUNG

Steps	Ingredients
1	3 eggs, beaten
	1 tablespoon light soy sauce
	⅛ teaspoon black pepper
	1 teaspoon sesame oil
	4 cups bean sprouts, washed and drained
	1 to 2 stalks green onions (scallions), thinly sliced
2	½ tablespoon oil
	½ tablespoon oil

Steps	Instructions
1	Combine ingredients in a bowl. Mix well.
2	Add ½ tablespoon oil to a pan and heat over medium-high heat until hazy. Spoon in enough egg mixture to make a 3-inch-diameter pancake. Repeat until the pan is filled. Cook until browned. Turn and brown the other side. Remove to a serving platter and keep warm. Continue making pancakes, adding the remaining ½ tablespoon oil as needed.

Yields 4 Servings   *Per Serving:* 145 calories, 376 mg. sodium, 191 mg. cholesterol

Further Modifications in Sodium: Reduce sodium to *202 mg. per serving* by substituting lower sodium soy sauce for the regular light soy sauce.

Further Modifications in Cholesterol: Reduce cholesterol to *64 mg. per serving* by using 1 whole egg plus 3 egg whites.

芽菜芙容蛋

8

Helpful Nutrition Guide

SAMPLE MENUS

Sample menus have been created for women and men desiring to lose weight while following a sensible sodium (not more than 2,000 mg. per day) or low-sodium (not more than 1,000 mg. per day) diet. The standard caloric levels used are: 1,200 calories for weight reduction in women, 1,500 calories for weight reduction in men, and 1,800 calories for weight maintenance in men and women. For those following the maintenance plan, adjustments with slightly more or less food (chosen from the Basic Four Food Groups) may be necessary since an individual's caloric needs can vary markedly. For example, if you notice a steady weight gain or loss of one pound every one to two weeks, adjust by increasing or decreasing 1 serving of bread or starch, 1 teaspoon fat, 1 fruit, and 1 ounce of meat, fish, or poultry each day. You may also wish to keep an accurate diary of your food intake for two weeks and compare it with the suggested sample menu for possible variations. If you have any doubt about the calorie value of a food, just check the composition tables in the appendix.

Good nutrition, with an emphasis on moderation and variety, is built into the menu's format. Also included in the plan are heart-healthy principles, including a low-cholesterol intake (weekly average of less than 300 mg. cholesterol per day) and reduction in total fat consumption to less than 30 percent of the daily caloric allowance. You will notice that the use of special low-calorie, low-sodium products is kept to a minimum for practical and economic reasons.

Food should be prepared without salt or high-sodium seasonings. Although you will find a few high-sodium foods and condiments, such as cheese and ketchup, in our menus, please don't be alarmed! Small amounts of these items, carefully calculated into the daily menu, will add variety and appeal and yet not exceed the desired sodium level.

REDUCING DIET WITH A SENSIBLE
SODIUM LEVEL FOR WOMEN

(1,200 calories, not more than 2,000 mg. sodium per day)

MONDAY

Breakfast
½ fresh grapefruit
¾ cup Rice Krispies
½ cup skim milk
 Coffee or tea

Lunch
Carrot-raisin salad:
½ cup shredded carrots
1 tablespoon raisins
2 teaspoons low-calorie imitation
  mayonnaise
Turkey sandwich:
2 slices whole wheat bread
3 ounces white meat turkey
1 teaspoon margarine
2 lettuce leaves
2 slices tomato
½ cup skim milk

Dinner
1 serving Cold Bean Sprouts
1 serving Oyster Sauce Beef
1 serving Asparagus with Chicken
½ cup rice
 Hot tea

Evening Snack
½ cup skim milk

Total Day's Intake:
         1,217 calories
      1,963 mg. sodium
         173 mg. cholesterol
       23 percent fat

TUESDAY

Breakfast
1 fresh tangerine
¾ cup Oatmeal with Raisins and
  Spice
1 teaspoon margarine
1 cup skim milk
 Coffee or tea

Lunch
Stuffed tomato:
1 medium tomato
3½ ounces low-sodium,
   water-packed tuna mixed with
¼ cup chopped celery
1½ tablespoons low-calorie
   imitation mayonnaise
3 lettuce leaves
3 radish roses
5 carrot curls
1 slice French bread
½ tablespoon margarine
1 cup skim milk

Dinner
1 serving Stewed Chicken
1 serving Spinach with
  Fermented Bean Cake
½ cup rice
 Hot tea

Evening Snack
1 bran muffin
1 teaspoon margarine
1 cup hot tea with lemon

Total Day's Intake:
         1,197 calories
      1,950 mg. sodium
         134 mg. cholesterol
       22 percent fat

REDUCING DIET WITH A SENSIBLE
SODIUM LEVEL FOR WOMEN

(1,200 calories; not more than 2,000 mg. sodium per day)

WEDNESDAY

Breakfast
¼ of a 5-inch cantaloupe
1 soft-cooked egg
1 cup Total
½ cup skim milk
Coffee or tea

Lunch
Middle Eastern chicken sandwich:
2 ounces sliced white meat
    chicken
1 ounce American cheese
2 lettuce leaves
2 slices tomato
¼ cup alfalfa sprouts
1 tablespoon low-calorie
    Thousand Island dressing
1 whole wheat pita bread
½ cup mixed fresh fruit salad
Iced tea

Dinner
1 serving Sweet and Sour Pork
    Cantonese
1 serving Steamed Chinese
    (Napa) Cabbage
½ cup rice
Hot tea

Evening Snack
½ cup skim milk

Total Day's Intake:
            1,197 calories
        1,997 mg. sodium
            391 mg. cholesterol
        26 percent fat

THURSDAY

Breakfast
⅔ cup fresh strawberries
⅓ cup All-Bran
½ cup skim milk
Coffee or tea

Lunch
Hamburger sandwich:
    3-ounce broiled lean beef patty
    Hamburger bun
2 lettuce leaves
2 slices tomato
1 teaspoon ketchup
1 teaspoon low-calorie imitation
    mayonnaise
5 carrot sticks
5 celery sticks
½ cup skim milk

Dinner
1 serving Kung Pao Chicken
1 serving Steamed Fuzzy Melon
1 serving Vegetarian Fried Rice
Hot tea

Evening Snack
½ cup skim milk

Total Day's Intake:
            1,198 calories
        1,938 mg. sodium
            201 mg. cholesterol
        25 percent fat

REDUCING DIET WITH A SENSIBLE SODIUM LEVEL FOR WOMEN

(1,200 calories; not more than 2,000 mg. sodium per day)

FRIDAY

Breakfast
1 medium orange
1 whole English muffin
½ tablespoon margarine
1 teaspoon strawberry jam
½ cup skim milk
Coffee or tea

Lunch
Chef's salad bowl:
  2 cups romaine lettuce
  1 ounce American Swiss cheese
  1 ounce lean roast beef strips
  1 ounce roast turkey strips
  3 green pepper rings
  ½ small cucumber, sliced
  6 small cherry tomatoes
1½ tablespoons low-calorie
      Thousand Island dressing
  1 slice whole wheat bread
  1 teaspoon margarine
  1 medium peach
  1 cup skim milk

Dinner
1 serving Steamed Salmon
1 serving Stir-Fried Broccoli
½ cup rice
Hot tea

Evening Snack
½ cup skim milk

Total Day's Intake:
        1,196 calories
    1,997 mg. sodium
      115 mg. cholesterol
    25 percent fat

SATURDAY

Breakfast
½ cup unsweetened grapefruit
    juice
⅔ cup Raisin Bran
½ cup skim milk
Coffee or tea

Lunch
Cottage cheese and fruit salad:
  ¼ cup low-fat cottage cheese
  1 fresh apricot
  3 ounces lean roast leg of lamb
  ½ cup parsley-buttered potato
    (using 1 teaspoon margarine)
  ¾ cup steamed zucchini squash
  ½ teaspoon margarine
  Iced tea

Dinner
1 serving Stir-Fried Pressed Tofu
1 serving Dry-Fried String Beans
1 serving Cauliflower with
    Chicken in Black Bean Sauce
½ cup rice
Hot tea

Evening Snack
2 plain graham crackers
½ cup skim milk

Total Day's Intake:
        1,196 calories
    1,997 mg. sodium
      56 mg. cholesterol
    26 percent fat

REDUCING DIET WITH A SENSIBLE
SODIUM LEVEL FOR WOMEN

(1,200 calories; not more than 2,000 mg. sodium per day)

SUNDAY

Brunch
  1 serving Spring Rolls
  1 serving Stir-Fried Bean Sprouts
  1 serving Bok Choy Stir-Fried
     with Beef
  Coffee or tea

Afternoon Snack
  1 serving Cantonese
     Chicken Salad
  ⅓ cup plain low-fat yogurt
  ¾ cup fresh diced papaya
  Iced tea

Dinner
  1 serving Pan-Fried Fish with
     Lemon Sauce
  1 serving Stir-Fried Mixed
     Vegetables
  ½ cup rice
  Hot tea

Total Day's Intake:
           1,202 calories
           1,946 mg. sodium
           177 mg. cholesterol
           27 percent fat

REDUCING DIET WITH A SENSIBLE
SODIUM LEVEL FOR MEN

(1,500 calories; not more than 2,000 mg. sodium per day)

MONDAY

Breakfast
  ½ fresh grapefruit
  1 large Shredded Wheat biscuit
  1 teaspoon brown sugar
  1 slice whole wheat toast
  1 teaspoon margarine
  ¾ cup skim milk
  Coffee or tea

Lunch
Carrot-raisin salad:
  ½ cup shredded carrots
  2 tablespoons raisins
  ½ tablespoon low-calorie imitation
     mayonnaise
Turkey sandwich:
  2 slices whole wheat bread
  3 ounces white meat turkey
  ½ tablespoon margarine
  2 lettuce leaves
  2 tomato slices
  ½ cup skim milk

Dinner
  1 serving Cold Bean Sprouts
  1 serving Oyster Sauce Beef
  1 serving Asparagus with Chicken
  1 cup rice
  Hot tea

Evening Snack
  2 medium dried apricots
  ½ cup skim milk

Total Day's Intake:
           1,497 calories
           1,980 mg. sodium
           176 mg. cholesterol
           22 percent fat

REDUCING DIET WITH A SENSIBLE
SODIUM LEVEL FOR MEN

(1,500 calories; not more than 2,000 mg. sodium per day)

TUESDAY

Breakfast
  1 fresh tangerine
  ¾ cup Oatmeal with Raisins and
      Spice
  2 teaspoons margarine
  1 teaspoon orange marmalade
  1 cup skim milk
    Coffee or tea

Lunch
Stuffed tomato:
  1 medium tomato
  3½ ounces low-sodium, water-
      packed tuna mixed with
  ¼ cup chopped celery
  1½ tablespoon low-calorie imitation
      mayonnaise
  3 lettuce leaves
  3 radish roses
  5 carrot curls
  1 slice French bread
  2 teaspoons margarine
  1 medium pear
  1 cup skim milk

Dinner
  1 serving Stewed Chicken
  1 serving Spinach with Fermented
      Bean Cake
  1 cup rice
    Hot tea

Evening Snack
  1 bran muffin
  1 teaspoon margarine
  ½ cup peach nectar

Total Day's Intake:
        1,489 calories
    1,997 mg. sodium
      135 mg. cholesterol
    21 percent fat

WEDNESDAY

Breakfast
  ¼ of a 5-inch cantaloupe
  1 poached egg
  1 slice whole wheat toast
  ½ cup Total
  1 teaspoon brown sugar
  ½ cup skim milk
    Coffee or tea

Lunch
Middle Eastern chicken sandwich:
  3 ounces sliced white meat
      chicken
  1 ounce American cheese
  2 lettuce leaves
  2 tomato slices
  ¼ cup alfalfa sprouts
  1 tablespoon low-calorie
      Thousand Island dressing
  1 whole wheat pita bread
  ¾ cup mixed fresh fruit salad
    Iced tea

Dinner
  1 serving Sweet and Sour Pork
      Cantonese
  1 serving Steamed Chinese (Napa)
      Cabbage
  1 cup rice
    Hot tea

Evening Snack
  2 cups unsalted popcorn
  ½ cup skim milk

Total Day's Intake:
        1,494 calories
    1979 mg. sodium
      415 mg. cholesterol
    24 percent fat

REDUCING DIET WITH A SENSIBLE
SODIUM LEVEL FOR MEN

(1,500 calories; not more than 2,000 mg. sodium per day)

THURSDAY

Breakfast
 1 cup fresh strawberries
 ¾ cup Wheatena
 1 teaspoon honey
 1 teaspoon margarine
 1 cup skim milk
   Coffee or tea

Lunch
Hamburger sandwich:
   3-ounce broiled lean beef patty
   Hamburger bun
 2 lettuce leaves
 2 tomato slices
 1 teaspoon ketchup
 1 teaspoon mustard
 ½ tablespoon low-calorie imitation
   mayonnaise
 5 carrot sticks
 5 celery sticks
 1 medium peach
 1 cup skim milk

Dinner
 1 serving Kung Pao Chicken
 1 serving Steamed Fuzzy Melon
 1 serving Vegetarian Fried Rice
   Hot tea

Evening Snack
 2 plain graham crackers
 ½ cup skim milk

Total Day's Intake:
       1,488 calories
       1,968 mg. sodium
        206 mg. cholesterol
        23 percent fat

FRIDAY

Breakfast
 1 medium orange
 1 whole English muffin
 ½ tablespoon margarine
 ½ tablespoon strawberry jam
 1 cup skim milk
   Coffee or tea

Lunch
Chef's salad bowl:
 2 cups romaine lettuce
 1 ounce American Swiss cheese
 1 ounce lean roast beef strips
 1 ounce roast turkey strips
 3 green pepper rings
 ½ small cucumber, sliced
 6 cherry tomatoes
   Oil and vinegar dressing using
 1 tablespoon oil and vinegar as
   desired
 2 slices whole wheat bread
 1 teaspoon margarine
20 Thompson (seedless) grapes
 ½ cup skim milk

Dinner
 1 serving Steamed Salmon
 1 serving Stir-Fried Broccoli
 1 cup rice
   Hot tea

Evening Snack
 ½ cup skim milk

Total Day's Intake:
       1,495 calories
       1,955 mg. sodium
        115 mg. cholesterol
        28 percent fat

REDUCING DIET WITH A SENSIBLE SODIUM LEVEL FOR MEN

(1,500 calories; not more than 2,000 mg. sodium per day)

SATURDAY

Breakfast
½ cup unsweetened grapefruit
   juice
⅔ cup Raisin Bran
½ cup skim milk
   Coffee or tea

Lunch
Cottage cheese and fruit salad:
¼ cup low-fat cottage cheese
1 pineapple ring (canned in juice)
3 ounces lean roast leg of lamb
½ cup parsley-buttered potato
   (using 1 teaspoon margarine)
¾ cup steamed zucchini squash
½ teaspoon margarine
1 slice whole wheat bread
1 teaspoon margarine
½ cup skim milk

Afternoon Snack
3 fresh apricots

Dinner
1 serving Stir-Fried Pressed Tofu
1 serving Dry-Fried String Beans
1 serving Cauliflower with
   Chicken in Black Bean Sauce
1 cup rice
   Hot tea

Evening Snack
¾ cup hot apple juice with a
   cinnamon stick

Total Day's Intake:
      1,500 calories
      1,990 mg. sodium
      142 mg. cholesterol
      23 percent fat

SUNDAY

Brunch
1 serving Spring Rolls
1 serving Cantonese
   Chicken Salad
1 serving Bok Choy Stir-Fried
   with Beef
   Coffee or tea

Afternoon Snack
1 cup plain low-fat yogurt
1 teaspoon honey
¾ cup fresh diced papaya
1 slice whole wheat bread
½ teaspoon margarine
   Iced tea

Dinner
1 serving Pan-Fried Fish with
   Lemon Sauce
1 serving Stir-Fried Mixed
   Vegetables
1 cup rice
   Hot tea

Evening Snack
¾ cup skim milk

Total Day's Intake:
      1,502 calories
      1,974 mg. sodium
      186 mg. cholesterol
      23 percent fat

MAINTENANCE DIET WITH A SENSIBLE
SODIUM LEVEL FOR WOMEN AND MEN

(1,800 calories; not more than 2,000 mg. sodium per day)

MONDAY

Breakfast
½ fresh grapefruit
1 large Shredded Wheat biscuit
1 teaspoon brown sugar
1 slice whole wheat toast
1 teaspoon margarine
1 cup low-fat milk
  Coffee or tea

Lunch
Carrot-raisin salad:
½ cup shredded carrots
3 tablespoons raisins
2 teaspoons low-calorie imitation
    mayonnaise
Turkey sandwich:
2 slices whole wheat bread
3 ounces white meat turkey
2 teaspoons low-calorie imitation
    mayonnaise
2 lettuce leaves
2 slices tomato
½ cup low-fat milk

Afternoon Snack
1 medium pear

Dinner
1 serving Cold Bean Sprouts
1 serving Oyster Sauce Beef
1 serving Asparagus with Chicken
1 cup rice
  Hot tea

Evening Snack
3 medium dried apricots
½ cup low-fat milk

Total Day's Intake:
      1,799 calories
      1,963 mg. sodium
        201 mg. cholesterol
        23 percent fat

TUESDAY

Breakfast
5 stewed prunes without sugar
1 cup regular oatmeal
1 teaspoon margarine
1 teaspoon brown sugar
1 slice whole wheat toast
1 teaspoon margarine
1 cup low-fat milk

Lunch
Stuffed tomato:
1 medium tomato
3½ ounces low-sodium, water-
    packed tuna mixed with
¼ cup chopped celery
1 tablespoon low-calorie imitation
    mayonnaise
3 lettuce leaves
5 carrot curls
2 slices French bread
½ tablespoon margarine
1 cup cubed watermelon
1 cup low-fat milk

Afternoon Snack
1 fresh tangerine

Dinner
1 serving Stewed Chicken
1 serving Spinach with
    Fermented Bean Cake
1 cup rice
  Hot tea

Evening Snack
1 bran muffin
1 teaspoon margarine
½ cup peach nectar

Total Day's Intake:
      1,797 calories
      1,988 mg. sodium
        154 mg. cholesterol
        25 percent fat

MAINTENANCE DIET WITH A SENSIBLE SODIUM LEVEL FOR WOMEN AND MEN

(1,800 calories; not more than 2,000 mg. sodium per day)

WEDNESDAY

Breakfast
¼ of a 5-inch cantaloupe
1 poached egg
2 slices whole wheat toast
1 teaspoon margarine
1 teaspoon orange marmalade
1 cup low-fat milk
  Coffee or tea

Lunch
Middle Eastern chicken sandwich:
3 ounces sliced white meat
  chicken
1 ounce American cheese
2 lettuce leaves
2 tomato slices
¼ cup alfalfa sprouts
1 tablespoon low-calorie
  Thousand Island dressing
1 whole wheat pita bread
1 cup mixed fresh fruit salad
  Iced tea

Afternoon Snack
1 cup fresh cherries

Dinner
1 serving Sweet and Sour Pork
  Cantonese
1 serving Steamed Chinese (Napa)
  Cabbage
1 cup rice
  Hot tea

Evening Snack
2 cups unsalted popcorn
⅔ cup unsweetened pineapple
  juice

Total Day's Intake:
    1,783 calories
  1,985 mg. sodium
    425 mg. cholesterol
  27 percent fat

THURSDAY

Breakfast
½ cup fresh strawberries
¾ cup Wheatena
1 teaspoon honey
1 slice raisin toast
1 teaspoon margarine
1 cup low-fat milk
  Coffee or tea

Lunch
Hamburger sandwich:
  3-ounce broiled lean beef patty
  Hamburger bun
2 lettuce leaves
2 tomato slices
½ tablespoon low-calorie imitation
  mayonnaise
5 carrot sticks
5 celery sticks
20 Thompson (seedless) grapes
1 cup low-fat milk

Dinner
1 serving Kung Pao Chicken
1 serving Steamed Fuzzy Melon
1 serving Vegetarian Fried Rice
  Hot tea

Evening Snack
Open-faced sandwich:
1 slice whole wheat bread
1 teaspoon honey
½ large banana, sliced
½ cup low-fat milk

Total Day's Intake:
    1,803 calories
  1,980 mg. sodium
    231 mg. cholesterol
  30 percent fat

MAINTENANCE DIET WITH A SENSIBLE
SODIUM LEVEL FOR WOMEN AND MEN
(1,800 calories; not more than 2,000 mg. sodium per day)

FRIDAY

Breakfast
1 medium orange
1 whole English muffin
½ tablespoon margarine
1 tablespoon strawberry jam
1 cup low-fat milk
Coffee or tea

Lunch
Chef's salad bowl:
2 cups romaine lettuce
1 ounce lean roast beef strips
2 ounces roast turkey strips
3 green pepper rings
½ small cucumber, sliced
6 cherry tomatoes
1½ tablespoon low-calorie
Thousand Island dressing
1 bran muffin
1 tablespoon honey
1 teaspoon margarine
1 medium peach
1 cup low-fat milk

Afternoon Snack
1 medium pear

Dinner
1 serving Steamed Salmon
1 serving Stir-Fried Broccoli
1 cup rice
Hot tea

Evening Snack
2 graham cracker squares
½ cup low-fat milk

Total Day's Intake:
1,813 calories
1,994 mg. sodium
160 mg. cholesterol
27 percent fat

SATURDAY

Breakfast
½ cup unsweetened grapefruit
juice
¾ cup Roman Meal
1 teaspoon honey
1 slice whole wheat toast
1 teaspoon margarine
1 teaspoon apple jelly
1 cup low-fat milk
Coffee or tea

Lunch
Cottage cheese and fruit salad:
¼ cup low-fat cottage cheese
2 pineapple rings (canned in juice)
3 ounces lean roast of lamb
½ cup parsley-buttered potato
(using 1 teaspoon margarine)
¾ cup steamed zucchini squash
½ teaspoon margarine
1 slice whole wheat bread
1 teaspoon margarine
½ cup low-fat milk

Afternoon Snack
3 fresh apricots

Dinner
1 serving Stir-Fried Pressed Tofu
1 serving Dry-Fried String Beans
1 serving Cauliflower with
Chicken in Black Bean Sauce
1 cup rice
Hot tea

Evening Snack
½ cup hot apple juice with a
cinnamon stick

Total Day's Intake:
1,788 calories
1,995 mg. sodium
159 mg. cholesterol
28 percent fat

MAINTENANCE DIET WITH A SENSIBLE SODIUM LEVEL FOR WOMEN AND MEN

(1,800 calories; not more than 2,000 mg. sodium per day)

SUNDAY

Brunch
1 serving Cantonese
    Chicken Salad
1 serving Spring Rolls
1 serving Bok Choy Stir-Fried
    with Beef
½ cup rice
    Fresh orange
    Coffee or tea

Afternoon Snack
1 cup plain low-fat yogurt
1 cup fresh diced papaya
1 slice raisin toast
1 teaspoon margarine
    Iced tea

Dinner
1 serving Pan-Fried Fish with
    Lemon Sauce
1 serving Stir-Fried Mixed
    Vegetables
1½ cups rice
    Hot tea

Evening Snack
1 cup skim milk

Total Day's Intake:
    1,788 calories
    1,993 mg. sodium
    187 mg. cholesterol
    18 percent fat

REDUCING DIET WITH A LOW SODIUM LEVEL FOR WOMEN

(1,200 calories; not more than 1,000 mg. sodium per day)

MONDAY

Breakfast
½ fresh grapefruit
1 slice low-sodium bread
1 teaspoon margarine
¾ cup skim milk
    Coffee or tea

Lunch
Carrot-raisin salad:
½ cup shredded carrots
1½ tablespoons raisins
2½ teaspoons low-calorie imitation
    mayonnaise
Open-faced turkey sandwich:
1 slice low-sodium bread
3 ounces white meat turkey
1 teaspoon margarine
2 lettuce leaves
2 tomato slices
½ cup skim milk

Dinner
1 serving Oyster Sauce Beef*
1 serving Asparagus with
    Chicken*
½ cup rice
    Hot tea

Evening Snack
6 dried apricots
½ cup skim milk

Total Day's Intake:
    1,189 calories
    994 mg. sodium
    169 mg. cholesterol
    23 percent fat

*Refer to the low-sodium version located at the end of each recipe.

REDUCING DIET WITH A LOW SODIUM
LEVEL FOR WOMEN

(1,200 calories; not more than 1,000 mg. sodium per day)

TUESDAY

Breakfast
1 fresh tangerine
¾ cup regular oatmeal
1 teaspoon margarine
1 teaspoon brown sugar
1 slice low-sodium bread
1 teaspoon margarine
½ cup skim milk
Coffee or tea

Lunch
Stuffed tomato:
1 medium tomato
3½ ounces low-sodium, water-
    packed tuna mixed with
¼ cup chopped celery
1 tablespoon low-calorie imitation
    mayonnaise
3 lettuce leaves
3 radish roses
5 carrot curls
4 unsalted Melba toasts
1 teaspoon margarine
1 cup skim milk

Dinner
1 serving Stewed Chicken*
1 serving Spinach with
    Fermented Bean Cake*
½ cup rice
Hot tea

Evening Snack
1 cup popcorn, popped
    with 2 teaspoons oil

Total Day's Intake:
        1,190 calories
        984 mg. sodium
        110 mg. cholesterol
        21 percent fat

WEDNESDAY

Breakfast
⅔ cup fresh strawberries
1 cup Puffed Rice
1 scrambled egg (cooked in 2
    teaspoons margarine)
1 cup skim milk
Coffee or tea

Lunch
Chicken sandwich:
2 ounces sliced white meat
    chicken
2 lettuce leaves
2 tomato slices
¼ cup alfalfa sprouts
1 tablespoon low-calorie imitation
    mayonnaise
2 slices low-sodium bread
1 cup mixed fresh fruit salad
    Iced tea

Dinner
1 serving Sweet and Sour
    Pork Cantonese*
1 serving Steamed Chinese (Napa)
    Cabbage*
½ cup rice
    Hot tea

Evening Snack
7 carrot sticks
½ cup skim milk

Total Day's Intake
        1,218 calories
        931 mg. sodium
        371 mg. cholesterol
        24 percent fat

*Refer to the low-sodium version located at the end of each recipe.

REDUCING DIET WITH A LOW SODIUM LEVEL FOR WOMEN

(1,200 calories; not more than 1,000 mg. sodium per day)

THURSDAY

Breakfast
¼ of a 5-inch cantaloupe
¾ cup Wheatena
1 teaspoon margarine
½ cup skim milk
Coffee or tea

Lunch
Hamburger sandwich:
3-ounce broiled lean beef patty
2 slices low-sodium bread
2 lettuce leaves
2 tomato slices
1 tablespoon low-calorie imitation mayonnaise
10 Thompson (seedless) grapes
½ cup skim milk

Dinner
1 serving Kung Pao Chicken*
1 serving Steamed Fuzzy Melon*
½ cup rice
Hot tea

Evening Snack
3 graham crackers
½ cup skim milk

Total Day's Intake:
1,186 calories
967 mg. sodium
140 mg. cholesterol
25 percent fat

FRIDAY

Breakfast
1 medium orange
1 cup Puffed Wheat
1 teaspoon brown sugar
1 slice low-sodium bread
½ tablespoon margarine
1 cup skim milk
Coffee or tea

Lunch
Chef's salad bowl:
2 cups romaine lettuce
1 ounce lean roast beef strips
1 ounce roast turkey strips
3 green pepper rings
½ small cucumber, sliced
6 cherry tomatoes
Oil and vinegar dressing using
2 teaspoons oil and vinegar as desired
1 slice low-sodium bread
½ tablespoon margarine
1 medium peach
½ cup skim milk

Dinner
1 serving Szechwan Beef Stew*
1 serving Stir-Fried Broccoli*
½ cup rice
Hot tea

Total Day's Intake:
1,208 calories
901 mg. sodium
114 mg. cholesterol
29 percent fat

*Refer to the low-sodium version located at the end of each recipe.

REDUCING DIET WITH A LOW SODIUM
LEVEL FOR WOMEN

(1,200 calories; not more than 1,000 mg. sodium per day)

SATURDAY

Breakfast
½ cup unsweetened grapefruit
   juice
½ cup Nutri-Grain cereal
1 teaspoon brown sugar
1 cup skim milk
Coffee or tea

Lunch
Small green salad:
3 lettuce leaves
½ tomato, sliced
   Oil and vinegar dressing using
1 teaspoon oil and vinegar as
   desired
3 ounces lean roast leg of lamb
½ cup parsley-buttered potato
   (using 1 teaspoon margarine)
¾ cup steamed zucchini squash
1 slice low-sodium bread
1 teaspoon margarine
8 carrot sticks
Iced tea

Dinner
1 serving Stir-Fried Pressed Tofu*
1 serving Cauliflower with
   Chicken in Black Bean
   Sauce*
½ cup rice
Hot tea

Evening Snack
½ cup skim milk

Total Day's Intake:
         1,181 calories
      910 mg. sodium
      135 mg. cholesterol
      26 percent fat

SUNDAY

Brunch
1 serving Spring Rolls*
1 serving Cantonese
   Chicken Salad*
1 serving Dry-Fried String Beans*
Coffee or tea

Afternoon Snack
⅓ cup plain low-fat yogurt
¾ cup fresh diced papaya
4 unsalted Melba toasts
1 teaspoon honey
Iced tea

Dinner
1 serving Pan-Fried Fish with
   Lemon Sauce*
1 serving Stir-Fried Mixed
   Vegetables*
½ cup rice
Hot tea

Evening Snack
½ cup hot apple juice with
   cinnamon stick

Total Day's Intake:
         1,200 calories
      1,000 mg. sodium
         138 mg. cholesterol
      25 percent fat

*Refer to the low-sodium version located at the end of each recipe.

REDUCING DIET WITH A LOW SODIUM
LEVEL FOR MEN

(1,500 calories; not more than 1,000 mg. sodium per day)

MONDAY

Breakfast
½ fresh grapefruit
1 slice low-sodium toast
1 teaspoon low-sodium margarine
1 teaspoon cherry preserves
1 cup skim milk
   Coffee or tea

Lunch
Carrot-raisin salad:
½ cup shredded carrots
3 tablespoons raisins
1 pineapple ring (canned in juice)
½ tablespoon low-calorie
   imitation mayonnaise
Turkey sandwich:
2 slices low-sodium bread
3 ounces white meat turkey
1½ teaspoons low-sodium
   margarine
2 lettuce leaves
2 tomato slices
½ skim milk

Dinner
1 serving Oyster Sauce Beef*
1 serving Asparagus with
   Chicken*
1 cup rice
   Hot tea

Evening Snack
3 medium dried apricots
½ cup skim milk

Total day's Intake:
       1,490 calories
       997 mg. sodium
       171 mg. cholesterol
       21 percent fat

TUESDAY

Breakfast
5 stewed prunes without sugar
1 cup regular oatmeal
½ tablespoon low-sodium margarine
1 teaspoon brown sugar
1 cup skim milk
   Coffee or tea

Lunch
Stuffed tomato:
1 medium tomato
3½ ounces low-sodium, water-
   packed tuna mixed with
¼ cup chopped celery
1½ tablespoons low-calorie
   imitation mayonnaise
3 lettuce leaves
3 radish roses
5 carrot curls
1 slice low-sodium bread
½ tablespoon low-sodium margarine
   Fresh tangerine
½ cup skim milk

Afternoon Snack
1 medium pear

Dinner
1 serving Stewed Chicken*
1 serving Spinach with
   Fermented Bean Cake*
1 cup rice
   Hot tea

Evening Snack
½ cup skim milk
3 tablespoons unsalted almonds

Total Day's Intake:
       1,480 calories
       925 mg. sodium
       112 mg. cholesterol
       21 percent fat

REDUCING DIET WITH A LOW SODIUM
LEVEL FOR MEN
(1,500 calories; not more than 1,000 mg. sodium per day)

WEDNESDAY

Breakfast
  ¼ of a 5-inch cantaloupe
  1 scrambled egg (using 1 teaspoon
     low-sodium margarine)
  1 slice low-sodium toast
  1 teaspoon low-sodium margarine
  1 cup skim milk
     Coffee or tea

Lunch
Chicken sandwich:
  3 ounces sliced white meat
     chicken
  2 slices low-sodium bread
  2 lettuce leaves
  2 tomato slices
  ¼ cup alfalfa sprouts
  1½ tablespoons low-calorie
     imitation mayonnaise
  1 cup mixed fresh fruit salad
  ⅓ cup plain low-fat yogurt
     Iced tea

Dinner
  1 serving Sweet and Sour
     Pork Cantonese*
  1 serving Steamed Chinese (Napa)
     Cabbage*
  1 cup rice
     Hot tea

Evening Snack
  ½ cup skim milk

Total Day's Intake:
           1,489 calories
            956 mg. sodium
            398 mg. cholesterol
             23 percent fat

THURSDAY

Breakfast
  1 medium orange
  ¾ cup Wheatena
  1 teaspoon honey
  ½ tablespoon low-sodium
     margarine
  1 cup skim milk
     Coffee or tea

Lunch
Hamburger sandwich:
  3-ounce broiled lean beef patty
  2 slices low-sodium bread
  2 lettuce leaves
  2 tomato slices
  1 tablespoon low-calorie imitation
     mayonnaise
  5 carrot sticks
  5 celery sticks
  20 Thompson (seedless) grapes
  1 cup skim milk

Dinner
  1 serving Kung Pao Chicken*
  1 serving Steamed Fuzzy Melon*
  1 cup rice
     Hot tea

Evening Snack
  2 pieces unsalted Melba toast
  1 teaspoon low-sodium margarine
  ½ cup skim milk

Total Day's Intake:
           1,484 calories
            921 mg. sodium
            143 mg. cholesterol
             23 percent fat

*Refer to the low-sodium version located at the end of each recipe.

REDUCING DIET WITH A LOW SODIUM
LEVEL FOR MEN

(1,500 calories; not more than 1,000 mg. sodium per day)

FRIDAY

Breakfast
⅔ cup fresh strawberries
1 cup Puffed Wheat
1 teaspoon brown sugar
1 slice low-sodium toast
½ tablespoon low-sodium
    margarine
½ cup skim milk
    Coffee or tea

Lunch
Chef's salad bowl:
2 cups romaine lettuce
1 ounce lean roast beef strips
2 ounces roast turkey strips
3 green pepper rings
½ small cucumber, sliced
6 cherry tomatoes
    Oil and vinegar dressing using
1 tablespoon oil and vinegar as
    desired
1 slice low-sodium bread
½ tablespoon low-sodium
    margarine
1 medium fresh peach
1 cup skim milk

Dinner
1 serving Steamed Salmon*
1 serving Stir-Fried Broccoli*
1 cup rice
    Hot tea

Evening Snack
3 graham cracker squares
1 cup skim milk

Total Day's Intake:
        1,498 calories
        949 mg. sodium
        113 mg. cholesterol
        24 percent fat

SATURDAY

Breakfast
½ cup unsweetened grapefruit
    juice
½ cup Nutri-Grain cereal
1 teaspoon honey
1 slice low-sodium toast
1 teaspoon low-sodium margarine
1 cup skim milk
    Coffee or tea

Lunch
Small green salad:
3 lettuce leaves
½ tomato, sliced
    Oil and vinegar dressing using
2 teaspoons oil and vinegar as
    desired
3 ounces lean roast leg of lamb
½ cup parsley-buttered potatoes
    (using 2 teaspoons
    low-sodium margarine)
¾ cup steamed zucchini squash
1 teaspoon margarine
1 cup skim milk

Dinner
1 serving Stir-Fried Pressed Tofu*
1 serving Cauliflower with
    Chicken in Black Bean Sauce*
1 cup rice
    Hot tea

Evening Snack
3 fresh apricots
    Decaffeinated coffee

Totals Day's Intake:
        1,484 calories
        930 mg. sodium
        139 mg. cholesterol
        27 percent fat

*Refer to the low-sodium version located at the end of each recipe.

REDUCING DIET WITH A LOW SODIUM
LEVEL FOR MEN
(1,500 calories; not more than 1,000 mg. sodium per day)

SUNDAY

Brunch
1 serving Vegetarian Fried Rice*
1 serving Spring Rolls*
1 serving Dry-Fried String Beans*
Fresh orange slices (½ of an
    orange)
Coffee or tea

Afternoon Snack
¾ cup plain low-fat yogurt
½ cup fresh diced papaya
3 unsalted Melba toasts
1 teaspoon low-sodium margarine
Iced tea

Dinner
1 serving Pan-Fried Fish with
    Lemon Sauce*
1 serving Stir-Fried Mixed Vegetables*
1 cup rice
Hot tea

Evening Snack
½ cup canned fruit cocktail
    in fruit juice

Total Day's Intake:
1,506 calories
983 mg. sodium
154 mg. cholesterol
23 percent fat

MAINTENANCE DIET WITH A LOW SODIUM
LEVEL FOR WOMEN AND MEN
(1,800 calories; not more than 1,000 mg. sodium per day)

MONDAY

Breakfast
½ fresh grapefruit
1 large Shredded Wheat biscuit
1 teaspoon brown sugar
1 slice low-sodium toast
1 teaspoon cherry preserves
1 cup low-fat milk
Coffee or tea

Lunch
Carrot-raisin salad:
½ cup shredded carrots
2½ tablespoons raisins
2 teaspoons low-calorie imitation
    mayonnaise
Turkey sandwich:
2 slices low-sodium bread
3 ounces white meat turkey
2 teaspoons low-calorie imitation
    mayonnaise
2 lettuce leaves
2 tomato slices
½ cup low-fat milk

Dinner
1 serving Oyster Sauce Beef*
1 serving Asparagus with
    Chicken*
1 cup rice
Hot tea

Evening Snack
1 medium pear
½ cup low-fat milk

Total Day's Intake:
1,788 calories
987 mg. sodium
197 mg. cholesterol
24 percent fat

MAINTENANCE DIET WITH A LOW SODIUM LEVEL FOR WOMEN AND MEN

(1,800 calories; not more than 1,000 mg. sodium per day)

TUESDAY

Breakfast
5 stewed prunes without sugar
1 cup regular oatmeal
1 teaspoon brown sugar
1 slice low-sodium toast
1 teaspoon low-sodium margarine
1 teaspoon orange marmalade
1 cup low-fat milk
  Coffee or tea

Lunch
Stuffed tomato:
1 medium tomato
3½ ounces low-sodium water-
    packed tuna mixed with
¼ cup chopped celery
1 tablespoon low-calorie
    imitation mayonnaise
3 lettuce leaves
3 radish roses
5 carrot curls
1 slice low-sodium bread
1 teaspoon low-sodium margarine
¾ cup unsweetened applesauce
1 cup low-fat milk

Afternoon Snack
1 fresh tangerine

Dinner
1 serving Stewed Chicken*
1 serving Spinach with
    Fermented Bean Cake*
1 cup rice
  Hot tea

Evening Snack
2 tablespoons unsalted
    roasted almonds
½ cup low-fat milk

Total Day's Intake:
    1,776 calories
     983 mg. sodium
     137 mg. cholesterol
      26 percent fat

*Refer to the low-sodium version located at the end of the recipe.

MAINTENANCE DIET WITH A LOW SODIUM
LEVEL FOR WOMEN AND MEN

(1,800 calories; not more than 1,000 mg. sodium per day)

WEDNESDAY

Breakfast
¼ of a 5-inch cantaloupe
1 poached egg
2 slices low-sodium toast
2 teaspoons honey
2 teaspoons low-sodium
   margarine
1 cup low-fat milk
  Coffee or tea

Lunch
Chicken sandwich:
  3 ounces sliced white meat
    chicken
  2 slices low-sodium bread
  2 lettuce leaves
  2 slices tomato
  ¼ cup alfalfa sprouts
  1 tablespoon low-calorie imitation
    mayonnaise
  ¾ cup mixed fresh fruit salad
  ½ cup plain low-fat yogurt
  Iced tea

Dinner
1 serving Sweet and Sour
   Pork Cantonese*
1 serving Steamed Chinese
   (Napa) Cabbage*
1 cup rice
  Hot tea

Evening Snack
2 cups unsalted popcorn
½ cup low-fat milk

Total Day's Intake:
     1,793 calories
     957 mg. sodium
     411 mg. cholesterol
    28 percent fat

THURSDAY

Breakfast
1 cup fresh strawberries
½ cup Wheatena
1 teaspoon honey
1 teaspoon low-sodium margarine
1 slice low-sodium toast
1 teaspoon low-sodium margarine
1 cup low-fat milk
  Coffee or tea

Lunch
Hamburger sandwich:
  3-ounce broiled lean beef patty
  2 slices low-sodium bread
  2 lettuce leaves
  2 slices tomato
  ½ tablespoon low-calorie imitation
    mayonnaise
  5 carrot sticks
  5 celery sticks
 20 Thompson (seedless) grapes
  1 cup low-fat milk

Dinner
1 serving Kung Pao Chicken*
1 serving Steamed Fuzzy Melon*
1 cup rice
  Hot tea

Evening Snack
Open-faced sandwich:
  2 graham cracker squares
  ½ large banana, sliced
  ½ cup low-fat milk

Total Day's Intake:
     1,798 calories
     972 mg. sodium
     167 mg. cholesterol
    30 percent fat

*Refer to the low-sodium version located at the end of each recipe.

MAINTENANCE DIET WITH A LOW SODIUM LEVEL FOR WOMEN AND MEN

(1,800 calories; not more than 1,000 mg. sodium per day)

FRIDAY

Breakfast
1 medium orange
1 cup Puffed Wheat
1 teaspoon brown sugar
1 slice low-sodium bread
1 teaspoon grape jelly
1 teaspoon low-sodium margarine
½ cup low-fat milk
Coffee or tea

Lunch
Chef's salad bowl:
  2 cups romaine lettuce
  1 ounce lean roast beef strips
  2 ounces roast turkey strips
  3 green pepper rings
  ½ small cucumber, sliced
  6 cherry tomatoes
  Oil and vinegar dressing using
  ½ tablespoon oil and vinegar as
    desired
2 slices low-sodium bread
1½ teaspoons low-sodium
    margarine
1 medium fresh peach
1 cup low-fat milk

Dinner
1 serving Szechwan Beef Stew*
1 serving Stir-Fried Broccoli*
1 cup rice
Hot tea

Evening Snack
2 graham cracker squares
½ cup low-fat milk

Total Day's Intake:
      1,801 calories
       969 mg. sodium
       156 mg. cholesterol
      28 percent fat

SATURDAY

Breakfast
½ cup unsweetened grapefruit juice
½ cup Nutri-Grain cereal
1 teaspoon brown sugar
1 slice low-sodium toast
1 teaspoon low-sodium margarine
1 teaspoon strawberry jam
1 cup low-fat milk
Coffee or tea

Lunch
Small green salad:
  3 lettuce leaves
  ½ tomato, sliced
  Oil and vinegar dressing using
  1 teaspoon oil and vinegar
3 ounces lean roast leg of lamb
1 large baked potato
2 teaspoons margarine
¾ cup steamed zucchini squash
1 teaspoon low-sodium margarine
1 cup low-fat milk

Afternoon Snack
2 fresh plums

Dinner
1 serving Stir-Fried Pressed Tofu*
1 serving Cauliflower with
    Chicken in Black Bean Sauce*
1 cup rice
Hot tea

Evening Snack
3 fresh apricots
Hot tea

Total Day's Intake:
      1,795 calories
       996 mg. sodium
       159 mg. cholesterol
      28 percent fat

*Refer to the low-sodium version located at the end of each recipe.

MAINTENANCE DIET WITH A LOW SODIUM
LEVEL FOR WOMEN AND MEN

(1,800 calories; not more than 1,000 mg. sodium per day)

SUNDAY

Brunch

1 serving Vegetarian Fried Rice*
1 serving Spring Rolls*
1 serving Dry-Fried String Beans*
  Fresh orange slices
    (1 medium orange)
  Coffee or tea

Afternoon Snack

¾ cup plain low-fat yogurt
1 cup diced papaya
1 slice low-sodium bread
1 teaspoon low-sodium margarine
  Iced tea

Dinner

1 serving Pan-Fried Fish with
    Lemon Sauce*
1 serving Stir-Fried Mixed
    Vegetables*
1 cup rice
  Hot tea

Evening Snack

½ cup canned fruit cocktail in
    fruit juice
5 unsalted Melba toasts

Total Day's Intake:

1,798 calories
993 mg. sodium
154 mg. cholesterol
22 percent fat

*Refer to the low-sodium version located at the end of each recipe.

THE NUTRITIONAL COMPOSITION
OF EACH RECIPE

CHICKEN DISHES	Calories	Sodium (mg.)	Cholesterol (mg.)	Modified Sodium (mg.)
Chicken Stir-Fried with Sweet Bean Sauce	166	329	51	236
Chicken with Cashew Nuts	299	335	51	236
Chicken Stir-Fried with Mushrooms	173	311	51	212
Cantonese Chicken Salad	188	346	51	254
Curried Chicken	244	318	51	219
Lemon Chicken	175	396	51	222
Lychee Chicken	221	359	51	235
Chicken Stir-Fried with Green Bell Pepper	174	347	51	202
Chicken Salad with Sesame Paste	294	396	51	222
Chicken Stir-Fried with Snow Peas	201	396	51	222
Kung Pao Chicken	187	331	51	249
Sweet and Sour Cold Chicken	162	308	51	209
Sesame Chicken	190	307	51	208
Tomato-Sesame Chicken	215	318	51	219
Sherry Chicken	121	396	51	222
Braised Chicken with Chestnuts	229	310	51	211
Stewed Chicken	145	382	51	208
Baked/Broiled Chicken	177	334	51	235
Red-Cooked Chicken	197	388	68	289
Clay Pot Chicken	237	316	68	214
Steamed Chicken with Mushrooms	118	382	51	208

SEAFOOD DISHES	Calories	Sodium (mg.)	Cholesterol (mg.)	Modified Sodium (mg.)
Poached Filet of Fish	143	351	57	206
Steamed Salmon	140	314	35	215
Steamed Whole Fish	139	396	56	222
Pan-Fried Fish with Lemon Sauce	185	357	57	212
Fish Slices with Bean Sprouts	197	384	57	247
Steamed Filet of Sole with Black Bean Sauce	126	322	57	256
Pan-Fried Fish Patties	170	377	57	232
Tomato Sauce Fish Slices	211	375	57	230
Pan-Fried Oysters with Cocktail Sauce	126	343	28	244
Green Onion and Ginger Oysters	111	339	28	240

BEEF AND LAMB DISHES	Calories	Sodium (mg.)	Cholesterol (mg.)	Modified Sodium (mg.)
Mongolian Beef	197	316	58	191
Beef with Satay Sauce	214	380	58	292
Tomato Beef	246	336	58	237
Curried Beef	197	319	58	220
Beef Stir-Fried with Almonds	289	343	58	244
Oyster Sauce Beef	184	399	61	283
Dry-Fried Beef, Szechwan Style	182	348	58	249
Curry-Tomato Beef	234	326	58	227
Ginger Beef	197	326	58	227
Beef Stir-Fried with Dried Mushrooms	204	317	58	218
Pepper-Beef with Black Bean Sauce	207	348	58	224
Szechwan Beef Stew	235	383	58	334
Beef Stir-Fried with Shoestring Potatoes	189	333	58	234
Steamed Beef Patty	157	398	58	224
Lamb Stir-Fried with Green Onions	212	343	60	244
Lamb with Sweet Bean Sauce	161	319	60	270
Cold Cut Lamb	169	317	60	218

PORK DISHES	Calories	Sodium (mg.)	Cholesterol (mg.)	Modified Sodium (mg.)
Boy Scout Pork	214	316	53	180
Sweet and Sour Pork Cantonese	304	321	53	222
Fragrant Pork	227	276	53	227
Twice-Cooked Pork	203	294	53	203
Boiled Pork with Hot Pepper Sauce	188	324	53	258
Pork with Sweet Bean Sauce	224	321	53	224
Stewed Pork with Peanuts and Fresh Mushrooms	257	321	53	222
Pork with Red Fermented Bean Cake	204	298	53	215
Sweet and Sour Pork, Northern Style	203	343	53	244
Pork with Dried Bean Curd Sticks in Fermented Bean Cake Sauce	234	339	44	290
Pork with Fermented Bean Cake	197	314	53	215
Steamed Pork with Shrimp Paste	158	359	57	199

TOFU AND SOY PRODUCTS DISHES	Calories	Sodium (mg.)	Cholesterol (mg.)	Modified Sodium (mg.)
Tofu Stir-Fried with Ground Pork	205	288	27	189
Tofu and Pork with Oyster Sauce	230	313	27	255
Ma Po Tofu	195	324	22	216
Kung Pao Tofu	217	283	22	192
Stir-Fried Pressed Tofu	191	325	22	226
Stuffed Tofu	174	355	24	268
Tofu Beef with Chee Hou Sauce	174	330	29	228
Steamed Bean Curd Rolls	180	374	18	200
Frozen Dried Tofu with Pork	186	283	22	184
Tofu Pork Patty	153	261	35	145
Vegetarian Chicken	269	306	0	207
Tofu with Fresh Mushrooms and Dried Shrimp	145	308	7	209
Steamed Tofu with Pork	137	351	18	177
Bean Curd Sticks with Pork	231	306	27	207
Tofu with Tomatoes	135	270	0	171

VEGETABLE DISHES

	Calories	Sodium (mg.)	Cholesterol (mg.)	Modified Sodium (mg.)
Bok Choy Stir-Fried with Beef	157	321	39	222
Stir-Fried Broccoli	83	263	0	164
Asparagus with Chicken	166	283	34	217
Cabbage with Bean Threads	145	333	13	218
Stir-Fried Bean Sprouts	77	331	0	157
Cauliflower with Chicken in Black Bean Sauce	153	267	34	201
Dry-Fried String Beans	81	255	0	156
Cold Bean Sprouts	74	373	5	199
Stir-Fried Cabbage	64	270	0	171
Steamed Chinese (Napa) Cabbage	34	385	5	211
Bean Threads with Ground Pork	133	264	18	165
Stir-Fried Mixed Vegetables	103	283	0	184
Szechwanese Eggplant	94	273	0	207
Stir-Fried Chinese (Napa) Cabbage	56	345	0	171
Law Bak with Pork	159	316	27	217
Steamed Winter Melon with Ground Pork	114	359	27	185
Stuffed Fuzzy Melon	174	343	38	219
Spinach with Fermented Bean Cake	72	397	0	258
Steamed Fuzzy Melon	28	338	1	164
Chinese Cabbage in Milk Sauce	66	373	3	199
Bitter Melon with Beef in Black Bean Sauce	122	276	29	210

DEEM SUM DISHES	Calories	Sodium (mg.)	Cholesterol (mg.)	Modified Sodium (mg.)
Pot Stickers	323	298	35	199
Ground Pork Dumplings	248	212	22	125
Spring Rolls	290	252	27	136
Green Onion Pancakes	154	168	0	81
Beef Dumplings	231	295	39	196
Chicken Chow Mein	391	395	51	296
Vegetarian Fried Rice	316	343	64	169

DISCRETIONARY DISHES	Calories	Sodium (mg.)	Cholesterol (mg.)	Modified Sodium (mg.)	Modified Cholesterol (mg.)
Prawns in Tomato Sauce	104	255	84	180	—
Chinese Broccoli Stir-Fried with Prawns	110	313	63	197	—
Chinese Broccoli with Crab in White Sauce	119	387	38	271	—
Moo Shu Pork	387	321	154	192	27
Lobster Cantonese	161	393	58	302	—
Scrambled Eggs with Tomatoes	122	275	191	159	64
Shrimp Dumplings	206	208	42	121	—
Steamed Eggs with Ground Pork	134	386	205	212	77
Steamed Tofu and Eggs	131	261	136	145	73
Custard	80	70	68	—	1
Scallops with Bean Sprouts	132	375	20	259	—
Bean Sprout Egg Foo Yung	145	376	191	202	64

NUTRITIONAL COMPOSITION TABLES

Bold type indicates the BEST CHOICES. These items are the best choices within each food category. They are comparatively lower in total fat, saturated fat, cholesterol, sodium, and calories. Some items may be low in calories and sodium but are not designated best choices due to their higher fat and/or cholesterol content.

tr   Indicates that trace or very small amounts of the substance are present in the portion of food specified.

—   indicates that values were not available.

CALORIE AND SODIUM CONTENT OF FOOD

DAIRY PRODUCTS	Portion Size*	Calories	Sodium (mg.)
Cheeses (Natural)			
Blue	1 oz.	100	396
Brie	1 oz.	95	178
Camembert	1 oz.	85	239
Cheddar	1 oz.	114	176
Cottage			
Creamed	4 oz.	117	457
Dry curd (unsalted)	4 oz.	96	14
Low-fat (2 percent fat)	4 oz.	101	459
Cream	1 oz.	99	84
Feta	1 oz.	75	316
Monterey	1 oz.	106	152
Mozzarella from whole milk	1 oz.	80	106
Mozzarella from part skim milk	1 oz.	72	132
Parmesan, grated	1 oz.	129	528
Parmesan, hard	1 oz.	111	454
Ricotta from whole milk	½ c	216	104
Ricotta from part skim milk	½ c	171	155
Roquefort	1 oz.	105	513
Swiss	1 oz.	107	74
Cheeses (Pasteurized Process)			
American	1 oz.	106	406
American cheese spread	1 oz.	82	381
Swiss	1 oz.	95	388
Cream			
Half-and-half	1 T	20	6
Light or coffee	1 T	29	6
Light whipping	1 T	44	5
Heavy whipping	1 T	52	6
Sour cream, cultured	1 T	26	6

*Abbreviations: c — cup; med. — medium; oz. — ounce; pkt. — packet; sl. — slice; sm. — small; T — tablespoon; t — teaspoon.

DAIRY PRODUCTS (continued)	Portion Size	Calories	Sodium (mg.)
Eggnog	½ c	171	69
Frozen desserts			
Ice cream, vanilla, hardened			
Regular (approx. 10 percent fat)	½ c	135	58
Rich (approx. 16 percent fat)	½ c	175	54
Ice milk, vanilla			
Hardened	½ c	92	53
Soft serve	½ c	112	82
Sherbet, orange	½ c	135	44
Imitation dairy products*			
Nondairy coffee whiteners			
Liquid (frozen)	1 T	20	12
Powdered	1 T	33	12
Dessert toppings			
Pressurized	1 T	11	2
Semisolid (frozen)	1 T	13	1
Milk,			
Buttermilk, cultured, low-fat			
(1 percent fat)	½ c	50	129
Buttermilk, cultured (unsalted);			
low-fat (1 percent fat)	½ c	50	62
Chocolate, low-fat (2 percent fat)	½ c	90	75
Low-fat (2 percent fat)	½ c	61	61
Skim	½ c	43	63
Whole (3.7 percent fat)	½ c	79	60
Milk, Canned			
Condensed, sweetened	1 T	62	25
Evaporated, skim	1 T	13	19
Evaporated, whole	1 T	21	17
Yogurt			
Fruit flavored, low-fat	4 oz.	116	66
Plain, low-fat	4 oz.	72	80
Plain, skim	4 oz.	63	87

FISH AND SHELLFISH**

	Portion Size	Calories	Sodium (mg.)
Cod			
Raw	3½ oz.	78	70
Broiled in margarine	3½ oz.	170	109
Clams, raw, meat only			
Hard	3½ oz.	80	205
Soft	3½ oz.	82	36

*Note: Imitation dairy products often contain coconut or palm oil, both high in saturated fats.

**Best Choices for fish and shellfish, designated by bold type, are those purchased fresh and prepared without fat (i.e., poached or broiled).

FISH AND SHELLFISH (continued)	Portion Size	Calories	Sodium (mg.)
Crab			
Canned, drained	3½ oz.	101	500
Steamed, meat only	3½ oz.	93	369
Fish sticks, breaded, fried	3½ oz.	175	—
Flatfish, raw (flounder, sand dab, sole)	3½ oz.	79	78
Flounder, broiled in margarine	3½ oz.	200	237
Haddock			
Raw	3½ oz.	79	61
Fried	3½ oz.	165	177
Halibut			
Raw	3½ oz.	100	54
Broiled in margarine	3½ oz.	171	134
Lobster, boiled	3½ oz.	95	249
Oysters			
Raw	3½ oz.	66	133
Fried	3½ oz.	243	205
Scallops			
Raw	3½ oz.	81	255
Cooked	3½ oz.	112	265
Shrimp			
Raw, meat only	3½ oz.	91	161
Canned	3½ oz.	116	2,300
Fried	3½ oz.	225	187
Salmon			
Raw			
Pink (Humpback)	3½ oz.	119	64
King (Chinook)	3½ oz.	222	45
Salmon			
Broiled in margarine	3½ oz.	160	102
Canned			
Pink (Humpback)	3½ oz.	141	521
Red (Sockeye)	3½ oz.	171	387
Unsalted	3½ oz.	—	48
Sardines			
Canned in liquid	3½ oz.	311	—
Canned drained	3½ oz.	203	649
Tuna			
Canned in oil, in liquid	3½ oz.	288	357
Canned in oil, drained	3½ oz.	197	—
Canned in water	3½ oz.	127	339
Canned in water without salt	3½ oz.	127	41

POULTRY PRODUCTS

	Portion Size	Calories	Sodium (mg.)
Chicken, broilers or fryers			
Flesh and skin, raw	3½ oz.	215	70
Flesh only, raw	3½ oz.	119	77
Chicken, cut-up parts			
Breast, flesh and skin, raw	3½ oz.	172	63
Breast, flesh and skin, roasted	3½ oz.	197	71
Breast, flesh only, roasted	3½ oz.	165	74
Drumstick, flesh and skin, raw	3½ oz.	161	83
Drumstick, flesh and skin, roasted	3½ oz.	216	90
Drumstick, flesh only, roasted	3½ oz.	172	95
Leg, flesh and skin, raw	3½ oz.	187	79
Leg, flesh and skin, deep-fried*	3½ oz.	273	279
Leg, flesh only, roasted	3½ oz.	191	91
Thigh, flesh and skin, raw	3½ oz.	211	76
Thigh, flesh and skin, roasted	3½ oz.	247	84
Thigh, flesh only, roasted	3½ oz.	209	88
Wing, flesh and skin, raw	3½ oz.	222	73
Wing, flesh and skin, deep-fried*	3½ oz.	324	320
Wing, flesh only, roasted	3½ oz.	203	92
Duck, domesticated			
Flesh and skin, raw	3½ oz.	404	63
Flesh and skin, roasted	3½ oz.	337	59
Flesh only, roasted	3½ oz.	201	65
Turkey, fryer–roasters			
Flesh and skin, raw	3½ oz.	134	58
Flesh and skin, roasted	3½ oz.	172	66
Flesh only, roasted	3½ oz.	150	67
Turkey, cut-up parts			
Breast, flesh and skin, raw	3½ oz.	125	48
Breast, flesh and skin, roasted	3½ oz.	153	53
Breast, flesh only, roasted	3½ oz.	135	52
Leg, flesh and skin, raw	3½ oz.	118	69
Leg, flesh and skin, roasted	3½ oz.	170	80
Leg, flesh only, roasted	3½ oz.	159	81
Wing, flesh and skin, raw	3½ oz.	159	56
Wing, flesh and skin, roasted	3½ oz.	207	73
Wing, flesh only, roasted	3½ oz.	163	78

*Chicken deep-fried in a batter.

RED MEATS	Portion Size	Calories	Sodium (mg.)
Beef			
Beef for stew			
Lean with fat, braised	3½ oz.	327	45
Well trimmed, braised	3½ oz.	214	52
Chuck rib roasts			
Lean with fat, boned, braised	3½ oz.	427	39
Well trimmed, boned, braised	3½ oz.	249	50
Flank steak			
Raw, well trimmed	3½ oz.	144	76
Well trimmed, braised	3½ oz.	196	53
Porterhouse steak			
Lean with fat, broiled	3½ oz.	465	48
Well trimmed, broiled	3½ oz.	224	74
Sirloin steak			
Lean with fat, broiled	3½ oz.	387	56
Well trimmed, broiled	3½ oz.	207	79
Rib roast			
Lean with fat, roasted	3½ oz.	440	49
Well trimmed, roasted	3½ oz.	241	69
Round steak			
Lean with fat, broiled	3½ oz.	261	70
Well trimmed, broiled	3½ oz.	189	77
Ground beef			
Lean with 10 percent fat, broiled	3½ oz.	219	67
Lean with 21 percent fat, broiled	3½ oz.	286	59
Corned beef			
Boneless, cooked	3½ oz.	372	942
Canned	3½ oz.	216	1,051
Dried, chipped beef	3½ oz.	203	4,354
Lamb			
Leg			
Lean with fat, roasted	3½ oz.	279	62
Well trimmed, roasted	3½ oz.	186	70
Loin chop			
Lean with fat, broiled	3½ oz.	359	54
Well trimmed, broiled	3½ oz.	188	69
Rib chop			
Lean with fat, broiled	3½ oz.	407	49
Well trimmed, broiled	3½ oz.	211	67
Shoulder			
Lean with fat, roasted	3½ oz.	338	53
Well trimmed, roasted	3½ oz.	205	66

RED MEATS (continued)	Portion Size	Calories	Sodium (mg.)
Pork			
Bacon, cured			
Raw	3½ oz.	664	679
Broiled	3½ oz.	610	1,020
Canadian style, broiled	3½ oz.	277	2,553
Ham, fresh			
Lean with fat, baked	3½ oz.	374	56
Well trimmed, baked	3½ oz.	217	73
Ham, light cure			
Lean with fat, roasted	3½ oz.	289	748
Well trimmed, roasted	3½ oz.	187	905
Loin roast			
Lean with fat, roasted	3½ oz.	362	60
Well trimmed, roasted	3½ oz.	254	72
Shoulder (Boston butt)			
Lean with fat, roasted	3½ oz.	353	55
Well trimmed, roasted	3½ oz.	244	66
Spareribs			
Lean with fat, braised	3½ oz.	440	36

LUNCHEON MEATS AND SAUSAGES

	Portion Size	Calories	Sodium (mg.)
Bologna			
Beef	1 oz.	89	284
Pork	1 oz.	70	336
Turkey	1 oz.	57	249
Frankfurter			
Beef (1 frank)	2 oz.	184	584
Beef and pork (1 frank)	2 oz.	183	639
Turkey (1 frank)	1½ oz.	102	642
Ham			
Chopped, not canned	1 oz.	65	389
Chopped, canned	1 oz.	68	387
Sliced, extra lean	1 oz.	37	405
Sliced, regular	1 oz.	52	373
Italian sausage, cooked (1 link)	3 oz.	268	765
Liver sausage, liverwurst	1 oz.	93	—
Mortadella	1 oz.	88	353
Pastrami, turkey	1 oz.	40	297
Pepperoni	1 oz.	135	560
Polish sausage	1 oz.	92	248
Pork sausage, fresh, cooked	1 oz.	100	349

LUNCHEON MEATS AND SAUSAGES (continued)	Portion Size	Calories	Sodium (mg.)
Salami			
Beef	1 oz.	72	328
Beef and pork	1 oz.	71	302
Turkey	1 oz.	56	285
Salami, pork, dry or hard	1 oz.	115	639
Turkey ham	1 oz.	36	283
Turkey roll, light meat	1 oz.	42	139
Vienna sausage, canned (2 links)	1.14 oz.	90	304

ORGAN MEATS

	Portion Size	Calories	Sodium (mg.)
Brains (beef, calf, pork), raw	3½ oz.	125	125
Gizzard			
Chicken, cooked	3½ oz.	153	67
Turkey, cooked	3½ oz.	163	54
Heart			
Beef, braised	3½ oz.	188	104
Chicken, cooked	3½ oz.	185	48
Turkey, cooked	3½ oz.	177	55
Kidneys			
Beef, cooked	3½ oz.	252	253
Liver			
Beef, fried	3½ oz.	229	184
Calf, fried	3½ oz.	261	118
Chicken, cooked	3½ oz.	157	51
Pork, fried	3½ oz.	241	111
Lamb, fried	3½ oz.	261	85
Turkey, cooked	3½ oz.	169	64

MEAT SUBSTITUTES

Eggs

	Portion Size	Calories	Sodium (mg.)
Eggs, fresh			
Whole	1 large	79	69
White	1 white	16	50
Yolk	1 yolk	63	8
Egg substitute products			
Frozen	¼ c	96	120
Liquid	¼ c	53	111
Powder	¾ oz.	88	158

MEAT SUBSTITUTES (continued)

	Portion Size	Calories	Sodium (mg.)
Beans, Peas, and Lentils*			
Black-eye peas			
Cooked	1 c	178	12
Canned	1 c	179	602
Kidney beans			
Cooked	1 c	218	4
Canned	1 c	230	844
Lentils, cooked	1 c	212	4
Lima beans			
Cooked	1 c	189	4
Canned	1 c	163	401
Northern beans			
Cooked	1 c	212	5
Canned	1 c	212	1,181
Soybeans, cooked	1 c	234	4
Soybean curd (tofu) (¼ of block)	4 oz.	86	8
Soybean curd sheets or sticks (2 sheets)	1.6 oz.	207	56
Split peas, cooked	1 c	230	5

NUTS AND SEEDS

	Portion Size	Calories	Sodium (mg.)
Almonds			
Oil-roasted	½ c	492	156
Raw, shelled, whole nuts	½ c	425	3
Cashews			
Oil-roasted, unsalted	½ c	393	11
Dry-roasted, salted	½ c	—	600
Coconut meat, shredded	½ c	139	9
Peanuts			
Roasted, chopped, unsalted	½ c	419	4
Spanish, salted	½ c	421	412
Peanut butter			
Regular	2 T	188	162
Unsalted	2 T	188	2
Pecan, halves, unsalted	½ c	371	tr
Pumpkin seeds, hulled, raw	½ c	387	tr
Sunflower seeds, raw, hulled, unsalted	½ c	406	7
Walnuts, black, raw, chopped	½ c	393	4

*Note: cooked beans, peas, and lentils are prepared without fats or high-sodium seasonings.

FRUITS*

	Portion Size	Calories
Apple	1 med.	81
Apple juice, bottled	½ c	58
Applesauce		
Canned, unsweetened	½ c	53
Canned, sweetened	½ c	97
Apricots		
fresh	3 fruits	51
canned in water	6 halves	44
canned in juice	3 fruits	80
canned in heavy syrup	6 halves	140
dried, uncooked	10 halves	83
Apricot nectar, canned	½ c	70
Avocados, raw	½ med.	162
Bananas	½ med.	53
Blueberries,		
Raw	½ c	41
Canned in heavy syrup	½ c	112
Frozen, unsweetened	½ c	39
Cherries, sour red		
Raw, with pits	1 c	51
Canned in water	½ c	43
Canned in light syrup	½ c	94
Cherries, sweet		
Raw, with pits	½ c	52
Canned in water	½ c	57
Canned in juice	½ c	68
Canned in heavy syrup	½ c	107
Cranberry juice cocktail, bottled	½ c	74
Cranberry sauce, canned, sweetened	2 T	52
Currants, Zante, dried	2 T	51
Dates, dried	3	68
Figs		
Canned in water	3	42
Canned in light syrup	3	58
Canned in extra-heavy syrup	3	91
Fruit cocktail		
Canned in water	½ c	40
Canned in juice	½ c	56
Canned in heavy syrup	½ c	93

*The sodium value of most fresh, canned, frozen, and dried fruits ranges from 0 to 10 mg. per serving. An exception is dried fruit containing sodium bisulfite to preserve color. Such fruits will have a higher sodium level than other dried fruits. For example, dried apples containing bisulfite have 27 to 38 mg. sodium per ½ cup. Fruits canned in syrups are not Best Choices. Syrups add calories without adding any nutrients.

FRUITS (continued)	Portion Size	Calories
Grapefruit, pink	½	38
Grapefruit juice, from frozen concentrate, diluted	½ c	51
Grapes, American type	10	15
Grape juice, bottled	½ c	78
Guavas, raw	1 med.	45
Kiwi, raw	1 med.	46
Lemon, raw	1 med.	22
Lemon juice, raw	1 T	4
Lychees, raw	5	30
Melons, raw		
Cantaloupe	¼ melon	47
Casaba	⅒ melon	43
Honeydew	⅒ melon	46
Watermelon	1 c diced	50
Nectarine	1 med.	67
Orange, raw	1 med.	62
Orange juice, from frozen concentrate, diluted	½ c	56
Papaya, raw	½ med.	59
Peach	1 med.	37
Peach nectar	½ c	67
Pear, raw	1 med.	98
Pear nectar	½ c	75
Pineapple		
Raw	½ c diced	39
Canned in water	½ c	40
Canned in juice	½ c	75
Canned in extra-heavy syrup	½ c	109
Pineapple juice, canned	½ c	70
Plums, raw	2 med.	72
Prunes, dried, uncooked	3	60
Prune juice, canned	½ c	90
Raisins, seedless	2 T	55
Strawberries		
Raw	1 c	45
Frozen, unsweetened	1 c	52
Frozen, sweetened	1 c	200
Tangerine	1 med.	37

VEGETABLES	Portion Size	Calories	Sodium (mg.)
Asparagus			
Fresh, cut-up, cooked	½ c	15	1
Canned, drained	½ c	26	278
Canned, low-sodium	½ c	23	5
Bamboo shoots, canned without salt	½ c	20	6
Beans			
Lima, fresh, cooked	½ c	95	1
Lima, canned, drained	½ c	82	200
Lima, baby, frozen, cooked	½ c	106	116
Mung bean sprouts, raw	½ c	19	3
Mung bean sprouts, cooked	½ c	18	3
Snap, fresh, cooked	½ c	16	3
Snap, canned, drained	½ c	16	160
Snap, canned in liquid	½ c	22	282
Snap, canned, low-sodium, drained	½ c	15	2
Snap, frozen, cooked	½ c	17	1
Beets, red			
Fresh, diced, cooked	½ c	27	37
Canned, diced, drained	½ c	32	201
Bittermelon, raw	½ melon	22	3
Broccoli,			
Fresh, cooked	½ c	20	8
Frozen, cooked	½ c	24	14
Brussels sprouts			
Fresh, cooked	½ c	28	8
Frozen, cooked	½ c	26	11
Cabbage			
Common varieties, raw, shredded	½ c	9	7
Common varieties, fresh, cooked	½ c	15	10
Chinese, raw, chopped	½ c	6	15
Chinese, fresh, chopped, cooked	½ c	12	16
Carrots			
Raw	1 med.	30	34
Fresh, diced, cooked	½ c	23	24
Canned, in liquid	½ c	35	291
Canned, drained	½ c	23	183
Canned, low-sodium, drained	½ c	20	30
Cauliflower			
Raw, flowerbuds	½ c	14	7
Frozen, cooked	½ c	16	9
Celery, green			
Raw	1 lg. stalk	7	50
Fresh, diced, cooked	½ c	11	66

VEGETABLES (continued)	Portion Size	Calories	Sodium (mg.)
Chard, Swiss			
Fresh, chopped, cooked	½ c	13	63
Collard greens			
Fresh, chopped, cooked	½ c	21	18
Frozen, chopped, cooked	½ c	26	14
Corn			
Sweet	1 ear	70	tr
Canned, cream-style	½ c	105	302
Canned, whole kernel	½ c	87	248
Cucumber, raw	1 med.	35	14
Eggplant, fresh, diced, cooked	½ c	19	1
Kale, fresh, chopped, cooked	½ c	22	24
Law bak, Daikon radish, cubed	½ c	21	23
Lettuce			
Butterhead varieties, raw, chopped	½ c	4	3
Iceberg, raw, chopped	½ c	5	4
Lily root, dried	10 pieces	16	4
Mushrooms			
Raw, sliced	½ c	10	6
Chinese, dried	4	28	4
Mustard greens			
Fresh, chopped, cooked	½ c	16	13
Frozen, cooked	½ c	15	8
Onion			
Mature, raw, chopped	½ c	33	9
Green, raw	1 stalk	7	1
Peas, green			
Immature, fresh, cooked	½ c	57	1
Canned, immature, drained	½ c	75	201
Canned, immature, low-sodium, drained	½ c	67	3
Canned, sweet, drained	½ c	68	201
Frozen, cooked	½ c	55	92
Snow or sugar peas in pod	8 pods	11	3
Peppers			
Sweet, green, raw	½ pod	18	11
Mature, red, raw	½ pod	26	—
Potato			
Boiled	1 med.	88	3
Hashed brown (homemade with salt)	½ c	178	223
Mashed with milk, fat (homemade) and salt added	½ c	99	348
Scalloped or au gratin (homemade) with salt and cheese	½ c	178	548

VEGETABLES (continued)	Portion Size	Calories	Sodium (mg.)
Potato			
French fried, frozen, unsalted	10 strips	170	3
Potato chips	10 chips	114	200
Potato salad, homemade, cooked, with salad dressing and seasonings	½ c	124	660
Pumpkin, canned without salt	½ c	41	3
Radishes, raw, whole	10 large	14	15
Rutabagas, raw, cubed, cooked	½ c	30	4
Sauerkraut, in liquid	½ c	21	878
Spinach			
Raw, chopped	½ c	7	20
Raw, chopped, cooked	½ c	21	45
Canned, in liquid	½ c	22	274
Canned, drained	½ c	25	242
Canned, low-sodium, drained	½ c	27	40
Frozen, chopped, cooked	½ c	24	54
Squash			
Summer varieties, fresh, diced, cooked	½ c	15	1
Winter varieties, fresh, diced, cooked	½ c	65	1
Sweet potatoes			
Fresh, baked in skin	½ med.	81	7
Fresh, boiled, mashed	½ c	146	13
Candied	½ med.	176	44
Tomatoes			
Ripe	1 med.	27	4
Canned, solids and liquid	½ c	26	157
Ketchup, bottled	2 T	32	312
Juice	½ c	23	243
Juice cocktail	½ c	26	243
Paste, canned	2 T	27	13
Puree, canned	2 T	13	131
Puree, canned, low-sodium	2 T	13	2
Vegetables, mixed, frozen, cooked	½ c	58	48
Water chestnuts	4 whole	69	12
Winter melon, raw	3½ oz.	12	5
Wood ears, dried	4	28	6

GRAIN PRODUCTS	Portion Size	Calories	Sodium (mg.)
Biscuits, baking powder			
Regular (homemade)	1	103	175
Self-rising flour (homemade)	1	104	185
From mix	1	91	272
Bread			
French (5 inches by 2½ inches high by ½ inch thick)	1 sl.	51	102
French roll (submarine size, 11½ inches long by 3 inches wide by 2½ inches thick)	1 roll	392	783
Raisin	1 sl.	66	91
Rye			
American	1 sl.	61	139
Pumpernickel	1 sl.	79	182
White	1 sl.	74	134
Whole wheat	1 sl.	61	132
Bread crumbs, dry, grated	¼ c	98	184
Cereals			
Ready-to-eat			
All-Bran	1 oz. (⅓ c)	71	320
Alpha-Bits	1 oz. (1 c)	111	219
Apple Jacks	1 oz. (1 c)	110	125
Bran Buds	1 oz. (⅓ c)	73	174
Bran Chex	1 oz. (⅔ c)	91	263
Cheerios	1 oz. (1¼ c)	111	307
Corn Chex	1 oz. (1 c)	111	271
Corn Flakes (Kellogg's)	1 oz. (1¼ c)	110	351
Corn Flakes (Ralston)	1 oz. (1 c)	111	271
Corn Flakes (low-sodium)	1 oz. (1 c)	113	3
Crispy Wheats 'n Raisins	1 oz. (¾ c)	99	135
40% Bran Flakes (Post)	1 oz. (¾ c)	92	260
Frosted Mini-Wheats	1 oz. (4 bisc.)	102	8
Grape-Nuts	1 oz. (¼ c)	101	197
Heartland Natural, plain	1 oz. (¼ c)	123	72
Kix	1 oz. (1½ c)	110	339
Life (plain or cinnamon)	1 oz. (⅔ c)	104	148
Most	1 oz. (⅔ c)	95	150
Nature Valley, Granola (toasted oat mixture)	1 oz. (⅓ c)	126	58
Nutri-Grain, corn	1 oz. (⅔ c)	108	187
100% Natural Cereal, plain	1 oz. (¼ c)	133	12
Product 19	1 oz. (¾ c)	108	325
Raisin Bran (Kellogg's)	1 oz. (¾ c)	89	206

GRAIN PRODUCTS (continued)	Portion Size	Calories	Sodium (mg.)
Cereals			
Ready-to-eat			
Raisin Bran (Ralston)	1 oz. (¾ c)	90	246
Rice Krispies	1 oz. (1 c)	112	340
Rice, puffed, plain	1 oz. (2 c)	114	—
Team	1 oz. (1 c)	111	175
Total	1 oz. (1 c)	100	352
Wheat germ, toasted, plain	1 oz. (¼ c)	108	1
Wheat, puffed, plain	1 oz. (2 c)	104	2
Wheat, shredded	1 lg. biscuit	83	0
Dry cereals, cooked			
Corn grits, regular and quick	1 c	146	0
Corn grits, instant, plain	1 pkt. prepared	82	344
Cream of Rice	1 c	126	2
Cream of Wheat, regular	1 c	134	2
Cream of Wheat, quick	1 c	129	139
Cream of Wheat, instant	1 c	153	6
Farina	1 c	116	1
Malt-O-Meal, plain or chocolate	1 c	122	2
Oats, regular, quick and instant (non-fortified)	1 c	145	1
Oats, instant, fortified (Quaker Oats), plain	1 pkt. prepared	104	286
Oats, instant, fortified (Quaker Oats), with raisins and spice	1 pkt. prepared	161	225
Roman Meal, plain	1 c	147	3
Wheatena	1 c	135	5
Crackers			
Animal	5	56	40
Cheese	10 sm. squares	52	112
Graham, plain	2 squares	55	95
Rye wafers, whole grain	5	112	287
Saltine	5	62	175
Soda	5	63	156
Macaroni, cooked	½ c	96	1
Muffins			
Blueberry (homemade)	1	112	253
Bran (homemade)	1	104	179
Corn (homemade)	1	126	192
Corn from mix	1	130	192
English	½	69	147

	Portion Size	Calories	Sodium (mg.)
GRAIN PRODUCTS (continued)			
Noodles,			
Egg, cooked	½ c	100	3
Spaghetti, cooked	½ c	96	1
Pancakes			
Homemade	1, 4 in. diameter	62	115
From mix	1, 4 in. diameter	61	152
Rice, cooked			
White	½ c	112	tr
Brown	½ c	116	tr
Rolls, brown and serve	1 roll	84	138
Snacks			
Corn chips	1 oz.	—	231
Popcorn, plain	1 c	23	tr
Popcorn, oil, salted	1 c	41	175
Pretzels, 3-ring twists	5	59	252
Waffle			
From mix	1, 7 in. diameter	206	515
Frozen	1 (1.2 oz.)	86	219
Homemade	1, 7 in. diameter	209	356

FATS, OILS, SALAD DRESSINGS AND GRAVIES

	Portion Size	Calories	Sodium (mg.)
Fats			
Butter	1 T	102	117
Margarine (regular, soft, in tub)	1 T	101	152
Lard	1 T	116	0
Chicken fat	1 T	115	0
Beef tallow	1 T	116	0
Oils			
Safflower, sunflower, corn*	1 T	120	0
Peanut, olive**	1 T	119	0
Coconut, palm†	1 T	120	0
Salad dressings			
Blue cheese	1 T	77	—
French	1 T	67	214
French, low-calorie	1 T	22	128
Italian	1 T	69	116
Italian, low-calorie	1 T	16	118
Thousand Island	1 T	59	109
Thousand Island, low-calorie	1 T	24	153

*High in polyunsaturated fats.
**High in monounsaturated fats.
†High in saturated fats.

	Portion Size	Calories	Sodium (mg.)
FATS, OIL, SALAD DRESSINGS AND GRAVIES (continued)			
Salad Dressings			
Mayonnaise			
Regular, soy bean	1 T	99	78
Low-calorie, imitation, soy bean	1 T	35	75
Gravies			
Canned			
Au jus	1 T	2	—
Beef	1 T	8	—
Chicken	1 T	12	86
Mushroom	1 T	8	85
Dehydrated			
Au jus, prepared with water	1 T	1	36
Brown, prepared with water	1 T	5	—
Chicken, prepared with water	1 T	5	71
Mushroom, prepared with water	1 T	4	88
Onion, prepared with water	1 T	5	65

SOUPS

	Portion Size	Calories	Sodium (mg.)
Canned			
Bean, black, prepared with water	1 c	116	1,198
Beef, broth or bouillon, ready-to-serve	1 c	16	782
Cheese, prepared with whole milk	1 c	230	1,020
Chicken broth, prepared with water	1 c	39	776
Chicken, chunky, ready-to-serve	1 c	178	887
Chicken noodle, prepared with water	1 c	75	1,107
Chicken vegetable, prepared with water	1 c	74	944
Clam chowder, Manhattan, prepared with water	1 c	78	1,808
Clam chowder, New England, prepared with whole milk	1 c	163	992
Lentil with ham, ready-to-serve	1 c	140	1,318
Mushroom, cream of, prepared with water	1 c	129	1,031
Mushroom, cream of, low-sodium, prepared with water	1 c	129	27
Pea, green, prepared with water	1 c	164	987
Pea, green, low-sodium, prepared with water	1 c	164	33
Tomato, prepared with water	1 c	86	872
Turkey noodle, prepared with water	1 c	69	815
Turkey noodle, low-sodium, prepared with water	1 c	69	42

SOUPS (continued)	Portion Size	Calories	Sodium (mg.)
Vegetable with beef, prepared with water	1 c	79	957
Vegetable with beef, low-sodium, prepared with water	1 c	79	51
Dehydrated			
Beef noodle, prepared with water	1 c	41	1,041
Chicken broth or bouillon, prepared with water	1 c	21	1,484
Chicken, cream of, prepared with water	1 c	107	1,184
Minestrone, prepared with water	1 c	79	1,026
Onion, dehydrated	1 pkt, (1.4 oz.)	115	3,493
Onion, prepared with water	1 c	28	848

SWEETS AND DESSERTS*

	Portion Size	Calories	Sodium (mg.)
Cake			
Angel, 1/12 of cake	1 sl.	161	170
Devil's food with chocolate icing, 1/16 of cake	1 sl.	277	176
Yellow with icing, 1/16 of cake	1 sl.	274	156
Candy			
Caramel	1 oz.	113	64
Chocolate, milk, plain	1 oz.	147	27
Chocolate-coated almonds	1 oz.	151	23
Fudge, chocolate, plain	1 oz.	113	54
Hard candy	1 oz.	109	9
Cookies			
Brownie with nuts (1¾ inch square)	2	194	100
Chocolate chip	4	206	139
Macaroons	2	181	13
Danish pastry	1 (1½ oz.)	179	156
Doughnut			
Cake type, 3⅝ inch diameter	1	227	291
Yeast type, 3¾ inch diameter	1	176	99
Honey	1 T	64	1
Jams and preserves	1 T	54	2
Jellies	1 T	49	3
Marshmallows	1 oz.	90	11
Molasses, blackstrap	1 T	43	19
Pie			
Apple, ⅛ of pie	1 sl.	302	355
Lemon Meringue, ⅛ of pie	1 sl.	268	296
Peach, ⅛ of pie	1 sl.	301	316

*There are no Best Choices in this category. All are very low in nutrients.

SWEETS AND DESSERTS (continued)	Portion Size	Calories	Sodium (mg.)
Pudding, bread with raisins	½ c	248	267
Sugars			
Brown, packed	1 T	51	3
White	1 T	46	tr
Powdered	1 T	31	tr

CONDIMENTS*

	Portion Size		Sodium (mg.)
Baking powder	1 t		339
Baking soda	1 t		821
Catsup			
Regular	1 t		52
Low-sodium	1 t		1
Chili powder	1 t		26
Chinese condiments			
Bean cake, fermented (furu)	1 t		199
Bean cake, fermented, red (furu)	1 t		220
Bean sauce, brown	1 t		426
Bean sauce, hot	1 t		329
Bean sauce, sweet	1 t		165
Black beans, salted			
rinsed	1 t		100
unrinsed	1 t		123
Chee hou sauce	1 t		184
Hoisin sauce	1 t		160
Oyster-flavored sauce	1 t		334
Satay sauce	1 t		78
Soy sauce			
Dark	1 t		334
Light	1 t		433
Milder	1 t		202
Mushroom	1 t		442
Thick	1 t		250
Shrimp			
Dried, rinsed	1 t		22
Dried, unrinsed	1 t		92
Sauce	1 t		412
Vinegars, Chinese			
Brown	1 t		36
Red	1 t		36
Garlic			
Powder	1 t		1
Salt	1 t		1,850

*Calorie content of condiments unavailable; however, 1 teaspoon of a condiment will probably not exceed 10 to 15 calories.

CONDIMENTS (continued)	Portion Size	Sodium (mg.)
Horseradish, prepared	1 t	66
Meat tenderizer		
Regular	1 t	1,750
Low-sodium	1 t	1
MSG (monosodium glutamate)	1 t	492
Mustard, prepared	1 t	65
Olives		
Green	4 olives	323
Ripe	3 olives	96
Onion		
Powder	1 t	1
Salt	1 t	1,620
Parsley, dried	1 t	2
Pepper, black	1 t	1
Pickles		
Dill	1 pickle	928
Sweet	1 pickle	128
Relish, sweet	1 t	41
Salt	1 t	1,938
Sauces		
A–1	1 t	92
Barbecue	1 t	43
Chili	1 t	76
Tabasco	1 t	24
Tartar	1 t	61
Worcestershire	1 t	69
Vinegar, American	1 t	tr

SPICES AND HERBS

	Portion Size	Sodium (mg.)
Allspice, ground	1 t	1
Anise seed	1 t	tr
Basil, ground	1 t	tr
Bay leaf, crumbled	1 t	tr
Caraway seed	1 t	tr
Cardamom, ground	1 t	tr
Celery seed	1 t	3
Chervil, dried	1 t	tr
Chili powder	1 t	26
Cinnamon, ground	1 t	1
Cloves, ground	1 t	5
Coriander leaf, dried	1 t	1
Coriander seed	1 t	1

SPICES AND HERBS (continued)	Portion Size	Sodium (mg.)
Cumin seed	1 t	4
Curry powder	1 t	1
Dill seed	1 t	tr
Dillweed, dried	1 t	2
Fennel seed	1 t	2
Garlic powder	1 t	1
Ginger, ground	1 t	1
Mace, ground	1 t	1
Marjoram, dried	1 t	tr
Mustard seed, yellow	1 t	tr
Nutmeg, ground	1 t	tr
Onion powder	1 t	1
Oregano, ground	1 t	tr
Paprika	1 t	1
Parsley, dried	1 t	1
Pepper, black	1 t	1
Pepper, red or cayenne	1 t	1
Pepper, white	1 t	tr
Poppy seed	1 t	1
Poultry seasoning (without salt)	1 t	tr
Pumpkin pie seasoning	1 t	1
Pumpkin pie spice	1 t	1
Rosemary, dried	1 t	1
Saffron	1 t	1
Sage, ground	1 t	tr
Savory, ground	1 t	tr
Sesame seed, decorticated	1 t	1
Tarragon, ground	1 t	1
Thyme, ground	1 t	1
Turmeric, ground	1 t	1

CHOLESTEROL CONTENT OF FOODS

DAIRY PRODUCTS	Portion Size	Cholesterol (mg.)
Cheeses (natural)		
Blue	1 oz.	21
Brie	1 oz.	28
Camembert	1 oz.	20
Cheddar	1 oz.	30
Cottage		
Creamed	4 oz.	17
Dry curd (unsalted)	4 oz.	8
Low-fat (2 percent fat)	4 oz.	9
Cream	1 oz.	31
Feta	1 oz.	25
Monterey	1 oz.	—
Mozzarella from whole milk	1 oz.	22
Mozzarella from part skim milk	1 oz.	16
Parmesan, grated	1 oz.	22
Parmesan, hard	1 oz.	19
Ricotta from whole milk	½ c	63
Ricotta from part skim milk	½ c	38
Roquefort	1 oz.	26
Swiss	1 oz.	26
Cheeses (pasteurized process)		
American	1 oz.	27
American cheese spread	1 oz.	16
Swiss	1 oz.	24
Cream		
Half-and-half	1 T	6
Light or coffee	1 T	10
Light whipping	1 T	17
Heavy whipping	1 T	21
Sour cream, cultured	1 T	5
Eggnog	½ c	75
Frozen desserts		
Ice cream, vanilla, hardened		
Regular (approx. 10 percent fat)	½ c	30
Rich (approx. 16 percent fat)	½ c	44
Ice milk, vanilla		
Hardened	½ c	9
Soft serve	½ c	7
Sherbet, orange	½ c	7

DAIRY PRODUCTS (continued)	Portion Size	Cholesterol (mg.)
Imitation dairy products		
Nondairy coffee whiteners		
Liquid (frozen)	1 T	0
Powdered	1 T	0
Dessert toppings		
Pressurized	1 T	0
Semisolid (frozen)	1 T	0
Milk,		
Buttermilk, cultured low-fat (1 percent fat)	½ c	5
Buttermilk, cultured (unsalted) low-fat (1 percent fat)	½ c	5
Chocolate, low-fat (2 percent fat)	½ c	9
Low-fat (2 percent fat)	½ c	9
Skim	½ c	2
Whole (3.7 percent fat)	½ c	18
Milk, canned		
Condensed, sweetened	1 T	7
Evaporated, skim	1 T	1
Evaporated, whole	1 T	5
Yogurt		
Fruit flavored, low-fat	4 oz.	5
Plain, low-fat	4 oz.	7
Plain, skim	4 oz.	2

FISH AND SHELLFISH

	Portion Size	Cholesterol (mg.)
Cod, raw, meat only	3½ oz.	50
Clams, raw, meat only	3½ oz.	50
Crab		
Steamed, meat only	3½ oz.	100
Canned	3½ oz.	101
Flatfish, raw (flounder, sand dab, sole)	3½ oz.	50
Haddock, raw, meat only	3½ oz.	60
Halibut, raw, meat only	3½ oz.	50
Lobster, boiled	3½ oz.	85
Oysters, raw, meat only	3½ oz.	50
Scallops		
Raw, meat only	3½ oz.	35
Cooked	3½ oz.	53
Shrimp		
Raw, meat only	3½ oz.	150
Canned	3½ oz.	150

	Portion Size	Cholesterol (mg.)
FISH AND SHELLFISH (continued)		
Salmon, raw., meat only	3½ oz.	35
Sardines		
Canned, in liquid	3½ oz.	120
Canned, drained	3½ oz.	140
Tuna		
Canned in oil	3½ oz.	55
Canned in oil, drained	3½ oz.	65
Canned in water without salt	3½ oz.	63

POULTRY PRODUCTS

Chicken, broilers or fryers		
Flesh and skin, roasted	3½ oz.	88
Flesh only, roasted	3½ oz.	89
Duck, domesticated		
Flesh and skin, roasted	3½ oz.	84
Flesh only, roasted	3½ oz.	89
Turkey, fryer-roasters		
Flesh and skin, roasted	3½ oz.	105
Flesh only, roasted	3½ oz.	98

RED MEATS

Beef

Composite of retail cuts		
Lean with fat, cooked	3½ oz.	94
Well trimmed, cooked	3½ oz.	91

Lamb

Composite of retail cuts		
Lean with fat, cooked	3½ oz.	98
Well trimmed, cooked	3½ oz.	100

Pork

Composite of retail cuts		
Lean with fat, cooked	3½ oz.	89
Well trimmed, cooked	3½ oz.	88

	Portion Size	Cholesterol (mg.)
ORGAN MEATS		
Brains, beef, raw	3½ oz.	2000 or more
Heart		
Beef, cooked	3½ oz.	274
Chicken, cooked	3½ oz.	242
Turkey, cooked	3½ oz.	226
Kidneys, cooked (beef, calf, pork, lamb)	3½ oz.	804
Liver,		
Beef, calf, pork, lamb, cooked	3½ oz.	438
Chicken, cooked	3½ oz.	631
Turkey, cooked	3½ oz.	626
Gizzards, chicken, cooked	3½ oz.	194
LUNCHEON MEATS AND SAUSAGES		
Bologna		
Beef	1 oz.	16
Pork	1 oz.	17
Turkey	1 oz.	28
Frankfurter		
Beef (1 frank)	2 oz.	27
Beef and pork (1 frank)	2 oz.	29
Turkey (1 frank)	1½ oz.	48
Ham		
Chopped, not canned	1 oz.	15
Chopped, canned	1 oz.	14
Sliced, extra lean	1 oz.	13
Sliced, regular	1 oz.	16
Italian sausage, cooked (1 link)	3 oz.	65
Liver sausage, liverwurst	1 oz.	45
Mortadella	1 oz.	16
Polish sausage	1 oz.	20
Pork sausage, fresh, cooked	1 oz.	22
Salami		
Beef	1 oz.	17
Beef and pork	1 oz.	18
Turkey	1 oz.	23
Turkey roll, light meat	1 oz.	12
Vienna sausage, canned	2 saus. (1.14 oz.)	16

	Portion Size	Cholesterol (mg.)
MEAT SUBSTITUTES		
Eggs		
Eggs, fresh		
Whole	1 large	274
White	1 white	0
Yolk	1 yolk	272
Egg substitute products		
Frozen	¼ c	1
Liquid	¼ c	tr
Powder	¾ oz.	113
Beans, peas, and lentils		
All prepared without dairy or meat products		0
Nuts and seeds		
All prepared without dairy or meat products		0
FRUITS AND VEGETABLES		
All prepared without dairy or meat products		0
GRAIN PRODUCTS		
Noodles, egg type, cooked	½ c	25
Pancakes, from mix	1, 4-in. diameter	20
Waffle, from mix	1, 7-in. diameter	45

All breads, cereals, and other grain products contain no cholesterol if prepared without dairy or meat products.

FATS, OILS, SALAD DRESSINGS, AND GRAVIES		
Fats		
Butter	1 T	31
Margarine	1 T	0
Lard	1 T	12
Chicken fat	1 T	11
Beef tallow	1 T	14

FATS, OILS, SALAD DRESSINGS, AND GRAVIES (continued)	Portion Size	Cholesterol (mg.)
Oils		
Safflower, sunflower, corn*	1 T	0
Peanut, olive**	1 T	0
Coconut, palm†	1 T	0
Salad dressings		
French, low-calorie	1 T	1
Italian, low-calorie	1 T	1
Thousand Island, low-calorie	1 T	2
Mayonnaise		
Regular (soy bean)	1 T	8
Low-calorie, imitation (soy bean)	1 T	4
Gravies		
Canned		
Au jus	1 T	tr
Beef	1 T	tr
Chicken	1 T	tr
Mushroom	1 T	0
Dehydrated		
Au jus, prepared with water	1 T	tr
Brown, prepared with water	1 T	tr
Chicken, prepared with water	1 T	tr
Mushroom, prepared with water	1 T	tr
Onion, prepared with water	1 T	tr

SOUPS

Canned		
Bean, black, prepared with water	1 c	0
Beef, broth or bouillon, ready-to-serve	1 c	tr
Cheese, prepared with whole milk	1 c	48
Chicken broth, prepared with water	1 c	1
Chicken, chunky, ready-to-serve	1 c	30
Chicken noodle, prepared with water	1 c	7
Chicken vegetable, prepared with water	1 c	10
Clam chowder, Manhattan, prepared with water	1 c	2
Clam chowder, New England, prepared with whole milk	1 c	22
Lentil with ham, ready-to-serve	1 c	7

*High in polyunsaturated fats.
**High in monounsaturated fats.
†High in saturated fats.

	Portion Size	Cholesterol (mg.)
SOUPS (continued)		
Canned		
Mushroom, cream of, prepared with water	1 c	2
Mushroom, cream of, low-sodium, prepared with water	1 c	2
Pea, green, low-sodium, prepared with water	1 c	0
Tomato, prepared with water	1 c	0
Turkey noodle, low-sodium, prepared with water	1 c	5
Vegetable with beef, low-sodium, prepared with water	1 c	5
Dehydrated		
Beef noodle, prepared with water	1 c	2
Chicken broth or bouillon, prepared with water	1 c	1
Chicken, cream of, prepared with water	1 c	3
Minestrone, prepared with water	1 c	3
Onion, dehydrated	1 pkt. (1.4 oz.)	2
Onion, prepared with water	1 c	0
SWEETS AND DESSERTS		
Cake		
Angel, 1/12 of cake	1 sl.	0
Devil's food, 1/16 of cake	1 sl.	33
Yellow cake, 1/16 of cake	1 sl.	33
Cookies, brownie with nuts	1 (1¾ in. sq.)	17
Pie		
Apple, 1/8 of pie	1 sl.	0
Lemon meringue, 1/8 of pie	1 sl.	98
Peach, 1/8 of pie	1 sl.	0
Pudding, bread with raisins	½ c	85
Sugar, brown, white		0

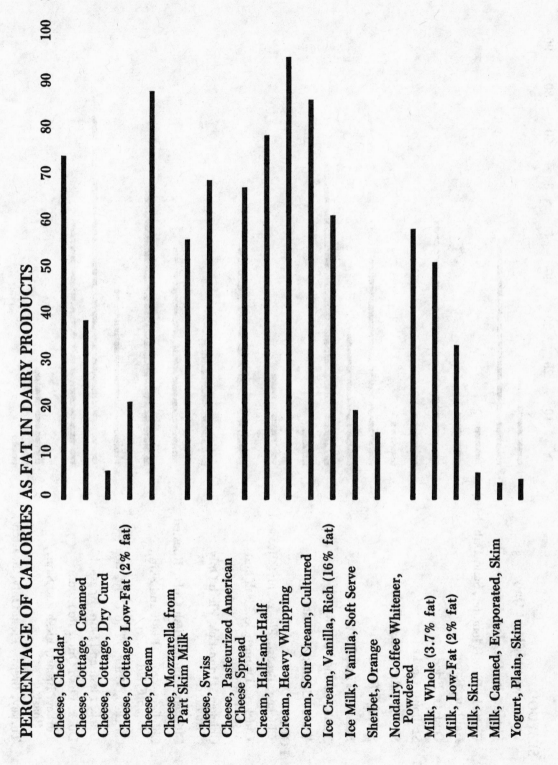

PERCENTAGE OF CALORIES AS FAT IN DAIRY PRODUCTS

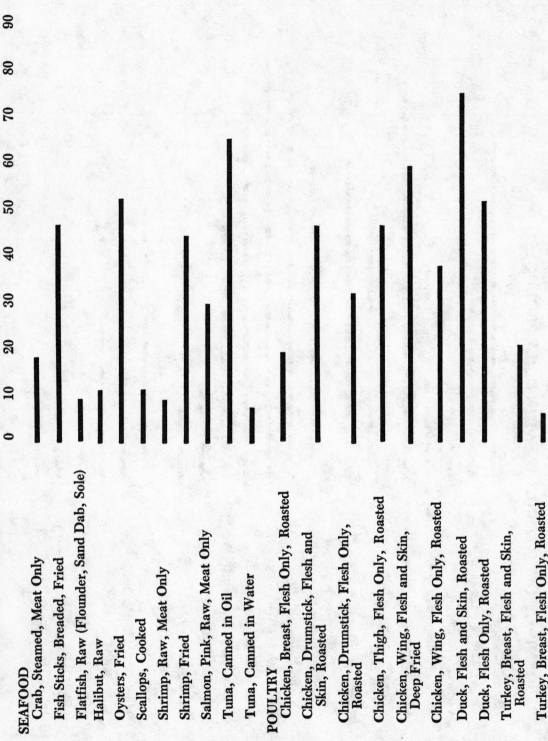

PERCENTAGE OF CALORIES AS FAT IN SEAFOOD AND POULTRY

SEAFOOD
  Crab, Steamed, Meat Only
  Fish Sticks, Breaded, Fried
  Flatfish, Raw (Flounder, Sand Dab, Sole)
  Halibut, Raw
  Oysters, Fried
  Scallops, Cooked
  Shrimp, Raw, Meat Only
  Shrimp, Fried
  Salmon, Pink, Raw, Meat Only
  Tuna, Canned in Oil
  Tuna, Canned in Water

POULTRY
  Chicken, Breast, Flesh Only, Roasted
  Chicken, Drumstick, Flesh and Skin, Roasted
  Chicken, Drumstick, Flesh Only, Roasted
  Chicken, Thigh, Flesh Only, Roasted
  Chicken, Wing, Flesh and Skin, Deep Fried
  Chicken, Wing, Flesh Only, Roasted
  Duck, Flesh and Skin, Roasted
  Duck, Flesh Only, Roasted
  Turkey, Breast, Flesh and Skin, Roasted
  Turkey, Breast, Flesh Only, Roasted

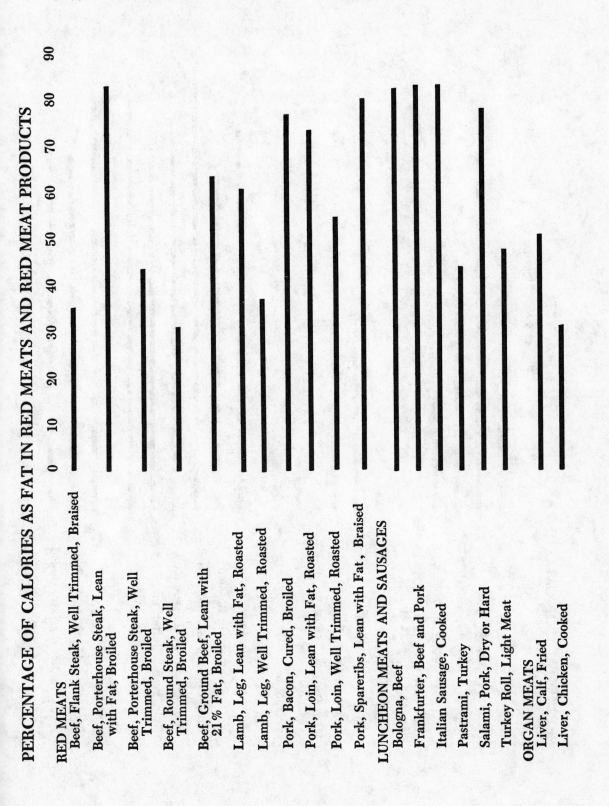

PERCENTAGE OF CALORIES AS FAT IN RED MEATS AND RED MEAT PRODUCTS

RED MEATS
Beef, Flank Steak, Well Trimmed, Braised

Beef, Porterhouse Steak, Lean with Fat, Broiled

Beef, Porterhouse Steak, Well Trimmed, Broiled

Beef, Round Steak, Well Trimmed, Broiled

Beef, Ground Beef, Lean with 21% Fat, Broiled

Lamb, Leg, Lean with Fat, Roasted

Lamb, Leg, Well Trimmed, Roasted

Pork, Bacon, Cured, Broiled

Pork, Loin, Lean with Fat, Roasted

Pork, Loin, Well Trimmed, Roasted

Pork, Spareribs, Lean with Fat, Braised

LUNCHEON MEATS AND SAUSAGES
Bologna, Beef

Frankfurter, Beef and Pork

Italian Sausage, Cooked

Pastrami, Turkey

Salami, Pork, Dry or Hard

Turkey Roll, Light Meat

ORGAN MEATS
Liver, Calf, Fried

Liver, Chicken, Cooked

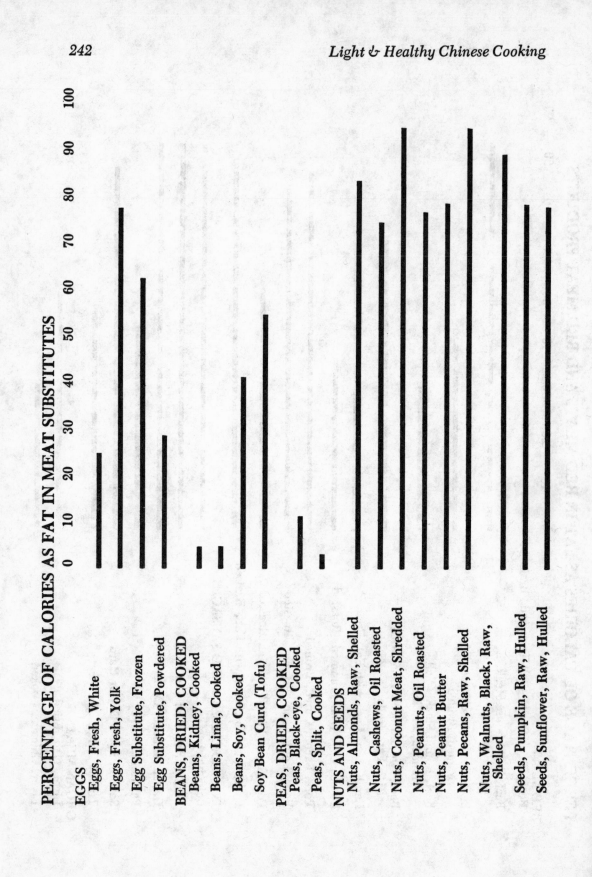

PERCENTAGE OF CALORIES AS FAT IN MEAT SUBSTITUTES

EGGS
Eggs, Fresh, White
Eggs, Fresh, Yolk
Egg Substitute, Frozen
Egg Substitute, Powdered

BEANS, DRIED, COOKED
Beans, Kidney, Cooked
Beans, Lima, Cooked
Beans, Soy, Cooked
Soy Bean Curd (Tofu)

PEAS, DRIED, COOKED
Peas, Black-eye, Cooked
Peas, Split, Cooked

NUTS AND SEEDS
Nuts, Almonds, Raw, Shelled
Nuts, Cashews, Oil Roasted
Nuts, Coconut Meat, Shredded
Nuts, Peanuts, Oil Roasted
Nuts, Peanut Butter
Nuts, Pecans, Raw, Shelled
Nuts, Walnuts, Black, Raw, Shelled
Seeds, Pumpkin, Raw, Hulled
Seeds, Sunflower, Raw, Hulled

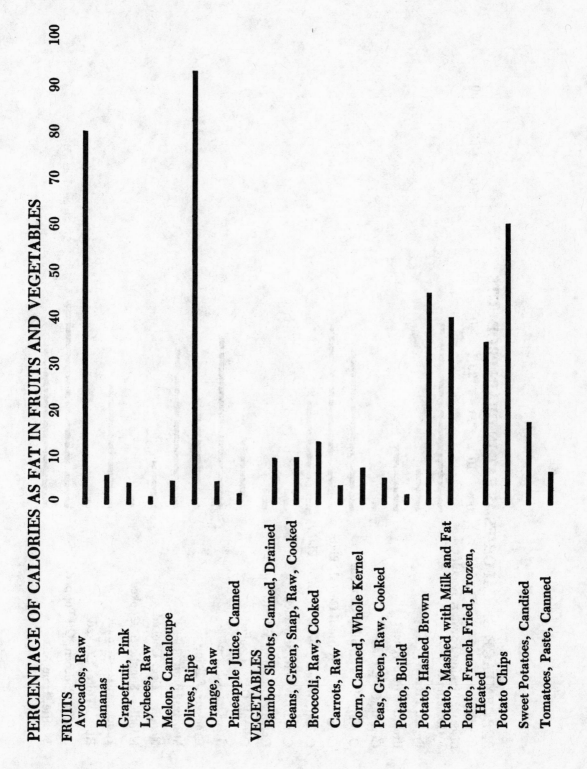

PERCENTAGE OF CALORIES AS FAT IN FRUITS AND VEGETABLES

FRUITS
Avocados, Raw
Bananas
Grapefruit, Pink
Lychees, Raw
Melon, Cantaloupe
Olives, Ripe
Orange, Raw
Pineapple Juice, Canned

VEGETABLES
Bamboo Shoots, Canned, Drained
Beans, Green, Snap, Raw, Cooked
Broccoli, Raw, Cooked
Carrots, Raw
Corn, Canned, Whole Kernel
Peas, Green, Raw, Cooked
Potato, Boiled
Potato, Hashed Brown
Potato, Mashed with Milk and Fat
Potato, French Fried, Frozen, Heated
Potato Chips
Sweet Potatoes, Candied
Tomatoes, Paste, Canned

PERCENTAGE OF CALORIES AS FAT IN GRAIN PRODUCTS

Biscuits, Baking Powder, Regular Homemade

Bread, French

Bread, Whole Wheat

Cereal, Corn Flakes

Cereal, Nature Valley Granola

Cereal, 100% Natural Cereal, Plain

Cereal, Wheat Germ, Toasted, Plain

Cereal, Wheat, Shredded

Cereal, Cream of Wheat, Cooked

Cereal, Oats, Cooked

Crackers, Cheese

Crackers, Saltine

Muffins, Bran

Noodles, Egg, Cooked

Noodles, Spaghetti, Cooked

Pancakes, Homemade

Rice, White, Cooked

Snacks, Popcorn, Oil Popped

Waffle, from Mix

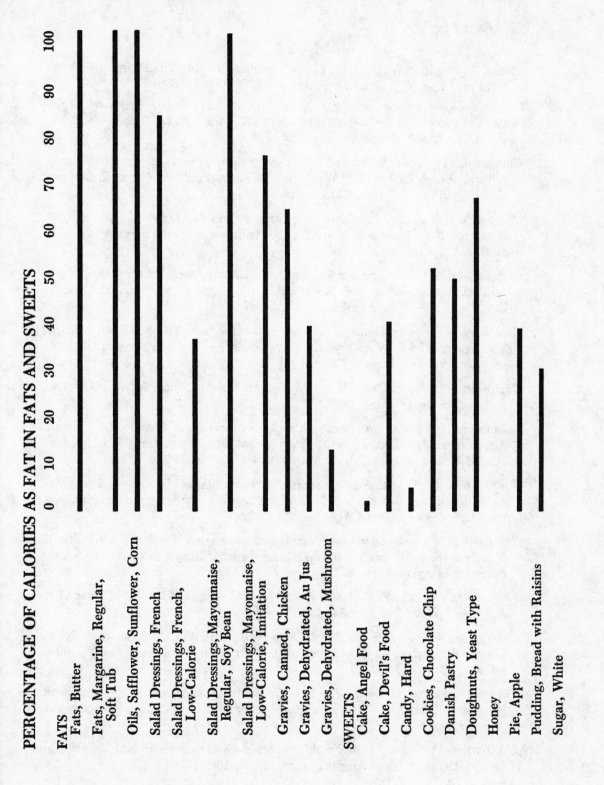

PERCENTAGE OF CALORIES AS FAT IN FATS AND SWEETS

FATS
Fats, Butter
Fats, Margarine, Regular, Soft Tub
Oils, Safflower, Sunflower, Corn
Salad Dressings, French
Salad Dressings, French, Low-Calorie
Salad Dressings, Mayonnaise, Regular, Soy Bean
Salad Dressings, Mayonnaise, Low-Calorie, Imitation
Gravies, Canned, Chicken
Gravies, Dehydrated, Au Jus
Gravies, Dehydrated, Mushroom

SWEETS
Cake, Angel Food
Cake, Devil's Food
Candy, Hard
Cookies, Chocolate Chip
Danish Pastry
Doughnuts, Yeast Type
Honey
Pie, Apple
Pudding, Bread with Raisins
Sugar, White

NUTRITIONAL COMPOSITION TABLES

Resource List

Chew, T. "Sodium Values of Chinese Condiments and Their Use in Sodium-Restricted Diets." J. Am. Diet. Assoc. Vol. 82:397, 1983.

Composition of Foods, Breakfast Cereals, Raw, Processed, Prepared. Agricultural Handbook No. 8-8. Washington, DC: Agricultural Research Service, U.S. Department of Agriculture, 1982.

Composition of Foods, Dairy and Egg Products, Raw, Processed, Prepared. Agricultural Handbook No. 8-1. Washington, DC: Agricultural Research Service, U.S. Department of Agriculture, 1976.

Composition of Foods, Fats and Oils, Raw, Processed, Prepared. Agricultural Handbook No. 8-4. Washington, DC: Agricultural Research Service, U.S. Department of Agriculture, 1979.

Composition of Foods, Fruits and Fruit Juices, Raw, Processed, Prepared. Agricultural Handbook No. 8-9. Washington, DC: Agricultural Research Service, U.S. Department of Agriculture, 1982.

Composition of Foods, Poultry Products, Raw, Processed, Prepared. Agricultural Handbook No. 8-5. Washington, DC: Agricultural Research Service, U.S. Department of Agriculture, 1979.

Composition of Foods, Raw, Processed, Prepared. Agricultural Service, U.D. Department of Agriculture, 1963.

Composition of Foods, Sausages and Luncheon Meats, Raw, Processed, Prepared. Agricultural Handbook No. 8-7. Washington, DC: Agricultural Research Service, U.S Department of Agriculture, 1980.

Composition of Foods, Soups, Sauces, Gravies, Raw, Processed, Prepared. Agricultural Handbook No. 8-6. Washington, DC: Agricultural Research Service, U.S. Department of Agriculture, 1980.

Composition of Foods, Spices and Herbs, Raw, Processed, Prepared. Agricultural Handbook No. 8-2. Washington, DC: Agricultural Research Service, U.S. Department of Agriculture, 1977.

Feely, R. M.; Criner, P. E.; and Watt, B. K. "Cholesterol Content of Foods." J. Am. Diet. Assoc. Vol. 61:134, 1972.

Food Composition Table for Use in East Asia. DHEW Publication No. (NIH) 73-465. Bethesda, Maryland: Department of Health, Education, and Welfare, 1972.

Nutritive Value of American Foods in Common Units. Agricultural Handbook No. 456. Washington, DC: Agricultural Research Service, U.S. Department of Agriculture, 1975.

The Sodium Content of Your Food. Home and Garden Bulletin No. 233. Washington, DC: U.S. Department of Agriculture, 1980.

Appendix

SHOPPING GUIDE

The condiments and ingredients used in this book are quite common and should be readily available in most Chinese grocery stores. This shopping guide, printed both in English and Chinese, may facilitate your shopping if you show it to your Chinese grocer.

In the event you are unable to purchase some of these items, we shall be glad to help you if you write to the following address:

Jue & Chew
718 Derby Ave.
Oakland, CA 94601

Be sure to enclose a stamped, self-addressed envelope.

Dried condiments

Dried Mushrooms 冬菇

Dried Red Chili Peppers 紅辣椒

Dried Shrimp 蝦米

Five Spice Powder 五香粉

Gum Jum (Dried Lily Flowers or Buds) 金針

Mook Yee (Dried Wood Fungus) 木耳

Salted Black Beans 豆豉

Star Anise 八角

Szechwan Peppers 花椒

White Ground Pepper 白胡椒粉

Fresh Condiments

Ginger 薑

Green Onions (Scallions) 蔥、

Sauces and Pastes

Bean Sauce 豆瓣醬

Chee Hou Sauce 柱侯醬

Fermented Bean Cake (Furu) 腐乳

Ground Bean Sauce (Mien See) 麵豉

Hoisin Sauce 海鮮醬

Hot Bean Sauce 辣豆瓣醬

Oyster Flavored Sauce 蠔油

Red Chili Oil 紅辣油

Red Fermented Bean Cake 南乳

Satay Sauce 沙茶醬

Sesame Paste 芝麻醬

Shrimp Sauce 鹹蝦

Sweet Bean Sauce 甜麵醬

Soy Sauces

Light Soy Sauce 生抽

Dark Soy Sauce 老抽

Thick Soy Sauce 珠油

Vinegars

Chinkiang Vinegar 鎮江醋

Chinese Red Vinegar 浙醋

Foodstuffs

Bamboo Shoots 竹筍

Beancurd Skins 腐竹

Beancurd Sticks 圓竹

Bean Threads 粉絲

Bitter Melon 苦瓜

Bok Choy 白菜

Chinese Broccoli 芥蘭

Fuzzy Melon 節瓜

Law Bak (Daikon)—Chinese White Turnip 蘿蔔

Napa or Chinese Cabbage 蔏菜

Snow Peas (Sugar Peas) 雪豆

Tofu, Regular 豆腐

Tofu, Soft 水豆腐

Water Chestnuts 馬蹄

Winter Melon 冬瓜

HELPFUL LITERATURE FROM NON-PROFIT ORGANIZATIONS

The following pamphlets, leaflets, and booklets may be obtained from their respective organizations. Single copies are free or available at minimal cost.

SUPERINTENDENT OF DOCUMENTS, U.S. GOVERNMENT PRINTING OFFICE, WASHINGTON, DC 20402

- *Food*, U.S. Dept. of Agriculture, 1979. Stock No. 001-000-03881-8. Home and Garden Bulletin No. 228, 64 pp.

- *The Hassle-Free Guide to a Better Diet*, U.S. Dept. of Agriculture, 1980. Stock No. 001-000-04130-4. Leaflet.

- *Nutrition and Your Health, Dietary Guidelines for Americans*, U.S. Dept. of Agriculture and U.S. Dept. of Health and Human Services, 1980. Home and Garden Bulletin No. 232, 19 pp.

- *Nutritive Value of Foods*, U.S. Dept. of Agriculture, 1978. Stock No. 001-000-03841-0, Home and Garden Bulletin No. 72, 34 pp.

- *The Sodium Content of Your Food*, U.S. Dept. of Agriculture, 1980. Home and Garden Bulletin No. 233, 35 pp.

HIGH BLOOD PRESSURE INFORMATION CENTER, 120/80 NATIONAL INSTITUTES OF HEALTH, BETHESDA, MD 20205

- *High Blood Pressure: Fact and Fiction*, U.S. Dept. of Health and Human Services, 1980. NIH Publication No. 80-1218, leaflet.

- *Questions about Weight, Salt, and High Blood Pressure*, U.S. Dept. of Health and Human Services, 1980. NIH Publication No. 80-1459, 6 pp.

- *Statement on the Role of Dietary Management in Hypertension Control*, 1980. U.S. G.P.O.: 1980 0-311-201/3129, 3 pp.

- *Watch Your Blood Pressure*, The Public Affairs Committee, 1979. Public Affairs Pamphlet No. 483B, 28 pp.

AMERICAN HEART ASSOCIATION, NATIONAL CENTER, 7320 GREEN-VILLE AVE., DALLAS, TX 75231

- *Eat Well But Eat Wisely — To Reduce Your Risk of Heart Attack*, 1979. Order No. 51-005-A, leaflet.

- *A Guide for Weight Reduction*, 1978. Order No. 50-034-A, 12 pp.

- *High Blood Pressure, What It Is, What It Can Do to You and What You Can Do about It*, 1980. Order No. 50-052-A, 9 pp.

- *How to Stop Smoking,* 1981. Order No. 51-013-Å, leaflet.

- *Nutrition Labeling, Food Selection Hints for Fat-Controlled Meals,* 1978. Order No. 50-040-A, 8 pp.

- *Recipes for Fat-Controlled, Low-Cholesterol Meals,* 1975. Order No. 50-020-B, 34 pp.

- *Reduce Your Risk of Heart Attack,* 1981. Order No. 50-021-B, 9 pp.

- *Save Food Dollars and Help Your Heart,* 1974. Order No. 50-032-A, 12 pp.

- *Seven Hopeful Facts about Stroke,* 1980. Order No. 51-016-C, leaflet.

- *Way to a Man's Heart, A Fat-Controlled, Low-Cholesterol Meal Plan to Reduce the Risk of Heart Attack.* 1972. Order No. 51-018-A, leaflet.

- *Weight Control Guidance in Smoking Cessation,* 1977. Order No. 51-026-A, 3 pp.

AMERICAN HEART ASSOCIATION, SAN FRANCISCO CHAPTER, 421 POWELL ST., SAN FRANCISCO, CA 94102

- *A Guide to Sodium: Why You Should Eat Less,* 1980. Order No. DT-8. 8 pp.

- *Shake the Salt Habit,* 1981. Order No. DT-6, leaflet.

SOCIETY FOR NUTRITION EDUCATION, 2140 SHATTUCK AVE., SUITE 1110, BERKELEY, CA 94704

- *Nutrition for Everybody:* An Annotated List of Resources, 1981, 24 pp.

PROFESSIONAL AND VOLUNTARY ORGANIZATIONS

The American Diabetes Association, 18 E. 48 St., New York, NY 10020

The American Dietetic Association, 430 N. Michigan Ave., Chicago, IL 60611

The American Heart Association, 7320 Greenville Ave., Dallas, TX 75231

The American Medical Association, 535 N. Dearborn St., Chicago, IL 60610

Center for Science in the Public Interest, 1755 S St., NW, Washington, DC 20009

Community Nutrition Institute, 1146 19 St., NW, Washington, DC 20006

High Blood Pressure Information Center, 120/80 National Institutes of Health, Bethesda, MD 20014

National Nutrition Education Clearing House (NNECH), The Society for Nutrition Education, 2140 Shattuck Ave., Suite 1110, Berkeley, CA 94707

Index